Turin

Genoa

Isola 2000

Alpes-Maritimes

Alassio

Sospel

River Var

Menton   **San Remo**   *Ligurian   Sea*

Monaco

Vence   **Nice**   Monte Carlo
Villefranche   Beaulieu
Grasse Villeneuve   Cap Ferrat
Vallauris   Cagnes-sur-mer
Juan-les-Pins   Antibes
Cannes   Golfe-
La Napoule   Juan   Cap d'Antibes

Fréjus

St Raphael

t Tropez   *d'Azur*

Côte

D1132896

```
0    10    20    30    40    50
```
Kilometres

When the Riviera was Ours

Other titles by Patrick Howarth

History and Criticism

The Year is 1851
Questions in the House
Squire: Most Generous of Men
Special Operations (*Editor*)
Play up and Play the Game

Novels

The Dying Ukrainian
A Matter of Minutes

Life-boat Service

The Life-boat Story
The Life-boat Service
How Men are Rescued from the Sea
Life-boats and Life-boat People

When the Riviera was Ours

Patrick Howarth

Routledge & Kegan Paul
London and Henley

First published in 1977
by Routledge & Kegan Paul Ltd
39 Store Street,
London WC1E 7DD and
Broadway House,
Newtown Road,
Henley-on-Thames,
Oxon RG9 1EN
Set in Baskerville by
Computacomp (UK) Ltd., Fort William, Inverness-shire
and printed in Great Britain by
Lowe and Brydone Ltd.
© Patrick Howarth 1977
No part of this book may be reproduced in
any form without permission from the
publisher, except for the quotation of brief
passages in criticism

ISBN 0 7100 8465 X

To Eva Welch

Contents

	Acknowledgments	xiii
1	The Early Travellers	1
2	The Railway Link	31
3	Before 1914: Establishing a Colony	49
4	Royal Presences	69
5	Political Leaders	90
6	The Rich and the Pleasure-loving	105
7	The Literary Scene	120
8	The Last Colonial Years	144
9	The American Impact	161
10	Russians, other Foreigners and the French	180
11	Epilogue: War and Aftermath	199
	Bibliography	216
	Index	223

Illustrations

Between pages 82-3

1 King Edward VII in the south of France: a caricature, 1901
  (Mary Evans Picture Library)
2 James Gordon Bennett (Mary Evans Picture Library)
3 Cora Pearl: the most celebrated courtesan of the Second
  Empire (Mary Evans Picture Library)
4 Duke of Connaught and the King of Sweden (By courtesy of
  Société des Bains de Mer)
5 Winston Churchill with Somerset Maugham at Villa
  Mauresque, Cap Ferrat, April 1959 (Keystone)
6 Marie Bashkirtseff (By courtesy of Nice Tourist Office and
  Michel de Lorenzo)
7 Renoir's house, Bas-de-Cagnes (By courtesy of Nice Tourist
  Office)
8 Mrs Frank Jay Gould (By courtesy of Société des Bains de
  Mer)

Between pages 114-15

9 La Croisette, Cannes (By courtesy of Grand Metropolitan
  Hotels)
10 Carlton Hotel, Cannes, whose cupolas recalled the shape of
  la Belle Otéro (By courtesy of Grand Metropolitan Hotels)
11 Dog's bar at the Carlton Hotel, Cannes (By courtesy of
  Grand Metropolitan Hotels and Traverso, Cannes)
12 The battle of the flowers, Cannes, 1889 (Mary Evans Picture
  Library)

13 Lloyd George demonstrating golf to Aristide Briand, Prime
    Minister of France, at Cannes in January 1922 (Popperfoto)

14 The Duke and Duchess of Windsor at the 'Bal des Petits Lits
    Blancs', Cannes, August 1939 (Popperfoto)

15 Cannes film festival — Gina Lollobrigida (By courtesy of
    Grand Metropolitan Hotels and Traverso, Cannes)

16 Boulevard des Anglais, Nice (By courtesy of Nice Tourist
    Office and Paul-Louis, Nice)

17 Russian church, Nice (By courtesy of Nice Tourist Office and
    Paul-Louis)

18 Queen Victoria, with Beatrice, Princess Henry of Battenberg
    (*back view*), Princess Helena Victoria of Schleswig-Holstein
    (*facing*), and Indian attendants Sheikh Ghulam Mustafa and
    Sheikh Chidda, Nice, April 1895 (Reproduced by gracious
    permission of Her Majesty The Queen)

19 Prince Leopold (*left*) and Prince Maurice of Battenberg, Nice,
    April 1895 (Reproduced by gracious permission of Her
    Majesty The Queen)

20 Monte Carlo, 1898 (Mary Evans Picture Library)

21 Roulette at Monte Carlo (By courtesy of Société des Bains de
    Mer)

22 Nijinsky and Karsavina dancing *Le Spectre de la Rose*. The first
    performance of the ballet was by Diaghilev's company at
    Monte Carlo in April 1911, with Nijinsky and Karsavina in
    the leading roles (Mary Evans Picture Library)

23 Monte Carlo, battle of the flowers, 1928 (By courtesy of
    Société des Bains de Mer)

24 Baron de Kehrling at Monte Carlo (By courtesy of Société des
    Bains de Mer)

25 Tennis at Monte Carlo, 1928 (By courtesy of Société des Bains
    de Mer)

26 *Le tir aux pigeons* (By courtesy of Société des Bains de Mer)

27 Monte Carlo rally, 1928 (By courtesy of Société des Bains de
    Mer)

Between pages 146-7

28 Shopping aboard the Mistral train (By courtesy of French
    Railways)

29 Mistral restaurant (By courtesy of French Railways)

30 Bay of Garavan, Menton (By courtesy of municipality of Mention and R. Judlin)

31 Anglican church, Menton (By courtesy of municipality of Menton and A. Chenier, Menton)

32 Queen Victoria at Grasse, April 1891, with (*left to right*) Long, Francis Clarke and Alexander Rankin (Reproduced by gracious permission of Her Majesty The Queen)

33 Lady Patricia Ramsay unveiling the statue of Queen Victoria at Menton (By courtesy of municipality of Menton and A. Chenier)

34 Menton lemon festival (By courtesy of municipality of Menton)

35 Isola 2000 skiing resort. The brainchild of an Englishman, Peter Boumphrey (By courtesy of 'Isola 2000')

Acknowledgments

Of the many people who have helped me with my researches for this book I would like to thank particularly Ernest Hildesheimer, Director of Archives for the Alpes Maritimes *département*, who gave me much valuable advice; Francis Cammaerts for perusing and commenting on the section on the Second World War in addition to other help; Richard Bancroft and the staff of the British Library; the staff of the London Library (as always); and the staffs of the Westminster and Kensington and Chelsea public libraries. I am grateful to Olive Walker and Tegwen Tyler for secretarial help.

Others who were kind enough to talk to me at length, to write to me or to help me in other ways were:

In Beaulieu, J. Potfer; in Cannes, Rev. Walter Barnes, M. Delhomme, Alan Kimber, Louise Mennetier, Bill Morris and D. Revertégat; in Isola 2000, Peter Boumphrey; in Le Cannet, Dorothy Prejger; in Menton, Francis Palméro and Anton Vogt; in Monte Carlo, Albert de Portu, Marcel Gamba, Josiane Mérino and Laurent Savelli; in Nice, Andrée Antonietti, Michael Hankins, Marie-France Reymond and William S. Tilney;

In England, Ivy Allen, Vera Atkins, François Batisse, Charles Bovill, Christine Brinkley, Lady Egremont, Roderick Junor, Dorothy King, Patricia Lindsell, Madeleine Masson, Peter Mills, Cyril Mitchell, Ethel Mitchell, Bryony Orme, Marba Stevens, Hubert Snowdon, Pauline Stone and Ethel Taylor;

In Scotland, Diane Morgan;

In Ireland, Katherine Guinness.

If there were others who helped me and whose names I have omitted I ask for their forgiveness.

1 The Early Travellers

In June 1763 Tobias Smollett set off on a journey through France and Italy. He reached Nice in December. The accounts of his experiences in and around Nice, which he wrote in letter form and which were later published in his *Travels through France and Italy*, provide the first detailed account in English by a writer of distinction of the region now known as the French Riviera.

Smollett had four companions on his journey: his wife, his servant Alexander Tolloush, who had been with him for more than twelve years and who insisted on accompanying him, and two girls to whom Mrs Smollett seems to have acted as a kind of governess. The Smolletts' only daughter had died in April 1763, and Smollett hoped the journey and the company of the two girls would afford his wife some consolation. For his own part he travelled mainly for the reason which in the next century was to drive large numbers of British people to the Mediterranean in winter, the state of his health. 'I hoped', he wrote, 'the mildness of the climate would prove favourable to the weak state of my lungs.' He certainly suffered from asthma and coughing fits, and he probably had a mild form of tuberculosis.

The journey was an adventurous one. On the way south Smollett encountered a general named Paterson who was returning from Nice, where he had been commandant of the garrison in the service of the King of Sardinia. From him Smollett obtained a letter of recommendation to the acting

British Consul in Nice, but otherwise he does not seem to have planned his travel arrangements with much care. The degree of comfort which he and his party could demand was modest. As a writer Smollett was well rewarded financially by eighteenth-century standards. He was a qualified surgeon, and his wife, whom he met in Jamaica, and whom he married partly in order to be able to relinquish the gruesome occupation of surgeon's mate in a naval vessel, had some money of her own. But Smollett himself had inherited virtually nothing, and for this reason he and his family could not hope to travel in the manner of young noblemen making the grand tour in the company of tutors.

For the journey from Paris to Lyons Smollett had a choice of three methods of travel. One was the *diligence* or stage-coach, which covered the distance in five days, the stretch from Châlons to Lyons being traversed by boat. There were eight seats in the coach, and Smollett decided not to 'run the risk of being stifled in very indifferent company'. To hire a coach and four horses and make the journey in ten days, would, he considered, be too expensive, and he therefore settled for hiring two post-chaises from stage to stage with two horses in each. From Paris to Dijon alone there were no fewer than fifty-nine stages. As Smollett disliked French cooking and 'abominated' garlic, the family laid in a stock of tea, chocolate, cured larks' tongues and Bologna sausages in Paris. These they supplemented with roast chickens, bread, wine and fruit, which they bought on the way.

From Montpellier to Avignon they travelled in a berlin drawn by three mules, and the journey through the Esterel was equally slow. Smollett commented that the bandits who had formerly frequented this area had been exterminated, but later travellers were, justifiably, less sanguine on this subject. Even after they had reached Cannes, described by Smollett as 'a little fishing town, agreeably situate on the beach of the sea', the party faced the formidable obstacle of the River Var, which then marked the frontier between France and the Kingdom of Sardinia. Here six men known as guides, their clothes tucked up above their waists and long poles in their hands, took charge of the coach and 'by many windings guided it to the opposite shore'.

The physical difficulties of travel were among the main reasons why the French Riviera, as it was later called, was known to relatively few British people before the nineteenth century.

Rather more than twenty years after Smollett's visit Arthur Young complained of the inadequacy of transport facilities in southern France. 'Will it be believed', he asked, 'that from Marseilles with 100,000 souls, and Toulon with 30,000, lying in the great road to Antibes, Nice, and Italy, there is no diligence or regular *voiture*? To a person accustomed to the infinity of machines that fly about England, in all directions, this must appear hardly credible.' Young estimated that in the 1780s nearly sixteen days were needed for the journey from Calais to Nice.

Another traveller who reached Nice in the late 1780s, James Smith, the botanist, on his way from Fréjus encountered three men returning from Nice who informed him 'with that *friendly* eagerness with which the common herd of mankind, when lately escaped from danger, warn those who are just entering upon it, that the road was infested with banditti', and that they were sure to be robbed. The alarm was a false one, but shortly afterward Smith underwent an experience similar to Smollett's when crossing the River Var. After describing this he added laconically: 'If any person be lost, the guides are hanged without mercy.' Whether this served as a deterrent or not, it suggests that the risk of loss was far from negligible.

The approach to Nice from the west was relatively comfortable in comparison with the overland routes from Nice across the Maritime Alps, or along the coast beyond the frontier which now divides France from Italy. Smollett reported that there were only two ways of crossing the mountains from Nice to Turin. One was by mule, and the other was to be carried in a kind of sedan chair. Six porters were normally employed to carry the chairs. 'Of these six men,' Smollett wrote, 'two are between the poles carrying like common chairmen, and each of these is supported by the other two, one at each hand; but as those in the middle sustain the greatest burden, they are relieved by the others in a regular rotation. In descending the mountain they carry their poles on their shoulders, and in that case, four men are employed, one at each end.' For the continuation of his journey through Italy there was of course the alternative of sea transport. Smollett wrote that the 'most agreeable carriage' to take from Nice was a felucca, or open boat, rowed by ten or twelve men and large enough to carry a post-chaise on board. No doubt for reasons of economy he himself hired for the journey to Genoa what he described as a gondola.

The railway did not reach the French Riviera until about a hundred years after Smollett's visit, and during all that period the routes from Nice to the modern Italian frontier and beyond were liable to be hazardous. In 1821, when the Sardinian king and his court travelled to Nice for a winter visit, the state of the roads obliged them to remain so long that the citizens of Nice had time to devise and present a new gala corso. Some forty years later an Italian diplomat stated that the roads serving Nice were as bumpy as a bridal bed, and even the journey from Nice to Menton was often an easier one by sea than by road in the mid-nineteenth century.

' "How did you get over the precipices?" is generally the first question asked of any one who arrives at Mentone.' These were the opening words of a book Augustus Hare wrote about the five months he spent in Menton as late as the winter and spring of 1860–1. He himself had arrived in the care of a driver who had delighted in showing off his skills by keeping as close as possible to the edge of a precipice. He had then had to cross 'a broad, white, foaming torrent' by a narrow footbridge of broken planks while the horses and carriage splashed through the shallows higher upstream. Menton was in darkness, nobody seemed to be able to guide him, and when eventually he found the house he had rented on the side of a steep hill overgrown with olives, he had great difficulty in persuading the driver to continue up the hill as there seemed little likelihood of finding a turning-point for the coach.

A few years before Augustus Hare's arrival in Menton the Marchioness of Bute, while travelling from Nice to Turin, was stopped by bandits, who relieved her of her diamonds. They also took some opium, which had been prescribed for her. This made them so sleepy that they were soon captured. Some surprise was expressed when it was learnt that a member of the bandits belonged to Nice's nobility.

Most modern tourists feel, as tourists have felt for a century and a half, that the beauty of mountain scenery more than compensates for any inconveniences the mountains themselves may afford. But when Smollett was writing, mountains were not readily associated with aesthetic pleasure. Describing the journey he made to Nice in 1789, Arthur Young was still expressing an orthodox view when he complained of 'that poverty in the robe of nature which always offends the eye where olives and fruits form the principal clothing'. 'Every view', he wrote, 'is meagre, on comparison with the rich foliage of our northern forests. The only singular features are the orange and lemon trees.'

The physical difficulties the countryside presented and the standards of taste for judging its aesthetic attractions being what they were, it is not surprising that until about two hundred years ago only enterprising travellers, and determined seekers after health, came from Britain as visitors to the region now known as the French Riviera. Nor was the commercial development such as to attract business men in appreciable numbers. Of all the towns to be found today along the coast from St Raphael to Menton, only Nice was a commercial centre of any importance in the eighteenth century, and even Nice had only about 12,000 inhabitants when Smollett arrived there.

Cannes was still a fishing village when Lord Brougham first saw it in 1834. Antibes had some standing as a garrison town in the eighteenth century, but it seems to have had limited attractions. The English writer of a guide-book published as late as 1847, although admitting that Antibes was 'a flourishing little sea-port', advised travellers to stop outside its gates and send in for horses. 'They will thus save time, and their carriage will escape the risk of accidents, in being twice dragged through the most odious streets.' Monaco had an old-established harbour and fortress, but Monte Carlo did not exist even in name until the second half of the nineteenth century. Menton, until comparatively recently, was considered primarily as a source of lemons. Legend states that when Adam and Eve were expelled from Paradise Eve secreted a lemon in her bosom. After a long search for the nearest approach to an earthly paradise she and Adam found the site of Menton, where all the lemon trees now stem from the lemon brought by Eve. A British ambassador in the mid-nineteenth century commented on the predominance of lemons rather more prosaically. On learning that Cavour was considering the purchase of the Principality of Monaco, including its then dependent townships of Menton and Roquebrune, he wrote that four million francs seemed 'quite a lot for a couple of places that produce nothing but lemons'.

Towns in what is now regarded as the hinterland of the

Riviera, such as Grasse and Vence, were relatively of more commercial importance in the eighteenth century than they are today. The scent industry of Grasse, which had been established by Florentines in the sixteenth century, had a powerful corporation formed by the master perfumers, and Arthur Young estimated that the area around Grasse furnished the scent essence for half of Europe. But of all the towns in the modern Alpes Maritimes, only in Nice did the British consider it necessary to establish a consulate.

Nice, like Antibes, had been a Greek settlement, and it is recorded as an episcopal see as early as the fourth century. From the late fourteenth to the late eighteenth century it was at different times under the control of the counts of Savoy and Provence and occupied by French and Spanish armies. In 1775 it came under Sardinian control, but it was incorporated in the French Republic after conquest in 1792. It reverted to Sardinian rule in 1814, Talleyrand stating later that if he had known how beautiful the countryside was he would not have agreed to its cession. Only after a plebiscite held in 1860 did Nice revert to being a part of France. The plebiscite, which took place after provisional agreement on the transfer had been reached, produced the remarkable result of 25,773 votes in favour of the decision and 160 against.

The 1860 plebiscite was powerful evidence of the French sentiments of the great majority of the people of Nice, but the town to which Smollett came was generally regarded as being predominantly Italian in character, and it was as an Italian city that most English visitors described it for several decades after Smollett's visit. The Nice to which Smollett came could also fairly be described as something of a backwater. In the fifteenth century Nice had had a distinguished school of religious painting, but in the mid-eighteenth it had little claim to distinction.

Smollett brought with him to this somewhat provincially minded township a number of prejudices acquired both in his native Scotland and in the England to which he had come to make a living. He also brought those powers of observation which, with his lively imagination and his wonderful talent for writing English prose, combined to make him one of the greatest of all eighteenth-century novelists.

Smollett had already expressed forthright opinions on what he had seen in France in the letters he wrote on his way to Nice. The *noblesse* of Boulogne were, in his judgment, 'helpless in themselves, and useless to the community; without dignity, sense, or sentiment; helpless from pride, and ridiculous from vanity'. He reported that if an English Protestant, who had gone to France with his wife for the sake of his health, were to die there with household effects to the value of a thousand guineas, the King of France would seize the whole property, the man's wife would be left destitute, and his body would be denied Christian burial. He did however record with some satisfaction that Scotsmen, and Swiss too, were exempt from this treatment. The state of French agriculture was typified for Smollett by the sight of a peasant 'ploughing the ground with a jackass, a lean cow, and a he-goat, yoked together'. The personal habits of a high proportion of Frenchmen would, he declared, be 'detestable even in the capital of North Britain'.

By the time he reached Nice Smollett was prepared for a variety of disagreeable encounters, and the people of Nice for their part do not seem to have greeted him, or indeed other British visitors, with much enthusiasm. The acting British Consul was a former army lieutenant named John Buckland, who served as agent for an absentee consul. Buckland had been at his post for thirty-four years without once eating or drinking in the home of a citizen of Nice. In 1765, towards the end of his stay, Smollett noted that the only friendships he himself had made were with other visitors. He admitted that the King of Sardinia took every opportunity 'to distinguish the subjects of Great Britain with particular marks of respect', but added that 'our nation is looked upon with an evil eye by the people of Nice; and this arises partly from religious prejudices, and partly from envy, occasioned by a ridiculous notion of our superior wealth.'

Smollett and his family occupied the ground floor of a house which he rented for £20 a year. His main domestic difficulty was to find a 'tolerable' cook. Maids too were 'all slovenly, sloths and unconscionable cheats'. In general the people of Nice struck him as being lazy. Rather than work for a moderate profit they chose 'to starve at home, to lounge about the ramparts, bask themselves in the sun, or play at bowls in the streets from morning till night.' He was shocked to find no public or private libraries and no bookseller. 'It is very surprising to see a people established between two enlightened nations, so devoid of taste and literature.'

Yet in spite of these complaints, most of which were predictable, Smollett was entranced by much of what he saw and experienced. The house he rented was comfortable and commodious. It had two gardens with 'plenty of salad, and a great number of oranges and lemons'.

> When I stand upon the rampart and look round me [he wrote], I can scarcely help thinking myself enchanted. The small extent of country which I see is all cultivated like a garden. Indeed, the plain presents nothing but gardens full of green trees loaded with oranges, lemons, citrons, and bergamots, which make a delightful appearance... roses, carnations, rananculas, anemonies, and daffodils, blowing in full glory, with such beauty, vigour, and perfume, as no flower in England ever exhibited.

He found the markets well stocked and particularly liked the wild boars and hares. He delighted in fresh anchovies fried in oil and in the water-melons, and he considered the Nice wine, when mixed with water, made an 'agreeable beverage'. He even gave the people of Nice credit for being law-abiding and sober. Murder, robbery and drunkenness, he reported, were 'unknown' and the police 'very well regulated'. At times he contemplated the prospect of living permanently in the area, and he came to the conclusion that if he did so he would spend the months from June to October in or near Grasse and the rest of the year in Nice. Indeed after his return to England he applied for the post of consul in Nice, and it was a measure of his inability to appreciate the offence his writings could give that he was both surprised and disappointed when his application was refused.

The climate was perhaps the greatest attraction which Nice had to offer Smollett. It allowed him to indulge his taste for bathing in the sea as early as May, a proceeding which aroused a good deal of curiosity locally. Some Swiss officers were the first to imitate him – there was then a Swiss garrison in Nice – and after a time a number of the native Niçois, either because they believed what Smollett, as a doctor, told them of the benefits they would derive or because of the very novelty of the pastime, also began to bathe.

Every day until April 1765 Smollett kept a record of the climatic conditions, and the publication of this in his *Travels through France and Italy* aroused immediate interest. The book was widely read in England, and not surprisingly curiosity was caused by such matter-of-fact statements as that January 1764 'had much fine, clear weather with almond-trees in blossom' or 'from the 1st to the 25th February, fine weather, clear sky, mild and warm in the day, wind easterly, sharp and piercing in the evening. Almonds, peaches, and apricots in blossom.'

French reception of Smollett's book was less enthusiastic, and it was violently attacked by a number of reviewers. More than a hundred years later Emile Négrin's guide to Nice described Smollett as 'un écrivain anglais qui a publié sur Nice des lettres assez acerbes', but in time the part played by Smollett in arousing the interest of the outside world in Nice as a holiday resort was officially recognized, and a street was given his name, or at least an approximation to it. As Rev. Hugh Macmillan, one of the numerous Anglican clergymen to write about the French Riviera in the nineteenth century expressed it, the rue Smolet was 'incorrectly spelt, as we should have expected from a people given to orthographical mistakes'.

II

In the quarter of a century following Smollett's visit, Nice and its immediate surroundings became increasingly fashionable among the upper strata of English society. A number of families who decided to winter in the area were drawn by the new social prestige which the presence of royalty had conferred on it. Two of King George III's brothers came to what is today the French Riviera in the 1760s. Both suffered from the incompatibility of the Royal Marriage Act with their own personal inclinations.

One of the royal visitors was the Duke of Gloucester, who in 1773 contracted a secret marriage with Maria Waldegrave, who was illegitimate. When rumours of what had happened began to circulate the King ordered an enquiry into the validity of the marriage. By this time the priest who had officiated was dead and there were no other witnesses, but the Duke and his bride insisted that the ceremony had taken place. He was therefore banished from the King's presence and spent much of his time abroad. Not until 1780 was he restored to the King's favour, and he subsequently filled a number of worthy but undistinguished offices. His brother, the Duke of York, came to a less fortunate end, dying suddenly in Monaco in September 1767. In the words of Horace Walpole,

> the poor Duke of York has ended his silly, good humoured, troublesome career in a piteous manner .... Scampered away as fast as he could ride for a drive all round the south of France, intending to visit a lady at Genoa that he was in love with .... Grew so ill that his gentlemen carried him to Monaco, where he arrived on the third, and languished with great suffering until the seventeenth.

The Monaco to which the Duke of York came was then, as now, an independent principality ruled by the remarkably tenacious Grimaldi family, whose associations with Monaco date back to the eleventh century. Their independence was buttressed by skilful handling of powerful neighbouring powers, a general tendency to side with France and a long-established right to levy 2 per cent of the value of merchandise in ships passing within sight of Monaco fortress. Prince Honoré of Monaco received the Duke of York with much kindness, which was duly recognized by both King George III and the Duke of Gloucester. They sent him as a present six horses which had belonged to their dead brother and invited him to London, where he stayed for two months. It was an example of courtesy to a ruler of a small power which the British royal family in their dealings with Monaco in the next century regrettably failed to emulate.

Evidence of the changes which British visitors helped to bring about in Nice and its surroundings in the two decades after Smollett's departure is to be found in the writings of three visitors to Nice in the late 1780s. All three were Norfolk men or had close associations with the county, all were men of exceptional distinction, and all wrote accounts of their journeys through France.

One of the three was James Edward Smith, who had studied

medicine at Edinburgh University with the intention of becoming a physician, but whose life was transformed when the herbarium, library and manuscripts of the younger Linnaeus came up for sale. They were offered for a thousand guineas to Sir Joseph Banks, who refused, and Smith bought them instead. This began him on a career which was to lead to the publication of two major standard works on English botany and English flora, a knighthood and the presidency of the Linnaean Society, which he largely helped to found. When Smith made his purchase in 1783 he was only twenty-three years old. Three years later he set off on a journey through France, which eventually brought him to Nice. There he stayed at the Hôtel des Quatre Nations, which he described as 'a decent and reasonable inn', but he added that he was 'soon disgusted with the gross flattery paid here to strangers, and the English in particular'. He went on to state: 'The whole neighbourhood has the air of an English watering-place. The whole town is much enlivened by the concourse of strangers, who resort hither for the sake of the climate in the winter .... In the environs of Nice there are several very pleasant villas, mostly destined to accommodate strangers.' He added that an apothecary named Faroudi had found it 'very worth his while to acquire our language'.

Smith also noted that there were a number of English families who wintered near Hyères, 'most of them invalids'. He found little to write in favour of Hyères itself, whose houses were 'mean, dirty, and crowded', but the Iles d'Hyères interested him, as they were still uninhabited and abounded in wild boar. Like other visitors he was charmed by the approaches to Cannes, and the town itself he described as 'a little sea-port, whose houses are bathed by the waves of the Mediterranean'.

Smith was inclined to be a pithy commentator, leaving his readers in suspense with such statements as: 'We passed the country house of a Mr E--, who murdered his wife at Aix some time ago.' As a descriptive writer he can hardly be compared with another of the visitors who came to Nice in the 1780s, Arthur Young.

Young was an astonishingly prolific writer. At school, at King's Lynn, he began to write a history of England, and at the age of nineteen he had already published four novels and two political pamphlets. He needed to produce these, he declared, in order to be able to indulge his taste for 'great foppery in dress for the balls'.

His monumental creation, the *Annals of Agriculture*, ran to forty-six volumes, and these and his books of travels give him a claim, which is not easily contested, to have been England's greatest writer on agriculture. Among the contributors to the *Annals* was King George III, who wrote in his role of Farmer Robinson and who was said never to travel without one of Young's volumes.

Young made three journeys to France, in 1787, 1788 and 1789, on one of them riding throughout on horseback and, somewhat unusually, travelling without a servant. His accounts of his journeys were considered by the French economist Lavergne, nearly a century later, to be the best record available of social conditions in France on the eve of the revolution.

Young came to Nice in 1789. At Hyères he recorded that the landlord of the Hôtel de Necker 'worried' him with the list of people who spent the winter in or near the town, and he noted the considerable number of new houses built for letting. Between Hyères and Nice he was impressed mainly by the poverty of the countryside. He spent one night en route on a mattress spread on a stone floor, and after starving all day dined off 'stale eggs, bad bread, and worse wine'. The next day three sailors carried his bags to a village where, it was believed, mules could be hired. In fact there were no mules, and his baggage was loaded on a donkey while he himself set off for St Tropez on foot. St Tropez he described as 'prettily situated, and tolerably well-built, on the banks of a noble inlet of the sea'.

The journey through the Esterel was 'through the same bad country, mountain upon mountain, not one mile in twenty cultivated. The only relief is the gardens at Grasse, where very great exertions are made.' Wherever he went he asked for milk, but he was told that the cows were all in the higher mountains, and not even goat's or sheep's milk was to be had. Butter, he learnt, was a contraband commodity which came from Nice. Between Cannes and Antibes there were certain improvements, with nine miles 'chiefly cultivated'. But he added: 'The mountains rise so immediately, that, in a general idea, all is waste.' In Nice itself Young, like James Smith, was conscious of the number of houses being built for foreigners, and a foretaste of what was to follow was given him when the innkeepers complained that the revolution was likely to prevent the English from coming to Nice for the winter.

The third Englishman to leave an account of his journey to Nice in the 1780s was Dr Edward Rigby, a physician, who, like Young, was interested in agricultural experiments and who is reputed to have introduced the practice of vaccination into Norwich. He also brought the flying shuttle to the attention of Norwich manufacturers and became the city's mayor. He wrote his account of his travels in letters which his daughter, Lady Eastlake, later edited.

Rigby arrived in Paris with three English companions in July 1789. They set off almost immediately for the south, and like others before him Rigby was struck by the poverty of the towns and countryside near the Sardinian frontier. 'There was nothing', he wrote, 'in the appearance of Fréjus to give us comfort. It is an old town evidently in decay .... Our inn was moreover a nasty one.'

By contrast, when they reached Nice the four companions, who stayed in a hotel kept by an Englishman, had a dinner '*tout à l'Anglaise*, which we relished much – plain roast beef and boiled potatoes, with some special good draughts of porter'. In a footnote to the word 'porter' Lady Eastlake added: 'This was an excess of former times, for my father was a strict water-drinker in the latter part of his life.'

Lady Eastlake described her father as 'a Whig of the old school, ardent in all movements for reform and enlightenment', and he and his companions clearly felt much sympathy with the revolutionary forces. 'I left France with regret', Rigby wrote from Nice. 'The late political event has been brought about by the courage and perseverance of the middle ranks, who appear to be more enlightened than with us.' In support of this opinion he stated that the people of Nice did not seem so 'merry' as in France, but then he added, no doubt trying to be fair, 'or perhaps I only supposed'. The British consul came to question the four English travellers about conditions in Paris, and the impression to be gained from Rigby's account is that the consul was almost the first person he encountered who was not in favour of the revolution.

The fears expressed by the Nice innkeepers to Arthur Young about the absence of the British were duly justified when revolution was followed by war. In May 1800 a party from a British frigate briefly captured the fortress of Monaco, but they were later repulsed by French troops brought from La Turbie, leaving behind them a trail of spilt gunpowder which exploded. British troops occupied Nice as well as Monaco in the concluding stages of the war, but for most of the war years a British presence seems to have been little felt. An insight into how one event affected British visitors was nevertheless provided by an adventurous woman traveller. This was Elizabeth, youngest daughter of the 4th Earl of Berkeley, who ended her days as the Margravine of Ansbach, or Anspach, as it was then generally spelt. She too wrote a book largely about her experiences on the continent of Europe, and a remarkable book it was, for she was a remarkable woman.

At the age of sixteen she married a man who later became Lord Craven. She bore him seven children, after which she discovered that another woman was passing herself off as Lady Craven. This was the former associate of a man described as 'a gay colonel', who had run up a large bill at the Crown Inn at Reading. Being unable to pay the bill the colonel had left his companion at the inn in lieu of settlement. Craven had found her there, as Tom Jones might have done, and began living with her. The real Lady Craven had therefore set off on an extensive tour of Europe, where she conducted herself in a manner which Horace Walpole described as '*infinitamente* indiscreet', but, he added, 'she is very pretty, has parts, and is good-natured to the greatest degree, has not a grain of malice or mischief.'

Walpole printed some of her verses on his press at Strawberry Hill, and she also wrote plays for which she composed the music. When listing her admirers she included Walpole with Dr Johnson, David Garrick and Sir Joshua Reynolds, who 'did not conceal his high opinion of me'. Of herself she wrote. 'The clearness of my ideas produced delight in all who knew me', adding 'nothing could excite vanity in me', and 'I defy my bitterest enemy to say that I was ever found guilty of falsehood.'

In the course of her travels in the 1780s Lady Craven reached St Petersburg, Moscow and Constantinople, and more than once she passed through Nice. Arthur Young stated that he had been sent by her 'on a wild-goose chase to Hyères' and complained that she took too romantic a view of the scenery.

After being accepted as the 'adopted sister' of the Margrave of Ansbach – she was also the adopted sister of the King of Prussia, to whom the Margrave sold his whole principality in 1791 in order to concentrate on breeding horses – Lady Craven duly married the Margrave shortly after the former Margravine and Lord Craven died, but her travels continued, and she left in her memoirs an account of the alarm felt by the British when Napoleon landed on the Riviera at Golfe Juan after his unexpected return from Elba. There seems to have been a fairly undignified scramble on the part of 'all the English' to leave the country, but the Margravine herself behaved with characteristic resourcefulness. She bought a carriage, had her arms and supporters painted on it, and, deciding that 'the Austrian was the best protection', approached the Austrian consulate at Marseilles as the Countess of Sayn. In this way she reached Genoa in some degree of comfort.

Another woman of strong character who came to Nice after the revolution had broken out in France was the future hostess of Holland House, whose maiden name was Elizabeth Vassall. In 1791 she arrived from Lausanne with her first husband, Sir Geoffrey Webster, who was more than three times her age. Webster soon returned to England, leaving her, as she complained in one of her letters, 'at twenty-years-old in a foreign land without a relation or any real friend'. But it was not long before she was writing that she had spent some of the happiest hours of her life in Nice while behaving, as she put it, with discretion 'even to prudery'.

The prudery probably began to wear a little thin after the arrival in Nice of a colourful party with whom she consorted. This included the beautiful Duchess of Devonshire, who was temporarily out of favour with the Duke because she had just given birth in Aix-les-Bains to a child by another man. Accompanying the Duchess was her close friend Lady Elizabeth Foster, two of whose children by the Duke had been accepted into her household by the Duchess.

Once the fears caused by the Hundred Days, and the need for hurried departures were no longer felt, the British began to return to Nice, to Hyères and to the countryside around them. Within a few years of the coming of peace they were making their presence felt in increasing numbers, with increasing authority and, not infrequently, with increasing arrogance.

III

By the early 1820s about a hundred English families were coming
to Nice for the winter. The need for an Anglican church in Nice
was increasingly felt, and an application to the Sardinian
Government for permission to build one was favourably
received. The church was opened for divine service on Advent
Sunday, 1822, one of the first sermons being preached by Rev.
Lewis Way.

The subject he chose was the condition of what he described as
'a body of simple and primitive Christians called the Vaudois'
living near Turin. Way expressed the opinion that these people
might well have received the gospel directly from St Paul, which
they had preserved as 'the true religion'. 'It cannot be shown', he
went on, 'that they have at any time conformed to the ritual of
the Romish Communion, notwithstanding the horrible
persecutions to which they have been subjected.' He then quoted
Milton's sonnet about their ancestral saints being 'slain by the
bloody Piedmontese'.

For a first venture in Anglican worship in a strongly Roman
Catholic kingdom it was an uncompromising performance, but
it was evidently well received by the congregation. Way appealed
for funds to provide for 'the maintenance of a regular clergy'
among the Vaudois and raised the considerable sum of £150. So
encouraged was he by his efforts that he repeated his sermon a
few months later in Rome.

Way was a forceful and persuasive character and for a number
of years was active on behalf of the London Society for
Promoting Christianity amongst the Jews. In this connexion he
visited every synagogue and talked to nearly every Chief Rabbi
on a journey from Rotterdam to Moscow, and he was even
received by the Russian Emperor in St Petersburg. 'It is', he
wrote in an open letter to the Bishop of St David's, 'the duty of
our favoured land to revive its character as "Defender of the
Faith", even in foreign lands.'

His powers of persuasion were not limited to missionary
activities. In the winter of 1821–2 a severe frost occurred which

killed large numbers of orange trees in the Nice area. To help the men thrown out of work and their families Way persuaded a number of the British residents to provide relief work in the construction of a coastal road. The road duly became known as the Promenade des Anglais, later to be gradually widened and lengthened until it stretched over six miles with, eventually, almost the highest traffic density of any road in France. The town which Smollett described had narrow streets, more of its windows being fitted with paper than with glass. Half a century later, at the end of the Napoleonic wars, its population had roughly doubled, and by the 1820s it was beginning to be transformed.

The Riviera towns and villages on the French side of the River Var were slower to attract the British after the coming of peace, but a change occurred in the 1830s as a result of a chance encounter, which followed an outbreak of cholera in Provence.

Late in 1834 Henry, Lord Brougham set out on a journey through France which, he intended, would bring him to Nice. He told Lord Wellesley his reason for going was to 'recreate' his health 'ruined after thirty-four years of slavery'. Brougham was fifty-six at the time. He still had some thirty-four years of active life in front of him, but he could already look back on virtually all his great achievements in the causes with which his name is generally associated: the abolition of the slave trade, the promotion of primary and secondary education, the raising of funds for the creation of London University, the exposure of the brutality of flogging in the army, the defence of Queen Caroline, the liberalization of the Whig Party.

He was certainly tired. Six years earlier he had become Lord Chancellor, an appointment which damaged his political career but whose emoluments he found welcome, and this had added hugely to his already prodigious labours. In a memorandum written to the Cabinet at the end of April 1834, in which he referred to himself in the third person, he called attention to 'the labour which he undergoes and cannot escape, and which, since the 2nd of November last, with the interruption of a fortnight more painfully passed' – he was referring here to the death of his brother – 'must be continued for three months longer'. He described how he spent seven hours daily in court, was never in bed before two and in the last six months had written about seventy long judgments with his own hand which would fill two large printed volumes. 'He is far from desiring to boast of hard work,' he added, 'but he makes the statement as an irrefragable proof that he must have a singular taste to love such an existence.'

Another of the reasons for his proposed journey to Nice was the health of his daughter, who accompanied him. A friend of the family later declared that the daughter did not suffer from tuberculosis, but she had been sickly since childhood, and her father believed a mild climate would suit her.

Travelling in a berlin drawn by six horses, Brougham and his daughter reached the Sardinian frontier at the River Var, near where Nice airport is today, on 28 December 1834, but were told they could not continue. Cholera had broken out in Provence, and only those who had visas from their consuls certifying that they had undergone the necessary period of quarantine were allowed to continue.

Brougham was not accustomed to being thwarted, and he was a man of impressive presence. A political opponent could describe him as 'that gin-drinking, straddling, corduroy scoundrel' and even apply to him, with equal malevolence, the epithet 'American-minded', but Macaulay once stated that 'there is no other man whose entrance into any town would be so certain to be greeted with huzzaing.' He did not therefore take kindly to being stopped, and after finding that his acquaintance with the works of Dante was not sufficient to enable him to persuade the Italian-speaking frontier guards to let him pass, he summoned the nearest mayor, complaining later of the conduct of the 'beast-ridden and priest-ridden Government of Sardinia'.

After some discussion it was suggested that Brougham and his daughter might stay at an inn in Antibes, but this was full of soldiers and could not be considered. Finally they agreed to put up at the Hôtel Pinchinat on the Fréjus road from Cannes, where Chateaubriand, Victor Hugo and Pope Pius VII had all stayed.

Once he had recovered from his irritation Brougham was so enchanted by Cannes that within about a week of his arrival he had bought a plot of land. Here a villa, on which building began without delay, was completed four years later in the Italianate style. In honour of his daughter Brougham named it the Villa Eléonore. A garden was also laid out, Brougham, in the words of a modern historian of the Côte d'Azur, Jean-Jacques Antier, 'stupéfiant les Cannois en créant d'immenses pelouses toujours vertes'.

Cannes soon became Brougham's second home. He regularly spent his winters there, writing books on politics, philosophy and history, and analysing the habits of bees. He found that in Cannes there were only three days out of 111 on which he could not carry out certain experiments with light which interested him, whereas at Brougham Hall in Westmorland at the same time of year, there were only about three days out of 111 on which he could.

In Paris, on his way out in the autumn or on his return journey to England in the spring, he would sometimes attend meetings of the Academy or the Academy of Science. He spoke French well, and he became increasingly attached to the country in which he had chosen to spend his winters. In 1848 he even applied to the Minister of Justice to become a French citizen and abandoned the project only when he learnt that if he did so he would have to renounce his British citizenship. One reason for the warmth of Brougham's feelings towards France was his personal friendship with King Louis-Philippe. The King would ask guidance on such questions as whether William IV attended cabinet meetings and in turn would entertain Brougham with imitations of Danton or Robespierre.

On the strength of this friendship Brougham, deciding shortly after he had bought his property that Cannes needed a harbour, made a personal application to the King for the necessary funds. A sum of 995,000 francs was promptly made available, although the annual budget of the municipality of Cannes at that time was 29,600 francs, and work on the harbour began in 1838. At the opening ceremony the Prefect of Var told the people of Cannes, quite correctly, that a new existence was beginning for them, and a poem composed for the occasion extolled both the King and 'Brougham l'orateur'.

Another important service which Brougham rendered to the economy of Cannes was to persuade a number of his friends to imitate his example by buying land and building villas. Several of them were men of both distinction and wealth – like Brougham they could afford to have turf brought by boat from England which they renewed every year – and a highly cultivated society of regular winter residents soon developed.

Brougham died in Cannes on 8 May 1868. In the period of less than thirty-four years since his first arrival the population of Cannes had increased from some 3,000 to about 10,000. The former wholly French fishing village had in the winter eighteen practising doctors, only ten of whom were French. Five were British, one was an American, one was a German, and one was a Pole.

Ten years after his death the municipality of Cannes erected a statue in recognition of Brougham's services to the town. A poem written by Stéphen Liégeard, who is believed to have been the man who first used the name 'Côte d'Azur', is inscribed on it. This contains the lines:

> 'Il enlace au palmier la rose d'Angleterre
>   et semble dire: c'est ici.'

Not far away from Brougham's statue in Cannes is one to King Edward VII, the near juxtaposition of the two symbolizing the extraordinary part which the British have played in Cannes's history.

IV

Among Lord Brougham's near neighbours when he was living at the Villa Eléonore was a man whose influence in changing the social structure and the physical appearance of Cannes in the mid-nineteenth century was probably second only to his own. This was Thomas Robinson Woolfield, who after travelling for seven years in Spain, Greece and the Near East, first saw Cannes on a May evening in 1838. A few years later he too decided to make Cannes his winter home.

Woolfield was much concerned with what he considered the lack of provision for the spiritual welfare of the English in Cannes. He had arrived there with a letter of recommendation from an evangelically minded publicist named James Evans, who had founded a periodical called *The Record* in England and, rather more ambitiously, another one called *Espérance* in France. Evans's letter was addressed to an Evangelist from Geneva named

Charbonnet, who, after appearing fourteen times before tribunals in France, was ordered to leave the country within twenty-four hours. This edict caused some uneasiness among the French in Cannes, as it was felt it might deter foreigners from settling there.

To make good the deficiencies Woolfield in 1847 fitted out a chapel in his own grounds for the holding of Protestant services. A French Protestant minister was asked to officiate, but the first time he tried to do so, as soon as the numbers of the hymns had been given out, the local commissioner of police appeared with two gendarmes and dissolved what was held to constitute an unlawful assembly. Woolfield appealed against the decision successfully, and for a few years, on Sundays, French Protestant services were held in the chapel in the morning and English services in Woolfield's drawing-room in the afternoon.

As the number of English visitors grew, more and more of them, Woolfield recorded, said to him, 'if only there was an English church at Cannes we should not run away from you'. In 1855 therefore he asked the French Government for permission to build an Anglican church at his own expense and on his own property. In preparing his petition he had the help of Prosper Mérimée, to whose anglophilia and passionate anti-clericalism, which was directed exclusively against the Roman Catholic church, the enterprise had a natural appeal. The petition was successful, and in 1855 on Queen Victoria's birthday the corner-stone of Christ Church, Cannes, was laid.

Gardens and fruit-growing were among Woolfield's many interests, and the sweet potato and the gooseberry, the eucalyptus and the acacia may all reasonably be regarded as among his gifts to the Riviera. Acacia seeds were, it is true, first planted in Cannes by a Frenchman named Tripet, but the first acacia trees to flourish grew on each side of an avenue in Woolfield's grounds, and they were regarded as such curiosities that visitors came from Nice and Menton to see them.

The introduction of croquet to Cannes was attributed by Woolfield to Prince Leopold, Duke of Albany, the son of Queen Victoria, but Woolfield himself did much to promote interest in the game and also in another pastime which succeeded croquet. 'In 1874', Woolfield wrote, 'the passion for crôquet had so subsided that part of the grounds was made into a good lawn-tennis court – the first and only one that existed for some time in Cannes. So enthusiastic were the players that they commenced at 8 a.m.' On certain days, he recorded, the public were invited to watch the matches.

'Mr and Mrs Woolfield', a visitor to Cannes in the 1850s wrote, 'are universally liked and respected; their hospitality and kindness and helpfulness are unbounded.' The Woolfields and a number of the friends whom they entertained at their Villa Victoria formed one element of Cannes society, an element which was distinguished by acts of philanthropy, acquisition of property and the establishment of British institutions, and which became most conspicuous when events connected with these institutions called for public worship, public mourning or public celebration. One such event was the death of the Prince Consort in 1861. Lord Brougham and Lord Dalhousie both delivered orations, a third speaker being another well-known figure in Cannes society, Admiral Pakenham, who had at one time found himself in trouble in Tuscany for distributing copies of the Bible and had had to leave hurriedly. The admiral told his audience that the Prince Consort had been no seaman.

A less stable element, that of short-term visitors or tourists, had by the middle of the century become so numerous that the publication of guide-books for their benefit was already a profitable enterprise. One such was the *Hand-Book for Travellers in France* published by John Murray in 1847, which was based on journeys undertaken at different times between 1830 and 1841.

This contains a section on the route from Avignon to Nice. Provence is described as 'too arid to deserve general praise', but an exception is made of 'that favoured terrace at the foot of the Alps along the shore of the Mediterranean'. Fréjus is dismissed as a 'small and dirty town'; the Var is 'an unmanageable stream, rolling enormous masses of shingle down into the sea'; but Cannes is once again singled out for favourable comment. A 'neat and cheerful small town, finely situated at the bottom of a beautiful bay', it is described as the port of Grasse.

The hand-book also gives guidance on personal conduct and warnings of dangers to be avoided. These are presented in such a way as to suggest that many English travellers may have been in need of them. In general, readers are informed, 'the inns of France are very inferior to those of Germany and Switzerland, in

the want of general comfort, and above all of cleanliness.'
Warnings are issued against those inns which 'make some
pretension to study English tastes and habits ... and, being
frequented by Englishmen, are very exorbitant in their charges.'
Women readers, in particular, are told that they should be
'cautious of presenting themselves at a French *table-d'hôte*, except
in first-rate hotels, where English guests form a considerable part
of the company'. Otherwise they may be in danger of mingling
with '"commis voyageurs", Anglice bagmen, but of a stamp
very inferior to those of the same class in England.... A more
selfish, depraved and vulgar, if not brutal set, does not exist.' The
authority of Lady Chatterton is cited for an incident she
witnessed at a *table-d'hôte*, when a Frenchman, after helping
himself to all the best parts of a roast fowl, turned to the lady
sitting beside him and said 'with a most insinuating smile
"Madame ne mange pas de volaille."'

Having offered his readers guidance on how to avoid
disagreeable encounters, the compiler of the hand-book
continues: 'It may not be amiss here to consider the causes which
render the English so unpopular on the continent; as to the fact
of their being so, it is to be feared there can be no doubt.' The
first of the causes he lists is the number of 'ill-conditioned
persons', who, 'not being in condition to face the world at home,
scatter themselves over foreign lands.' The 'morose sullenness'
sometimes attributed to the English is thought to derive from
nothing more reprehensible than ignorance of foreign
languages, but the compiler concedes that Englishmen
sometimes caused offence in Roman Catholic churches by
'talking loud, laughing and stamping their feet while the service
is going on'. He adds: 'Our countrymen have a reputation for
pugnacity in France: let them therefore be especially cautious
not to make use of their fists.'

Whether it was by building Protestant churches or stamping
their feet in Roman Catholic ones, by cultivating gardens or
using their fists, the British had by the mid-nineteenth century
made a considerable impact on the territory now known as the
French Riviera. In 1851 Alexandre Dumas stated that the
inhabitants of Nice regarded all visitors as Englishmen, to whom
sunshine was something known only by hearsay, who knew
oranges and pineapples only by name, and whose experience of

ripe fruits was confined to cooked apples. A Nice innkeeper told him that some new arrivals were certainly English, adding that he was not sure whether they were French or German.

The period immediately preceding the coming of the railway was, like the years shortly before 1789, rich in memoirs by visitors from Britain who for one reason or another chose to spend a winter on the Riviera. Two writers in particular have, between them, left colourful accounts of how life was lived by the British in Cannes, in Nice and in Menton between 1856 and 1861. One of these was Margaret Maria Brewster, the other was Augustus Hare.

V

Margaret Maria Brewster was the daughter of the eminent Scottish physicist, Sir David Brewster, whose fame derived principally from his discoveries in connexion with the polarization of light. He invented the kaleidoscope, was one of the founders of the British Association for the Advancement of Science, and was Vice-Chancellor of Edinburgh University when Lord Brougham was installed as Chancellor. His daughter became a prolific writer of books under her later married name of Gordon.

Margaret Brewster's *Letters from Cannes and Nice* were offered to the public as a supplement to the existing and, in her opinion, inadequate guide-books and were based on the experiences of herself and her father during the winter of 1856–7.

She came to Cannes, as her letters show, with prejudices as uncompromising as any of Smollett's. After travelling from Paris with a Roman Catholic priest she wrote from Fontainebleau: 'I should like to know how much he believes of that strange delusion he professes to look on as religion.' The sight of Sisters of Charity working in a hospital caused her to ask: 'What is their *motive?*' In an attempt to compare the relative merits of Britain and France she stated: 'Nothing strikes a greater difference between the two countries, than the different aspect of their soldiers; ours, noble-looking, well appointed, well buckled in – models of order and discipline; and the French so completely the reverse – untidy, shabby, and slouching.'

None of this prevented her from being immediately enchanted by Cannes. In the first letter she wrote after her arrival there in November 1856 she described the mountains as 'really very grand'. Four days later she declared 'Cannes is the loveliest of all lovely places'. The air, she decided, was so like champagne that it would be advisable 'to leave off all the stimulants that in England are considered necessary'.

Among the British, as her letters show, Cannes was becoming more popular every year, with 'a great demand for houses, many having been taken by telegraph, and the prices of course rising in consequence'. French owners were said to be reluctant to sell their houses because they could make more money by letting them, yet there was already an impressive list of British proprietors, a high proportion of whom had titles.

Facilities for the British to worship as they chose were now 'of a most liberal disposition', and through the good offices of Admiral Pakenham, who had built a chapel, Scottish Free Church services were held twice a week. Margaret Brewster was severely shocked to find a company of strolling players on an open-air stage in Cannes performing 'the most blasphemous and revolting representation of the crucifixion', but to offset this there were quiet social evenings held every Monday by the Duchess of Gordon, when a passage from the Scriptures was read and then discussed 'in a candid and friendly manner', after which there were prayers and sacred music.

Shops too were growing in number, a new 'fashionable' draper and a confectioner having recently opened up premises, but in addition to the 'house shops' there were still a number of 'out-of-door shops', which were presumably booths. The Croisette, later to become Cannes' equivalent of the Promenade des Anglais in Nice, was still a 'long narrow promontory which shoots out towards the islands, about two miles to the east of Cannes'.

Such complaints as Margaret Brewster had to make about Cannes were concerned mainly with domestic service, mosquitoes and heat. 'The native female servants', she wrote, 'are stupid, idle, ignorant and far from cleanly.' Their wages were thought to be excessively high, particularly as they expected free wine and coffee, and they had an aggravating habit of shaking hands with their employers. One lady, Margaret

Brewster wrote, 'was so fatigued by the constant shakings of hands expected by her cook and other domestics, that she was obliged to put a stop to it.'

Mosquitoes, which for many years to come were to be one of the most disagreeable features of the Riviera in the summer, were found to be troublesome in November, and in the same month Margaret Brewster wrote of 'the extreme caution which is necessary to protect the head from the sun' and recommended the use of white umbrellas, wide hats lined with white paper and thick veils. She did, it is true, come from the east of Scotland, but even so it is curious to find her writing from Nice on 7 February that 'the sun is of Bengal heat'. By 20 April the weather in Cannes was such that she considered it 'almost dangerous to move out' between 8 a.m. and 6 p.m.

In January 1857 the Brewsters went to Nice for about two months before returning to Cannes. Margaret Brewster was moved on her arrival in Nice to comment: 'It cannot fail that one's first thought and words, in crossing the frontier, ever are, "God bless Italy".' In Nice, she wrote, 'there is no mistaking that one is out of France', but she observed an increase of French influence in the 'new town', where signs in Italian had French translations underneath.

Nice in the mid-1850s was a town of some 35,000 inhabitants, well served by hotels and with a number of English shops. The way of life of the British winter visitors tended to be more formal and sophisticated than it was in Cannes. Importance was attached to relations with the Sardinian court, and Sir David Brewster was selected with Lord Stopford and the British consul to present an address to the King from the British residents. The King, Margaret Brewster commented, 'ought to have been very much flattered, for certainly one Scotch philosopher is worth a good many kings'.

The manners of the people of Nice impressed her, and she even wrote in one of her letters that 'you mannerless, soul-less Northlanders will not appreciate the improved manners which visitors to these regions take away with them.' Cimiez, the ancient Roman settlement on a hill, which was then outside Nice, was 'the pleasantest spot in the whole world – out of Scotland'. Here invalids who could not sleep in the urban surroundings of Nice were sent. Yet, for all the amenities which Nice offered,

Margaret Brewster was happy to return to 'dear little Cannes'. Her feelings towards the two towns were well summed up in a letter shortly before her return to England.

> There is so little temptation [she wrote] for 'gay' invalids to settle at Cannes, that they and their friends generally go on to Nice. At Cannes there is no Corso, no gay Boulevards du Midi – no fashionable lounges, no balls, no theatres, no fine shops, no billiard-tables, no smartly-dressed ladies and gentlemen – all of which being found at Nice, render it as suitable for those pining for rest and freedom from excitement as Piccadilly or the Rue Rivoli. At Cannes we have country quiet, less exciting air, tranquil companionship, and many religious privileges.

In contrast with the simple piety which Margaret Brewster shared with her father, who had himself been licensed as a preacher by the Edinburgh presbytery, Augustus Hare, the author of an informative work on Menton, was somewhat heterodox in outlook.

Hare's upbringing, like that of so many upper-class Englishmen in the first half of the nineteenth century, was such that he could hardly fail to become at least mildly eccentric. At the age of one he had been adopted by his godmother, his parents renouncing all claims on him. In completing the transaction his mother, who already had a large number of children, wrote to the godmother: 'If anyone else would like one, would you kindly remember that we have others?' The infant Augustus was conveyed to his new home in a green carpet-bag with two nightshirts and a red coral necklace. As a child he dined every day off roast mutton and rice pudding except when he went to stay with his Aunt Esther, who, believing herself to be a deeply religious woman, forced him to eat sauerkraut because the smell of it made him sick.

Augustus Hare was expected to take holy orders, but this he declined to do. Instead, with the encouragement of John Murray, he devoted much of his energies to writing guide-books, for which he had early shown an exceptional flair. In time he acquired some reputation as a man of letters, and Somerset Maugham, who, as a rising young author, was entertained by him, wrote a memorable description of him in his later years. By that time Hare made a practice of reading aloud to his household from the Book of Common Prayer but omitting all passages glorifying God. In explanation he told Maugham: 'God is certainly a gentleman, and no gentleman cares to be praised to his face.' He also reproached Maugham for vulgarity when, after returning from a walk and feeling thirsty, Maugham said he would like a drink. 'A gentleman', Hare explained, 'does not ask for a *drink*, he asks for *something to drink*.' He had the delicacy to convey this guidance in writing.

Hare spent a number of years travelling in Italy and France with his godmother, to whom he was devoted and of whom he later wrote a biography entitled *Memorials of a Quiet Life*, which ran to eighteen editions. He spent the months from November 1860 to May 1861 in Menton, and this provided him with the material for his book, *A Winter at Mentone*. When he came to Menton Hare was aged twenty-six. He was also a virgin, a condition in which, if we are to believe his statement to Somerset Maugham, he was to continue for another nine years.

The countryside around Menton Hare described as still largely unexplored by English travellers, but in the town itself there was already a lending library with Tauchnitz editions of books and English newspapers. There was also an Anglican church, though the sound of the sea from both sides sometimes distracted the congregation. The surrounding hills were said to be 'sprinkled' with English villas, an English grocer named Willoughby also acted as a house agent, Mr Edward Binyon gave drawing lessons and sometimes consented to go sketching with his pupils, and there was no shortage of music teachers. This combination of anglicization and gentility had served to inflate prices, and Hare noted that his first meal in the Pension Anglaise in Menton cost four times as much as he had paid for a first-class dinner in Rome. Eventually he found a restaurant, 'from whence we get a dinner which is very tolerable, after it has been stripped of its oil and garlic, and has had some extra cooking bestowed upon it by our own servants.'

Like other British travellers to this frontier region Hare was manifestly Italian rather than French in his political and personal sympathies, and for the principality of Monaco he seems to have had no sympathy at all. The period from 1815 to 1848, when

Menton had formed part of the principality, had, he wrote, been one of permanent police surveillance, high taxes and monopolies enjoyed by the Prince. After thirty-three years of 'patient submission' the people of Monaco and Roquebrune had 'unfurled the flag of Italy' and 'brought about a revolution, which, though perhaps the smallest, was certainly the most unanimous, which has ever occurred in history'. The plebiscite of 1860, whereby Menton and Roquebrune had voted for incorporation in France by 833 votes to 54, Hare found less easy to explain. Some people told him that it was largely due to the influence of the French wife of the Syndic. Others simply said 'Ah! Signor ... Citroni!' By this they meant that union with France had been expected to improve the prospects for the lemon market.

An English friend of Hare's on one occasion listened to a number of local inhabitants in a café complaining of the miseries they suffered as a result of the change to French rule. They had been speaking French, but on a signal from the landlord warning them that a stranger was present, they switched at once to the local patois. Hare drew the obvious conclusion about the degree of political liberty allowed, but he considered economic standards in Menton to be reasonably high. 'Compared with the state of the English poor', he wrote, 'there is very little real poverty here; almost every one has some little olive ground or orange garden which they can call their own.'

Local customs and English tastes occasionally clashed. At carnival time for instance, it was the accepted practice for local people, wearing masks, to enter any house where they could gain admittance and to stay as long as they chose, whether they were acquainted with the occupants or not. One English lady, who answered the doorbell herself, was startled by the appearance of four masks with long birds' beaks which concealed the faces of her dressmaker and three of the dressmaker's young friends. After that, Hare wrote, British residents felt 'obliged to keep their doors constantly locked'. François the donkeyman also occasioned some comment when he rode through the streets dressed as an English lady.

On another occasion an Englishwoman tried the experiment of reading the Bible to her cook, who roared with laughter at what she considered the ludicrous passages in this unfamiliar work. The British for their part gained some reputation among the people of Menton for intrepidity, if not foolhardiness, by their readiness to scale the surrounding hills. Hare, who was an accomplished water-colour painter, was a member of a mountain sketching party of both sexes when an angry mule was successfully kept at bay by having white umbrellas poked into its face. At a ball that evening he learnt that until that day 'no lady at Mentone had ever been up the Gran' Mondo, and very few gentlemen.'

The last picture Hare gave of relations between visitors and local inhabitants is as attractive as any in his book. He had already commented on the politeness shown to strangers and had described how a servant of one of his neighbours, on learning that the English were accustomed to seeing grass in their own country, had gone up to a village in the mountains and brought back two pots of grass as a present. Now, when the time came for his own departure, he told of the 'showers of bouquets from every one, rich and poor' and of the repeated statements that on every fête day prayers would be offered for the return of Hare and his party to Menton.

Hare did return, but when he wrote of Menton again in a guide-book published nearly forty years after his first visit it was to give a drier and more matter-of-fact description of a much more sophisticated community.

2 The Railway Link

I

When Augustus Hare was in Menton during the winter of 1860–1 the route followed by most British travellers who came there was from Toulon, either by diligence in twenty hours or by vetturino with two overnight stops, one of which was usually in Cannes. Some travellers preferred to take the steamer from Marseilles to Nice. The south-eastern terminus of the railway was then Toulon, which, according to Hare, could be reached from England in thirty-two hours.

Before the Second Empire, railway development in France was relatively slow in comparison with what was happening in England, in Belgium and in parts of Germany. As in England the earliest French railway lines tended to be built in mining areas. A decree of Louis XVIII's in 1823 permitted mine-owners to construct a line near St Etienne, and nine years later in the same area fare-paying passengers were conveyed for the first time. In the south the first trains did reach Sète from Montpellier in 1839, but economic difficulties in the early 1840s and revolution in 1848 damaged confidence and made capital for investment in railways harder to obtain.

The long-term benefits of these delays were considerable. As an English historian of French railways, Lord Monkswell, pointed out in a work published in 1911, 'it was possible to take stock of the situation and profit by the mistakes of other countries before railway building in France was seriously taken in hand'. As a result the French railway system was, he considered, among the best planned in the world. In the late 1850s agreements were reached between the French Government and the principal railway companies for the construction of the new lines deemed to be needed, subsidies in some instances being provided by the State. One of the companies was the Paris-Lyon-Méditerranée, whose lines brought the first trains to Cannes in 1863.

To the villa-owning British residents the prospect of trains coming into Cannes and disturbing their peace was most unwelcome, and Thomas Robinson Woolfield even learnt that the railway company planned to drive their line through his grounds. Richard Cobden happened to be in Cannes when news of this threat was received. He agreed to join Woolfield, Brougham and Lady Oxford in a protest to the French Government, and Prosper Mérimée again helped. The protest succeeded, the route was changed, and the railway company later complained to Woolfield that his efforts had cost the company £20,000.

To a number of the native citizens of Cannes the railway was the beginning of a new age of prosperity, and the changes it brought about were both sudden and spectacular. A dozen years before the coming of the railway Cannes had had only two hotels. In 1864 a winter visitor to Cannes wrote that a new hotel, the Grand, had been built which was almost as big as the Louvre and was always full. Woolfield himself wrote that after the coming of the railway 'the old hotels were enlarged, new ones built with marvellous rapidity'. There was a good deal of speculation and 'a rapid increase in the price of land, altogether unparalleled in its wildness for a time'. Several years later, he recorded that at the height of the season many hotels had to turn visitors away. One year after the coming of the railway the Cercle Nautique founded by the Duke of Vallambrosa, which was to become Cannes' most exclusive club, was opened, and three years later horse racing was brought to Cannes, the first meeting being held in April 1867.

In Nice too the impact of the railway was immediate, the Emperor Alexander II of Russia and his Empress arriving a week after the line was opened in 1864. By that time the long association of Russians with Nice had already begun on a small scale. Margaret Brewster had seen the Empress sweep by in a barouche. She had also reported the presence of the Grand Duchess Helena with 'rheumatic gout, like the whole winter population of Nice'. The Grand Duchess was, she wrote, 'up to all the politics of Europe', but added that unfortunately this was not considered a lady-like accomplishment. But it was only after the coming of the railway that the regular migration began of Russian families, some of whom came to Nice for the winter and some of whom, having sampled the delights of southern Europe, decided to take up more or less permanent residence there. One of the families to remain was that of Marie Bashkirtseff, three generations travelling together, with a Polish doctor in tow for whose services the family somehow omitted to pay.

With the steady increase of visitors Nice carnival became more and more elaborate and costly. In 1873 Marie Bashkirtseff wrote that 'almost the whole of society' was to be seen in carriages with white dominoes and iron masks, one carriage bearing 'society ladies dressed in violets of Nice'. Parts of the town were even illuminated by electric light, a new experiment which drew large crowds in the evening. Three years later the practice of throwing flowers was separated from the main carnival and the first battle of flowers took place on the Promenade des Anglais. Twenty years after that Augustus Hare was to quote with approval a comment that 'Nice is a home for the millionaire and the working-man. The intermediate class is not wanted. Visitors are expected to have money, and if they have to look at pounds, shillings and pence, had much better remain at home.'

Menton in the early 1860s was already acquiring a reputation as a health resort and as such benefited hugely once it was known that invalids could make the journey by rail instead of having to undergo the kind of experience Augustus Hare had had on his arrival. James Henry Bennet, an English doctor who did more than any other man to publicize Menton abroad, made a detailed study of how invalids from England could make their way to Menton by rail.

'Railways', he wrote in the 1875 edition of his book, *Winter and Spring on the Shores of the Mediterranean*, 'have all but annihilated space, and the facilities they afford to rapid travelling are so great that a traveller may leave the London Bridge station at 7.40 on Monday morning, by mail train for Paris, and be at Nice or

Mentone for supper the following day.'

This he described as a 'cannon-ball style of travelling', for which invalids were liable to pay a severe penalty, 'not least from contrast of climate'. Instead he recommended a night spent in Dover or Folkestone followed by a week or ten days in Paris. Travellers taking the morning express from Paris at 11 a.m. were advised to leave it at Lyons at 10.15 p.m., to have a good night's rest, and then take the omnibus train to Valence or Avignon at the convenient hour of 10.30 a.m. After spending another night, preferably at Valence, before the journey to Marseilles was resumed, Bennet's travelling invalids were recommended to have a final break of two days at Toulon. The French railway companies, he admitted, did not allow travellers to break their journey in this way on through tickets, but, he added comfortingly, 'Mr Cook has acquired the concession'. Bennet also recommended certain French carriages which had '*coupé lits*'. These, he explained, were 'carriages without divisions, so that an invalid can lie at full length throughout the journey. There are three seats in these carriages, and the charge is for four.'

Bennet appreciated, better perhaps than anyone else, the changes the coming of the railway had brought to Menton. The first edition of his book had been published in 1861. At that time Menton, he wrote, was 'a quiet little Italian town on the sunny shore of the Riviera, with two or three small hotels, principally used by passing travellers, and half a dozen recently erected villas.' Fourteen years later it had become 'a well-known and frequented winter resort, with thirty hotels, four times that number of villas, and a mixed foreign population of above sixteen hundred.'

What the railway had begun would, he felt sure, be continued. 'I believe the time is fast approaching', he wrote, 'when tens of thousands from the north of Europe will adopt the habits of the swallow' and transform all the towns and villages on the Riviera into 'sunny winter resorts'. The Riviera was, he observed, 'the first point of the Mediterranean shore where birds of passage from the north make a halt for the winter.'

The economic benefits which the railway brought to Cannes, Nice and Menton, substantial though they were, were neither so immediate nor so indisputable as those it brought to the principality of Monaco. In the 1850s Prince Charles III of Monaco had become increasingly concerned with the difficulties of raising enough money to support both his administration and his family, difficulties which seemed likely to be increased by the cession of Menton and the consequent loss of revenue from the lemon trade. The treaty he signed with the French Government in February 1861 did provide for a payment of four million francs as compensation for the loss of Menton and Roquebrune, but this was a once-for-all settlement and regular revenue was needed. That it came was a direct consequence of the provisions of the treaty. By its terms the French Government undertook to provide a carriage-road along the coast from Nice to Monaco as soon as possible, and the Prince for his part agreed to let the projected railway line from Nice to Genoa pass through his territory. It was to become, almost literally, his lifeline.

For some years before the treaty was signed the Prince had considered a casino as a possible source of revenue, and reports had reached him of the successful operation of one in Baden-Baden. Public gaming-tables had been prohibited in France in the reign of Louis-Philippe, and they had not been legalized subsequently, but the ban did not of course extend to Monaco. In April 1856, therefore, two men named Léon Langlois and Albert Audet were granted a thirty-five-year monopoly for the operation of a casino in Monaco. In return they were to pay a quarter of their profits to the principality with a guaranteed minimum amount. They also undertook to provide facilities for sea-bathing, build a hotel and organize services by both steamer and horse omnibus between Nice and Monaco.

The experiment was a disaster. No new transport services were organized, such visitors as did come from Nice having the choice between a four-hour coach journey on hilly and sometimes dangerous roads and a trip in a sailing-boat, which, when the sea was rough, remained, probably rightly, in harbour. During one week in March 1857 only one visitor seems to have visited the Monaco casino – he won two francs – and after about a year Langlois and Audet had given up their concession.

The concessionaires who immediately followed them were not much more successful, and the early croupiers seldom had to exert themselves. They would spend much of the day sitting on a terrace, one of their number being deputed to watch the approaches to the casino through a telescope. Only when he spotted a vehicle thought likely to contain a gambler would his colleagues take their places round the gaming-table.

The last of the unsuccessful concessionaires, Lefebvre and Co., did build two hotels. They also got a price for their concession from François Blanc, who had already operated a casino in Bad Homburg, where he had been rescued from financial disaster by the Rothschild family. The story has often been told of how on 31 March 1863 François Blanc went to Monaco, stated his terms for buying the casino concession, said he would return for his answer at 3.30 p.m., as he intended catching the 4 o'clock steamer to Nice, kept to his schedule, and bought the concession for 1,700,000 francs. The story may well be true.

The company which operated the casino under the direction of François Blanc was called the Société des Bains de Mer et du Cercle des Etrangers. The casino was a new one built on a hill which in the early 1860s was still covered with lemon and olive trees. In honour of the Prince the township which sprang up on the hill was officially named Monte Carlo on 1 June 1866. The building of an opera house followed, and on 25 January 1879 it was formally opened with Sarah Bernhardt reciting a prologue.

François Blanc was to succeed where the other concessionaires had failed, his success being interrupted only briefly by the Franco-Prussian war of 1870, when the casino was closed for nearly three months. The explanation of Blanc's success is to be found in the railway line. When he bought his concession the railway had already reached Cannes, and he knew it was to continue. The stretch of line between Nice and Menton, which passes through Monaco, was in fact opened to the public on 19 October 1868. The following February the Prince announced that rates and taxes in the principality had been abolished.

The story of success continued. In 1868 there were two hotels in the principality; thirty years later there were forty-eight. In 1878 there were three jewellers; twenty years later there were fifteen. Three years after the coming of the railway visitors to the principality numbered 140,000, and more attractions and entertainments were offered for their enjoyment. Making the reservation that it was 'lamentable to think that so much loveliness should originate in such a source', Dr Bennet had to admit that under Blanc's auspices Monaco had become 'a fairy-land'.

The band [he wrote] plays twice a day, from half-past two to four, and from half-past eight to ten. It is composed of seventy-four thoroughly good musicians, selected from Germany and Italy, and discourses really 'sweet music' in a noble music-hall or ball-room. On a fine sunny winter's day it is a most charming excursion to drive over to Monaco, to lunch at the luxurious Hôtel de Paris, or *al fresco* in pic-nic style on the road; to saunter over the gardens, to listen for an hour to the fairy-like music, and then to return leisurely home, before sunset chills the air.

In the years immediately following the coming of the railway to Monaco a new kind of sovereign state was in effect coming into being, a state based on the profits derived from allowing visitors to gamble. In time citizenship of that state was to become one of the most sought after of any in the world; to millions who never saw the inside of either, the terms 'Monte Carlo' and 'casino' were to become almost synonymous; and control of the casino became such a rich prize that until the principality finally took charge itself ownership was the privilege of men of almost inconceivable wealth such as Sir Basil Zaharoff and Aristotle Onassis. A new tradition of opera and ballet was also established, one which enabled Diaghilev in Monte Carlo to surround himself with, and dominate, a number of the greatest artists of his time.

The Blanc family, understandably, were to take their own share of the spoils, which included palatial houses and fast racehorses. One of François Blanc's daughters married a Radziwill, another married a Bonaparte. A granddaughter married Prince George of Greece. There was indeed much truth in the saying that *rouge gagne quelquefois, noir gagne souvent, mais Blanc gagne toujours.*

II

Before 1860 British subjects were not allowed to enter France without passports, and they were liable to be subjected to a variety of inconveniences imposed by regulations. Smollett, for instance, had had all his books impounded on his arrival and sent to Amiens for examination by the *chambre syndicale*. The British ambassador interceded to have the books released.

In the 1840s British passports had to be signed by the French Minister of the Interior before their holders could use them for travel within France or for leaving French territory. Visitors arriving for the first time had their passports removed at their point of entry and sent to Paris for scrutiny. They were then issued with temporary travel documents.

Heavy tolls too were imposed on travellers who used their own transport. Any foreigner entering France in a carriage not of French make had to pay a substantial deposit, one quarter of which was recoverable if the traveller left France within three years. Payment of the deposit could be avoided only if a respected French householder guaranteed that the carriage would be taken out of France within six days. The conditions on many of the roads being what they were, such a guarantee must at times have been a risky undertaking.

With the unprecedented mobility which the railway age brought there was a growing body of opinion which considered passports and regulations restricting travel to be anachronisms. Nor did they seem consistent with the Emperor Napoleon's policies of liberalization and of strengthening ties with Britain. On 18 December 1860 therefore it was decreed that British subjects need no longer carry passports when entering France or travelling within the country. *The Times* compared this victory for enlightenment with the capture of Pekin and wrote: 'Six months hence both nations will be wondering how an institution so preposterously mischievous could ever have been maintained.' Nearly a hundred years later Ernest Bevin, when British Foreign Secretary, was to say that his ambition, which was never of course fulfilled, was to be able to go down to Victoria station and buy a ticket to anywhere he chose.

With the advent of fast trains and the removal of official restrictions the British first-class traveller to the Riviera in the late 1860s and early 1870s lacked only one provision for the full enjoyment of his journey. This was comfortable overnight accommodation on the trains themselves.

In the development of the sleeping-car Europe lagged behind the United States, as the Belgian Georges Nagelmackers discovered, and it was a study of American innovations which led Nagelmackers to found the Compagnie Internationale de Wagons-Lits in Belgium in 1872. This was five years after the incorporation of Pullman's Palace Car Company in Chicago. Once agreement had been reached with Pullman's for the elimination of any possible rivalry, the Wagons-Lits company had a virtual monopoly over the routes on which it operated, and its sleeping-cars eventually became one of the most readily recognized symbols of European luxury travel.

The train known as the Calais-Nice-Rome Express, equipped with sleeping-cars, came into operation on 8 December 1883, about six months after the inauguration of the Orient Express. There was no difficulty during the season in filling the trains as far as the French Riviera, but the Italian section of the line was not so much used, and after six years the train was turned round at the frontier at Ventimiglia. It then became known as the Calais-Mediterranean Express.

The Calais-Mediterranean Express was planned as a service for the British. For a number of years it did not stop at the Gare de Lyon, and some trains even by-passed Paris. By 1897 the train was running three times weekly, and in that year the Compagnie Internationale de Wagons-Lits decided to open a hotel in Monte Carlo, to be known as the Riviera Palace and described by the company as 'the most luxurious hotel in the world'. To indicate that no trouble or expense was to be spared the company even brought its manager from the Gezireh Palace Hotel in Egypt to take charge.

How best to enjoy the luxury of the trains to the Riviera exercised the minds of a number of writers. In *Monte Carlo and How to Do It* published in 1891 W.F. Goldberg and G. Chaplin Piesse advised travellers to take the *train de luxe* rather than the *train rapide* as it offered 'incalculable advantages in the matter of comfort'. These included 'food and drink of the best', facilities for sending telegrams and messages, 'comfortable lavatories, card-rooms and smoking rooms', as well as an arrangement whereby there were 'at separate ends of the car, sleeping-rooms for ladies and gentlemen respectively'. The authors did not expect many travellers to choose the night train from London, which left at 8.15 p.m. and had one through carriage to Ventimiglia, observing that it was 'usually the way of the travelling Englishman to anchor for a day or two at Paris'.

In 1904 Arnold Bennett wrote that 'at the present moment probably the dearest bed of its size in the world is that to be obtained on the Calais-Mediterranean Express, which leaves Calais at 1.05 every afternoon and gets to Monte Carlo at 9.39 the next morning.' The bed cost more than £4 on top of the first-class fare, there was no 'drawing-room car', and what today would be called the sleeper was not as large as a whole first-class compartment on the trains between Manchester and Liverpool. The artistic taste shown in the decorations, with table-lamps fashioned in the curves of *art nouveau*, was, he added, deplorable.

Having made these rather limited reservations, he went on:

> However, it is the train of trains, outside the Siberian express, and the Chicago and Empire City Vestibule Flyer, Limited, and if decorations, silver, rare woods, plush, silk, satin, springs, cut-flowers, and white-gloved attendants will make a crack train, the International Sleeping Car Company has made one.

Travellers, Bennett wrote, entered the train with awe, knowing that by doing so they were enrolled for ever among the elite. The Riviera being, in his opinion, a winter playground for rich idlers, hypochondriacs and invalids, and for those who preyed on them, the train itself was 'a final instance of the specialization of transit to suit the needs of the aforesaid plutocrats and adventurers'.

The plutocrats, if not the adventurers, used the train for transporting not only themselves and their families but their servants and huge quantities of baggage too, and in time separate coaches were needed to convey these appendages. Nor did such complex train-loads come only from England. There was a very long-distance train known as the St Petersburg-Vienna-Nice-Cannes Express, in which some Russian travellers expected their servants to sleep outside the doors of their sleeping-cars. Other Russian travellers demanded even more. The Grand Duke Michael, for instance, was convinced that it would be bad for his heart to travel in a train at more than thirty miles an hour, and to meet his wishes the timetables of a number of European lines had to be rearranged.

There were also direct trains or carriages to the Riviera from

Berlin, Rome, Hamburg and Amsterdam, and after reaching the
Riviera visitors found local trains to cater for their pleasure and
convenience. In his guide-book entitled *The Rivieras*, Augustus
Hare wrote: 'Immediately opposite the main station at Hyères is
that of a delightful miniature railway, which, since 1894, has
opened out some of the greatest beauties of the Provençal coast,
without in the least interfering with the scenery.' Charles Graves,
one of the most entertaining writers on Riviera life, has
described how visitors to Cannes made use of the morning trains
to Monte Carlo to

> send a valet and lady's maid to the Hôtel de Paris with the
> gowns and dress clothes necessary for gala occasions. The
> distinguished visitors themselves followed on the afternoon
> train, then spent perhaps two hours dressing themselves
> before dining at the Hôtel de Paris as a prelude to going to
> the casino.

It was as a romantic in his attitude to luxury that Arnold Bennett
viewed the trains which bore his fellow-countrymen south to the
Mediterranean. H.G. Wells once wrote to him: 'You are always
taking surface values that I reject. Hotels are not luxurious, *trains-
de-luxe* are full of coal grit, *chefs* and pianists are not marvellous
persons.' Bennett thought differently, and the train of which he
was the first to write with such feeling later acquired fame and
distinction of a kind conferred on no other train in European
history, not even the Orient Express. This was after it had come
to be known as the Blue Train.

III

Sleeping-cars coloured blue and gold and built by a Leeds firm
first appeared as part of the Calais-Mediterranean Express on 9
December 1922. The name 'Blue Train' seems to have been
established by popular consent, for it was not shown on the
carriages themselves before 1949, when the form of nomenclature
chosen was 'train bleu'.

The earlier carriages were designed for fourteen passengers,
but in January 1929 a new *de luxe* carriage was brought into

service which accommodated only ten. This choice of comfort in preference to productivity was celebrated by a luncheon given in the Hôtel Ruhl in Nice. One of the *de luxe* carriages was later fitted with a special bath compartment for the exclusive use of the Duke of Windsor. It was blown up by the French resistance movement in the Second World War. Special dinner services were also a feature of the Blue Train, with white plates having the initials 'WL' traced in gold leaf. Fresh flowers were placed on every table.

In his book *The Big Spenders* published in New York in 1966 Lucius Beebe stated that some thirty or forty years earlier there had been a limited number of places in which a woman had had to be seen in order to acquire 'cosmopolitan status'. They included the Ritz and Colony restaurants in New York and the Everglades Club in Palm Beach, the Ritz in Paris, Claridge's in London and the Hôtel du Cap d'Antibes. The list was completed by the liners *Berengaria* and *Aquitania* (in May and June) and the Blue Train. One of the most prodigal of all the great spenders was James Gordon Bennett the younger, proprietor of the *New York Herald*, who was also one of the first Americans to make a major impact on the social life of the French Riviera, and a whirlwind impact it was. Bennett once gave his sleeping-car conductor on the Calais-Mediterranean Express a tip of 20,000 francs. His valet, having established what was thought to constitute a handsome tip, retrieved all but 1,000 francs of this, whereupon Bennett flew into one of his celebrated rages and restored to the conductor the remaining 19,000. The conductor shortly afterwards opened a restaurant in Boulogne. Henry Clews, the American sculptor, who was also a rich man, was also concerned in a curious incident involving the Blue Train. This arose from the tendency of his wife's white peacocks to stray on to the railway line and bring the Blue Train to a standstill. It happened so frequently that the Société Nationale des Chemins-de-Fer felt obliged to make a formal demand that the peacocks should not be allowed on the line.

As the fame of the Blue Train spread internationally it acquired in effect a personality of its own, and to travel on it, especially at the height of the season, became a privilege. In the *Menton and Monte Carlo News*, a weekly paper produced in the English language for Riviera visitors and residents, there appeared on 19 December 1925 the statement: 'The great and beautiful Blue Train arrived, fully conscious of its superiority.' Charles Graves described the Blue Train as 'that dowager duchess of crack expresses'. Arnold Bennett, after stating that the supreme rivalries in the business of organizing pleasure lay between certain towns on the Mediterranean shore, added: 'You continue to go south if and when you can obtain seats in the packed Blue Train.'

In January 1928, when the King and Queen of Afghanistan paid the first official visit by a reigning sovereign and his consort to Nice for many years, they were accorded full military honours before boarding the Blue Train. When Charles Chaplin arrived at Nice railway station in April 1931 to stay with Frank Jay Gould, the virtual founder of the modern Juan-les-Pins, he had a tumultuous reception. When two of the more successful casino concessionaires of the 1920s, François André, who had once worked for an undertaker, and Eugène Cornuché, brought sixteen of the brightest and prettiest girls from Maxim's in Paris to Cannes, where they were expected to pose as heiresses, the girls were all guaranteed first-class return tickets on the Blue Train. They did not all need them. One married a French duke, and others married successful industrialists.

More than one writer of distinction has described the journey by sleeper to the French Riviera, none perhaps more enchantingly than Katherine Mansfield in a passage in her journal written in April 1920. Dawn came up as the train neared Avignon, and an orchard in the first rays of sunlight shone with gold fruit. Then she heard an Englishman say to his wife: 'Bang on the door when you're ready, old girl.' They shared the last of their Dundee cake, the wife 'cutting it so tenderly that it almost seemed an act of cannibalism', and agreed they would never travel abroad without Dundee cake in future.

In Agatha Christie's *The Mystery of the Blue Train*, first published in 1928, it is the train which brings the principal characters together. One of them, Ruth Kettering, travels with her maid, she and the maid each having a single compartment with a communicating door between. The passenger list also, of course, includes Hercule Poirot, and it is through a detailed study of the timetable of the Blue Train, described as 'the millionaire's train', and of the lay-out of its compartments that Poirot is able to solve the mystery. E. Phillips Oppenheim used the arrival of the Blue Train at Monte Carlo – 'the Blue Train, still to the casual traveller the portent of romance' – for the opening of both the first and the last chapter of *The Colossus of Arcadia*, which was published in 1938. P.G. Wodehouse, with his unique gift for making time and mankind stand still, included in *Pearls, Girls and Monty Bodkin*, published in 1972, a confidence trickster known to his intimates as Soapy, who declares the Blue Train to be 'loaded to the roof with rich suckers just longing for a chance of parting with their money.' In what must surely be considered the greatest novel in the English language in which the scene is set largely on the French Riviera, F. Scott Fitzgerald's *Tender is the Night*, the action opens at an isolated railway station a mile from the sea. The year is 1925, and the time is summer. Outside Cannes station 'a dozen cabbies slept in their hacks.'

The quality of the Blue Train and the route it followed might reasonably have been expected to give rise to lyrical verse. Marie Bashkirtseff, for example, was so thrilled to be returning to Nice from Paris by train that she sang Niçois songs all the way from Antibes. But in fact the quantity of memorable verse inspired by the Blue Train has been slender. One writer who did use it as a theme for a poem was a being who could probably have lived and thought as she did only in the 1920s and 1930s, the period of the Blue Train's greatest fame. This was Nancy Cunard, who was almost certainly the original of both Lucy Tantamount in Aldous Huxley's *Point Counter Point* and Iris Storm in Michael Arlen's *The Green Hat*, both of them haunting figures. Nancy Cunard delighted in trains, and in a poem on a train journey entitled *Southward* she described the white highroads of Provence and the pictures in the compartment of Riviera holiday scenes. Sadly it is not very distinguished verse.

The most complex artistic creation inspired by the Blue Train was certainly the ballet entitled *Le Train bleu*, which was produced under Diaghilev's direction at the Théâtre des Champs-Elysées in Paris on 20 June 1924. The talents contributing to the production were formidable. Jean Cocteau provided the scenario, Darius Milhaud the music, Bronislava Nijinska the choreography, Coco Chanel the bathing costumes, and Pablo Picasso the curtain. But the figure on whom the attention of the audience was mainly riveted was the nineteen-year-old Patrick Healey-Kay, who had joined Diaghilev's company some three years earlier, using the unconvincing name of Patrikeef, but who by 1924 was already known as Anton Dolin.

Cocteau had seen Dolin performing the most complicated acrobatics in a theatre corridor, and this had given him the idea of a ballet revolving round the athletic hero of a seaside resort. Diaghilev instructed Milhaud to compose for a 'ballet musical comedy'. The subjects of the ballet were golf and tennis, gigolos and the Riviera. By his performance Dolin was acclaimed as a star of exceptional quality. Soon afterwards he left the company.

The young dancer from Sussex had been a puzzle to Diaghilev, who could not understand why he chose to spend his spare time in Monte Carlo playing tennis or having picnics rather than improving his mind by listening to the conversation of Picasso and Stravinsky. After Dolin left the company *Le Train bleu* does not seem to have been performed again.

IV

On 3 December 1921 the *Menton and Monte Carlo News* listed some of the changes which the visitor who had not been to the Riviera since before the 1914–18 war would most immediately notice. One was 'the absence of the Boche', a change which, though expected, was, the writer added, 'none the less pleasant for that'. Another was the 'great numbers of motor char-a-bancs starting out every afternoon from all the different Riviera towns.' Two years later the same paper described some of the different motor-cars by which visitors reached the Riviera; the Fiats, the Citroëns and the Talbots. Soon afterwards attention was drawn to a service provided for those returning from the Riviera, who could now book seats in 'luxurious half-open and half-shut cars'.

Such means of transport were at first mere supplements to the railways, as were the ocean-going liners which called with increasing frequency at the Mediterranean ports or the cruise-ships in which visitors to the Riviera were encouraged to return home in leisurely manner by way of Palma, Algiers and Lisbon. A direct challenge to railway supremacy was, however, thrown down by Woolf Barnato, whom W.O. Bentley considered the greatest British racing driver of his day, when at a party in

Cannes he made a bet that his motor-car would beat the Blue Train in a race back to London. He won his bet, driving straight through to Calais and arriving at his flat in London four hours before the boat train reached Victoria station.

When Woolf Barnato achieved this feat, to drive to and from the Riviera by car was no novelty. Frank Harris saw a motor-car for the first time in his life in Monte Carlo in the winter of 1895–6. It was a 7-horse power Georges Richard. He claimed, truthfully or otherwise, to have bought the car for about £600, driven it for a month around the Riviera and then returned home in it, taking seven days to reach Paris and another three to reach Calais. He certainly wrote about his experiences, 'the chief being the divine beauty of the Riviera, and the new power given to one by the motor-car.' But where Barnato had led, others began to follow. In an evocative novel about the lives of expatriates on the Riviera in the inter-war years entitled *A Door Ajar* Peter de Polnay wrote that 'doing Paris–Cannes in record time was a matter of prestige'. Woolf Barnato having taken fourteen hours, others could admit to taking fifteen, but 'not an hour more'.

In spite of these changes and innovations it was not until the mid-1930s that new measures were introduced to increase passenger traffic on the railways. In December 1936 it was announced that eleven trains would run daily from Paris to Nice and that for the next four months on certain specified days passengers would be allowed to travel at half fare. Even these concessions were made, not so much through fear of competition from other forms of transport, as in extension of a campaign which, since the depths of the economic recession of the early 1930s, the French tourist industry had conducted with an altogether new brand of professionalism. But, significantly, it was only a month after the concessions were announced that the French Air Ministry gave its consent to the building of an airport at Nice.

The French Air Ministry's decision came too late to deprive the railways of the supremacy they had enjoyed throughout the inter-war years. But war had the effect of greatly increasing the efficiency of aircraft as well as disrupting and damaging a large part of the French railway system.

In June 1948 British European Airways inaugurated a new

regular passenger service from London to Nice via Paris, and at that moment it might have been thought that in the business of transporting British visitors to the Riviera the railways would be entering on a period of decline. In fact the reconstruction of the railway system was one of the great industrial successes of France in the early post-war years. As Louis Armand, Director-General of the SNCF, expressed it, a peak period in the history of the railways in France was reached just when the country needed to give proof of its post-war revival. Some of the best of the new French trains linked Paris with the Mediterranean, one in particular, the Mistral, enjoying some of the distinction which Arnold Bennett had observed in the Calais-Mediterranean Express.

The Mistral, leaving the Gare de Lyon in Paris at 1.30 p.m. every day for the Riviera, offered the traveller a choice of four restaurant cars, in which cheeses, liqueur bottles and napkins were displayed as objects of art. The upholstery in the main carriages ranged from dove grey to olive green to crushed strawberry. A shop was provided as well as secretarial and hairdressing services. Yet for all the sense of well-being, of repletion, of privilege, afforded by the Mistral there was something missing which generations of passengers in the sleeping-cars had come to expect. Even at the height of summer, by the time the Mistral reached St Raphael darkness had fallen. To northern Europeans, particularly to those who, as had once been the fashion, travelled to the Riviera in the winter, one of the incomparable attractions of the Blue Train, and of its predecessors, was the contrast between departure from London on a cold grey day and waking the next morning to the sight of mimosa and orange trees, of the red rocks of the Esterel on one side of the line and the blue waters of the Mediterranean on the other.

People have come to the Riviera on foot, on horseback, by mule and in a variety of horse-drawn carriages. They have come by steamer and under sail, in liners and in private yachts. They have driven their own cars, thumbed lifts and arrived in motor-coachloads. They have flown in private aircraft and on scheduled airlines. They have landed as invading armies from vessels of war and been dropped clandestinely at night by parachute. But of all the means of transport it was the railway link which principally enabled the British, and to a lesser extent other foreigners, to establish on the French Riviera in the latter half of the last century and the first third of the present one, a way of life which was in some respects a unique experiment in colonization.

3 Before 1914:
Establishing a Colony

I

James Henry Bennet went to Menton in the autumn of 1859 in order, as he put it, 'to die in a quiet corner'. He had contracted tuberculosis, but to his surprise his condition soon improved, and attributing this to the effects of winter sunshine he decided the next year to go further south to Italy. Unfortunately, as he recorded, 'the unhygienic state of the large towns of that classical land undid the good previously obtained', and the following year he made Menton his permanent winter home. Before long he had established a regular rhythm, which consisted of practising as a doctor in Menton in the winter, taking a holiday in April and May, when he studied Mediterranean climate and vegetation, and resuming his medical practice in England in the summer.

As Smollett, also a doctor and also a sufferer from tuberculosis, had done a century earlier, Bennet kept careful meteorological records, and on the strength of these he dismissed as delusions the descriptions he had found in travel books of the Riviera as a land of perpetual spring or eternal summer. But he did state positively:

The fifteen years' experience I have had of pulmonary consumption in the south of Europe has led me to the conviction that there is a greater probability of the disease being arrested, of life being prolonged, and even of a cure being eventually effected if the patient can winter in the south than if he remains all winter in the north of Europe.

As living witnesses to the truth of this claim, he was, he stated, surrounded in Menton by 'a phalanx of cured and arrested consumption cases'.

In an age when tuberculosis was a scourge with which millions were familiar, but which few cared to mention, otherwise than by some euphemism such as 'a fell disease', statements of this kind brought new hope and comfort to people who lived in Britain and could afford to winter in the south of France. Bennet found that sufferers from other afflictions, bronchitis and asthma in particular, also benefited from the Menton winter, as did those who, 'without having any particular ailment', were 'weak, ailing, dyspeptic or below par'. Those who sought cures in Menton should, he emphasized, be prepared to come, not for one winter only, but repeatedly. 'The most satisfactory cases of arrested and of cured phthisis that I have seen', he wrote, 'have been among those who have had the power and the will to return again and again.'

Such assurances, coming from a qualified physician, not surprisingly drew people to Menton in the winter in increasing numbers, as Bennet noted with satisfaction. When he first arrived, there were few foreigners. For a time virtually all the visitors were either English or French. But the publication of a German translation of his book *Winter and Spring on the Shores of the Mediterranean* in 1863 brought a sudden influx of Germans, and after an edition had appeared in New York in 1870 he recorded: 'Our American cousins are finding their way to Menton in increasing numbers.'

Bennet did not claim that the climate alone would cure sufferers from tuberculosis. He did find statistical evidence that pulmonary tuberculosis was comparatively rare among the native inhabitants of Menton, being the cause of only one death in fifty-five, as compared with one in five in London and Paris and one in six in Geneva. Yet in Marseilles, which also had a southern climate but whose sanitary conditions were, in Bennet's judgment, even worse than those of Naples, the disease caused one death in four.

The full benefit of the Menton winter was to be had, Bennet believed, only by adherence to a regime which he defined with some precision. Fresh air was an important requirement both indoors and out. Old people were encouraged to go out 'on foot, in Bath or donkey-chairs, or in carriages', and the Swiss and the Germans were found to derive less benefit from the climate than other visitors because of their unwillingness to open their windows.Thick winter clothing was recommended, Bennet himself wearing a woollen Inverness cape whenever he went out. At night mosquito nets were required.

Bennet advised invalids not to remain in Menton in the summer, though he did call attention to an attempt being made by a Dr Farina to establish a nearby mountain station for summer visitors, for he considered 70 degrees Fahrenheit the highest temperature to which those suffering from tuberculosis should be subjected. 'The last ten days of October', he wrote, 'is quite early enough for arrival', and a suitable time for departure was the first week in May.

Bennet's regime served in effect as a blueprint for a way of life which the British, more determinedly than other visitors, established in Menton and maintained long after Bennet had ceased to practise. As a result Menton developed to a considerable extent into a kind of winter sanatorium for the British, giving rise to the well-known saying that Cannes was for living, Monte Carlo for gambling and Menton for dying. The authors of *Monte Carlo and How to Do It*, published in 1891, described Menton's residents and visitors as 'being of a bronchial nature, suggestive of Bournemouth, apt to cough and spit in a manner that does not act as a gin-and-bitters to your next meal.' 'We will', they wrote, 'have but a brief stay at Mentone.'

One of the many Englishmen who came to Menton in the last century in an advanced state of tuberculosis was Aubrey Beardsley, who arrived in November 1897. A month later he wrote in a letter: 'Every one in Menton is on a bicycle and bursting with health. I believe I am the only invalid in the place.' He was of course wrong, as he had begun to suspect when he wrote shortly afterwards: 'There is a horrid pseudo-Christmas gaiety spread over this our French town.' After a time he became acquainted with a number of other English invalids, including an Egyptologist named Joseph Tylor, 'who looks like a corpse, has looked like one for fourteen years, who is much worse than I am, and yet lives and does things.' Beardsley was not to live and do things. Within five months of coming to Menton he died, his extraordinary graphic talent extinguished before he was twenty-six.

There were other towns on the Riviera which also attracted invalids from Britain. Hyères had long done so. Beaulieu was increasingly recognized as having one of the mildest winter climates on the coast; the name 'Bournemouth of the Riviera' was sometimes applied to St Raphael; and in his book entitled *The Riviera*, published in 1885, Rev. Hugh Macmillan wrote: 'Antibes is a favourite residence with foreigners, and its numerous attractions are being more appreciated every year. It is more restful for the invalid than either Cannes or Nice, while the picturesque scenery in the neighbourhood is more accessible.'

No matter whether they treated the Riviera towns primarily as sanatoria or as convalescent centres, the British increasingly expected to be cared for by people of their own nationality. By 1890 not only were there five English doctors practising in Cannes, as well as a Scottish woman doctor, Miss Agnes McLaren, but the Holland Institution for English Trained Nurses was turning out a supply of other acceptable medical attendants. But for all the professional care provided, the toll of death among British residents and visitors was high. In the 1880s it was decided that no new interments were to take place in the Protestant churchyard in Nice, and a newer English cemetery a mile west of Nice's outer suburbs was already described as 'fast filling up, alas!'

II

One of the main reasons why in the nineteenth century the British on the Riviera were regarded as different beings from the local inhabitants, and regarded themselves as such, was that the form of the Christian faith most of them professed was not the one most prevalent in France and Italy. They were too generally convinced of the demonstrable superiority of their own brand. In this they did not necessarily differ from adherents of other Christian sects, but in propagating their faith many of them displayed the self-confidence which underlay so much of British conduct on the Riviera in the nineteenth century.

In *The Bible in Spain* George Borrow gave an account of an interview he had had with Menizabel, the Spanish Prime Minister. 'Ever since I have held the reigns of government', Menizabel, who was a Jew, said, 'I have been pestered in this manner, by English calling themselves Evangelical Christians. What strange infatuation is this which drives you over lands with Bibles in your hands?' In the 1850s some French authorities felt a similar concern. A Miss Marsh, author of a book called *Memorials of Hedley Vicars*, returning one day from Nice to Cannes, distributed a number of tracts and prayers which had been translated into French, and for some time afterwards British travellers, when crossing the frontier at the River Var, were subjected to a close examination of their luggage. Margaret Brewster does not seem to have suffered any official obstruction, but when she visited a girls' school in Nice, and presented one of the pupils with a copy of the *Sinner's Friend* translated into *patois*, the schoolmistress gave her 'a very sharp suspicious look'. In time, as Thomas Robinson Woolfield discovered, French officials, although they may have shared some of the Spanish Prime Minister's bewilderment, became reluctant to interfere with British missionary activity, and the British duly took advantage of the licence granted. In particular they engaged on an almost prodigal programme of church construction.

By 1890, when its total population was only about 19,000, Cannes had four English churches and one Scottish Presbyterian church. Holy Trinity, the one Anglican Church which has survived, although on a different site, was opened for divine worship on 19 December 1874 in the presence of the Mayor of Cannes. Among the earliest contributors to church funds were representatives of the banking families of Baring, Hambro and Hoare, the Duke of Bedford, the Marquis of Exeter, the Earl of Jersey and Mrs Brown of Rhode Island.

The first Anglican church in Menton was opened for worship in 1863 on the east side of the town. This was inconvenient to some of the winter residents, and within ten years another, and larger, Anglican church was opened on the west side.

In one Riviera town after another English churches sprang up, and where church buildings were lacking other provision was made. In 1890 there was a resident English chaplain in St

Raphael, although its population was only 3,500, and in Cannes weekly Bible classes were conducted for the benefit of English domestic servants. Even the Île St Honorat near Cannes, where a monastery had been founded in the fourth century and where St Patrick studied, became for a time the property of an Anglican clergyman named Sims, but he was later persuaded to dispose of it to the Bishop of Fréjus, who wanted to re-establish a religious community there.

The Anglican Church also provided an appreciable proportion of the English visitors who came to the Riviera in the winter for health or recreation. One of them, the Rev. John Wickes Tomlinson, wrote an enormously long 'historic and descriptive poem' entitled *The Rock of Nice*, which he dedicated to 'the Travellers, of my own country, who have visited or resided at Nice'. This appeared in 1855, and although for the most part it reveals little other than that talent for versification, combined with aridity, which was a common product of a certain kind of classical education ('Discern I Caesar, truncheoning a key?'), there are occasional unintended glimpses into the future:

And oh! can Nizza combat hordes *alone?* –
She smokes! First altar of barbarian ire.

In 1847 the Rev. Henry Francis Lyte had been advised by his doctor to journey south and, while in Avignon, had written part of his hymn *Abide With Me*. He spent his last days in the Hôtel de Grande-Bretagne in Nice at a time when Nice had no resident English clergyman. The Archdeacon of Chichester and Rector of Lavington in Sussex happened to be in Nice at the time, having also gone there on medical advice. He was described as being of ardent evangelical zeal and had been Gladstone's immediate predecessor as President of the Oxford Union. His name was Henry Edward Manning, and from his hands Lyte received for the last time the sacrament of the Lord's Supper according to the rites of the Church of England. Rather more than three years later Manning was received into the Roman Catholic faith, which he was to serve as Cardinal Archbishop of Westminster.

Among the Anglican clergymen who wrote books about the French Riviera one of the most colourful was the Rev. Sabine Baring-Gould, who had stayed for a time in southern France as a boy, when he had uncovered some mosaics at Pau, paying the workmen out of his pocket-money. Baring-Gould's published works comprised 130 volumes, many of them being novels, of which the average length was 170,000 words. For forty-three years he was parson and squire of Lew Tranchard in Devon, where he lived with his wife whom he had found when she was a mill-girl and had sent away to be educated before he married her. She bore him a large number of children, among the instructions he gave to his daughters being that they were not to read his novels or mention the Reformation.

Baring-Gould wrote the words of *Onward, Christian Soldiers*, the familiar version of Widdecombe Fair and biographies of 3,600 saints. He also wrote *Book of the Riviera*, which was published in 1905. This contains some fine writing, with vivid descriptions such as that of the Esterel: 'these flame-red crags shooting out of a sea the colour of a peacock's neck.' St Tropez he described as 'a charming little town', whose women were 'noted for their good looks due to the infusion of Italian blood', and from Cannes there stretched 'a veritable rosary of winter resorts from Hyères on one side to Alassio on the other'. But the place which he described as 'assuredly the loveliest spot on the entire Ligurian coast' was Monaco. It was also 'the moral cesspool of Europe'.

As a consequence of the operations of the casino an earthly paradise had, Baring-Gould declared, been 'given over to harlots and thieves, and Jew moneylenders, to rogues and fools of every description.' The Grimaldi palace he described as mean and ugly and the entire principality as no larger than the estate of a petty English squire. He even deprecatingly called attention to the fact that the Princess of Monaco had originally been 'a Heine of New Orleans', adding: 'The name is Jewish.'

Indignation did not prevent him from telling a number of anecdotes concerning the casino. One was of a nobleman who attended the Anglican chapel in Monte Carlo and noticed that the number of the last hymn before the sermon was 32. He decided to miss the sermon, went to the roulette table, backed 32 and won £500. The story of his success spread, others began to adopt the same method, and instructions were issued that from then onward the number of the last hymn before the sermon was never to be lower than 37. But on practical as well as moral grounds Baring-Gould preferred the Stock Exchange to the casino. It did, he pointed out, offer better odds.

Baring-Gould's attitude to the Monte Carlo casino was shared by many British people in the last century, and a number of voices were raised to denounce with vigour and, no doubt, pleasure the moral depravity which it was believed to have brought about. Some of these were lay voices. Dr Bennet wrote that in Monaco 'the company, male and female, is very bad in the evening. The four o'clock afternoon train from Nice brings daily a crowd of loose characters.' John Addington Symonds wrote in his diary on 22 March 1866: 'The croupiers are either fat, sensual cormorants, or sallow, lean-cheeked vultures, or suspicious foxes.' They did not compare favourably with 'Coutts' men'. 'These men of the gaming bank', he went on, 'show every trace of a dissolute youth and a vile calling, of low sensuality and hardened avarice.'

But it was from the clergy that the most persistent condemnation came and to the Church of England that opponents of the casino looked most hopefully for support. The Rev. Hugh Macmillan in his book *The Riviera*, published in 1885, stated that the casino had had the effect of increasing the cost of living enormously, and that while it had fostered habits of luxury and idleness it had not improved the opportunities of earning an honest living. 'The question of the abolition of the Casino', he wrote, 'is keenly argued at the present time, and popular opinion is daily gaining in favour of the removal of this plague-spot.'

The Riviera towns came within the Anglican diocese of Gibraltar. In the early days of François Blanc's casino concession certain citizens of Nice, fearing that the new resort would take trade away from them, petitioned the French Government for the closing of the casino. In this they had the active support of the Bishop of Gibraltar. The alliance of the Bishop and the Niçois was a brief one, for when they discovered the harm which the temporary closing of the Monte Carlo casino during the Franco-Prussian war did to their own hotel business the Niçois changed their attitude. But successive Bishops of Gibraltar battled on.

In 1876 the Bishop, whose name was Charles Sandford, sent a pastoral letter to all his clergy on the French Riviera which they were instructed to read to their congregations during Lent. This stated that because of the Monte Carlo casino many respectable families had been driven away from Nice and its surroundings. 'Unless public authority interpose to arrest this growing evil', the Bishop declared, 'these bright, picturesque and genial shores of the Mediterranean will be condemned as unfit places of sojourn for English families.' Members of the congregations were also to be reminded that 'if such an establishment existed in England they would never dream of being seen near the place.'

In 1882 a society for the abolition of the Monte Carlo casino was formed in London, which also operated in Paris. In London it had the enthusiastic support of *The Times*, which looked forward to the day 'when the last croupier shall have taken his last crown from the last Monaco gambler'. If this were to happen, a *Times* leader-writer argued, the economy of Monaco need not be seriously impaired. Every year the number of British and French visitors to the Riviera increased, and they did not go there in order to gamble. 'The mass of the three hundred thousand visits to Monte Carlo', he wrote, 'are merely visits of curiosity. The visitors would be in the neighbourhood whether the tables were there or not.'

The argument was of course as specious as the efforts of the abolitionists were unsuccessful, but it was not until 1922 that a Bishop of Gibraltar could bring himself to pay an official visit to Monte Carlo. By then the moral disapproval of British residents and visitors tended to be directed more towards the evils of pigeon-shooting than towards those of gambling.

To a number of other foreigners the strength of the British concern with the evils of gambling in Monte Carlo was puzzling. One of these was Hiram S. Maxim, ex-barman, ex-boxer and inventor of a mousetrap, as well as of the machine gun which bears his name, who made a detailed study of systems for playing roulette. Maxim considered the British ought to legalize roulette in their own country. If they did, he argued, it would increase their military strength. They would be able to pay off their national debt, and the 'useless racehorse' would disappear and be replaced by 'a useful animal suitable for military purposes'.

III

In the last years of the nineteenth century the economy of

Cannes was already large largely dependent on and determined by the influx of British visitors. In 1889, with a population of under 20,000, Cannes had thirty-six hotels and fourteen *pensions*. It had between seven and eight hundred villas, a high proportion of which were let to British and other foreign visitors in the winter, and a newspaper report of the time gave the number of English villa-owners as 140. Several of the largest and most famous hotels were still to be built, the Carlton, for instance, which was to acquire a fame comparable with those of the Hôtel de Paris in Monte Carlo and the Hôtel Negresco in Nice, being completed in 1912.

For many years virtually all British people who bought or rented property in and around Cannes turned to the same man if they needed the services of an agent. This was John Taylor, a Suffolk gardener turned house agent, who also became a banker and a wine merchant. To attract British clients he provided a reading-room next to his offices in Cannes which they could use free of charge. In 1884 Taylor was appointed British vice-consul, a position he was to fill with distinction for thirty-seven years. The Agence Taylor remains today one of Cannes's leading enterprises.

Nice in 1880 had some 65,000 inhabitants with an English quarter known as Newburgh. About 25,000 visitors came for the winter, and there were already a number of what would today be called tourist shops specializing in preserved fruit, candied sweets and souvenirs made of olive-wood inscribed with such statements as 'Je reviendrai'.

In Menton the hotels had to accept new standards in order to meet the requirements of the British. Dr Bennet estimated that the cost of living doubled in fifteen years and attributed this largely to British influence. 'As I have been told by Mentonian hotel keepers', he wrote, 'the dinners we positively require and exact every day at the hotels and "pensions" are to them festive dinners, which they never dream of unless to welcome friends for a marriage or a baptism. To provide this high standard of food to many hundred strangers, the country had to be ransacked for a hundred and fifty miles around.' In time a number of Menton's hotels became almost exclusively British preserves. Lord Clark, who knew Menton as a small boy shortly before the First World War, recalls that a French visitor who came to one of the larger hotels was regarded as something of a curiosity and was commonly referred to as 'the Frenchman'.

In Beaulieu a British Prime Minister, the Marquess of Salisbury, established a holiday home, and a number of well-to-do British followed his example. Cap Martin was developed by foreigners of various nationalities into one of the most exclusive of all the resorts. In Hyères in 1890 the services and facilities provided included, in addition to an Anglican church, a bank, a house agency and two public tennis-courts.

The British also perceptibly changed the landscape by the creation of gardens. The man who laid out Thomas Robinson Woolfield's garden in Cannes was John Taylor, the future house agent. Dr Bennet also made a garden with the help of 'an intelligent peasant' from a neighbouring village whom he raised, as he put it, 'to the dignity of head-gardener'. The local inhabitants of Menton were deterred by the high cost of watering from growing any flowers other than those which could be sold to scent factories, and they could not understand, Bennet wrote, 'anyone making a mere flower garden for pleasure on the mountain side, a mile or two from the town.' But he did exchange gardening experiences with Count Margaria and Baron Vigier in Nice and the Duke of Vallambrosa in Cannes. When he returned to Menton each year in October Bennet usually found that thyme, juniper, rosemary, cactuses and geraniums had flourished, and the chrysanthemums continued 'in full glory from then until Christmas'. His experiment in introducing snowdrops failed.

The most famous of the gardens open to the public in the nineteenth century with which visitors to the French Riviera were familiar, was the creation of Sir Thomas Hanbury. It was situated just across the Italian frontier, was a favourite haunt of Queen Victoria, and was the subject of a water-colour painting by Turner. Hanbury also erected a fountain near the frontier, to which visitors were brought by electric tram.

The creators of gardens were among those who established permanent second homes on the Riviera. In the early years of the twentieth century other British visitors to the Riviera tended more and more to experiment in their choice of a winter residence. The motor-car had increased their mobility, and the requirement for the fashionable was to spend a certain amount of time each year in some part of the Riviera rather than in any particular town. Princess Daisy of Pless, the English wife of the hereditary ruler of a small German principality, spent a few weeks at different times between 1904 and the outbreak of war in villas in Cannes, Beaulieu, Cap Martin, Monte Carlo, Cimiez, La Napoule and Mandelieu. One year, when she was pregnant, she even tried the experiment of living in a hotel in Cap Ferrat. 'I thought', she wrote in her diary, 'an hotel with only a few servants and no extra bills to pay, but just to live "en pension" would be cheaper and more restful than a villa. But it cost a hundred pounds a week, and one had no comfort or homeliness.' So she moved to a villa in Cimiez, which she rented for about £20 a week, and sent for 'the little German cook' to reinforce the 'few servants'. 'The old woman from the Café Kirche and her daughter Louise helped in the house.'

The only one of the resorts Princess Daisy visited which did not much appeal to her was Monte Carlo. Like some other English visitors, she found its size gave her a sense of being hemmed in. She could not go out without continually meeting people she knew, and in consequence living in sin, she explained, would not even have the merit of being scandalous, as it was 'all, so to speak, open and above-board'. The lack of privacy did however serve to enhance the reputation of certain well-known philanderers. One of these was General Sir John Cowans, and the story was told of a woman who in the course of her morning walk in Monte Carlo claimed to have met 'the reigning Lady Cowans, the Dowager Lady Cowans, the ex-Lady Cowans, the deputy Lady Cowans – and all their understudies'.

Princess Daisy did not usually reach the Riviera before February or March. She might still be in occupation of a rented villa in April or even early May, but not later than the second week in May she would return to Germany or to England for the accepted social round, escaping from the Riviera before the summer came, as did virtually all the other visitors. With the advent of summer most of the pensions closed. So did nearly all the hotels, those owned by the French as well as those, such as the Hôtel des Anglais in Nice, which were owned by English joint stock companies. In the last decade of the nineteenth century only one hotel of international repute remained open in the summer. This was the Hôtel d'Angleterre in Nice, whose proprietor was a German.

There were some good reasons why the British left the Riviera before the summer came. The chief of these was the prevailing standard of hygiene. Apart from the general unpleasantness which the heat accentuated, sanitary conditions in many parts of the Riviera were such that outbreaks of typhoid were not unusual occurrences. The British did much to remedy the defects. In 1866 the contract to build a canal to relieve the water shortage in Cannes was given to a British concern called the General Irrigation and Water Supply Co. of France. *A Handbook for Travellers in France* published by John Murray in 1890 stated in the section on Cannes: 'The drainage, formerly bad, is now considerably improved; many works have already been carried out, and others, more important, are about to be undertaken, according to Capt. D. Galton's plans and suggestions.' Hyères was recommended in the handbook as a health resort largely because 'pure water has been laid on to all parts of the town by a company'.

Pronouncements by Englishmen of standing on whether the sanitary arrangements in a particular town were or were not acceptable to their fellow-countrymen understandably carried weight, and the British consul conferred a real benefit on the economy of Nice when, in 1889, he made a favourable report on its standard of hygiene. Dr Bennet too merited the thanks of the people of Menton when he wrote: 'The hygienic state of Mentone is much better than that of any other sanatorium between Marseilles and Genoa, not from any peculiar forethought on the part of its inhabitants, but because its population, native and foreign, is smaller.'

Sanitary conditions and the lure of the London season, of Ascot and Goodwood and Cowes, explained in part why before 1914 British people virtually abandoned the Riviera when summer approached. Equally important was the general belief, which Bennet's regime had helped to foster, that in the height of summer the heat must be almost unbearable. That large numbers of the native inhabitants survived it does not seem to have aroused much comment. No doubt this was because to most British people it was a matter of relatively little concern.

IV

The most enduring exports which the British made to the territories they occupied in the last century – by treaty, by conquest or by assumption – were, for the most part, games and the English language. To the French Riviera they brought both with abundant self-assurance.

They even introduced cricket, the Cannes Cricket Club being founded in 1887. Although a number of enthusiasts were found who maintained a pitch in fairly good condition, the soil was unsuitable, and the club encountered other difficulties. One of these arose from the proximity of an ostrich farm. The boundaries of the cricket ground were rather short, and whenever, as frequently happened, the ball was hit for six into an ostrich pen one of the birds was liable to pick it up in its mouth and make off at high speed. It was then pursued by shouting cricketers, who had taken the precaution of arming themselves with stumps, until the ball was disgorged. In spite of all this, cricket continued to be played in Cannes in the early years of the present century.

Golf, another British export to be cultivated more intensively in other continents than on the mainland of Europe, put down firmer roots on the Riviera than cricket did. The Cannes Golf Club, the fourth oldest in France, was founded in 1891. Hyères quickly became a popular golfing centre. The first of its two courses was opened in 1894. In the section on Hyères in his guide-book published in 1897 Augustus Hare wrote: 'Many English families pass the winter here wholly for the sake of the golf.' Golf courses were also established at Valescure and Sospel before the First World War, and in 1908 the formidable task was begun of making a golf course for the tiny and hilly principality of Monaco at Mont-Agel. Before long reigning sovereigns and leading statesmen adopted the practice of lunching at the golf clubs, but the management of the clubs remained largely in the hands of British committees and British secretaries, with tuition being given by British professionals.

Yachting as a sport was also introduced by foreigners to the French Riviera. A society for organizing regattas was formed in Cannes in 1859, Lord Brougham being appointed honorary president. The next year the first regatta was held. Two bodies existed in Nice in the last century for the development of yachting, the Club Nautique and the Club de la Voile. They were amalgamated in 1898 under the presidency of the Duc de Rivoli. The permanent inhabitants seem to have taken little or no part in the conduct of the affairs of either. In the words of the historian Jean-Jacques Antier, 'la mer n'intéressait pas les niçois.' As in England, membership of a yacht club was a clear sign of social distinction, the Cercle Nautique in Cannes enjoying a pre-eminence which was not seriously challenged. As a result Cannes became known to a number of the British, the future King Edward VII among them, as 'the Cowes of the Mediterranean', a patronizing yet in some respects fairly accurate title which was still in common use in the 1920s.

Polo and horse racing were other sports traditionally patronized by the aristocracy which foreigners brought to the Riviera. A colourful picture of the state of racing in Nice in 1890 is to be found in *Monte Carlo and How to do It*. 'The fences, steeplechase or otherwise', the authors, Goldberg and Piesse, wrote, 'are mild, and anyone with a fast horse who could jump at all could pick up the lot; a good plater, with a turn of speed, could collar either or both of the prizes.' But, tempting though this might be to British owners, there were difficulties to be faced. Transporting a horse, a jockey, and a stable-lad to and from the Riviera cost about £200. If the British owner employed a so-called 'French' jockey he would be 'trusting a thief who had been kicked out of an English stable', and if he brought his own, 'these same Anglo-French blackguards will shut him in, jump on him at a fence, and do their best to kill him.'

Lawn tennis, an English invention of the 1870s, was flourishing on the Riviera a decade or two later. It was considered a particularly suitable pastime for English girls accompanying their parents to health resorts. In his 1897 guide-book Augustus Hare wrote that at Hyères 'there is a good deal of lawn-tennis and mild gaiety for young ladies.' In 1903 an event was staged for the first time which by the 1920s had become the first major event in the international tennis calendar. This was the Monte Carlo tournament, whose first organizer was A.E. Madge. The organizing committees of tennis clubs and tournaments were at first almost wholly British in composition, but it was a game in which the French challenge to British supremacy came

unexpectedly soon. One reason for this may have been that in
Nice a Frenchman filled a post which in other Riviera towns was
assumed to be the preserve of Englishmen. This was Charles
Lenglen, secretary of the Nice Lawn Tennis Club, whose
daughter became the greatest woman tennis player of her time.

Even in sports which they did not invent or introduce the
British on the Riviera enjoyed a peculiar position through
language or performance. When an ice-rink was built in Cannes
in 1912 the sport practised on it was known at first as 'le skating'.
Even the records of the popular Monégasque pastime of pigeon-
shooting show that of the nineteen contests for the annual *grand
prix* held between 1872 and 1890 ten were won by British
competitors, four by Italians and two by Belgians. There was one
American winner, one Hungarian and one French. To be
allowed to shoot pigeons in Monte Carlo a man had to prove a
certain social standing. Members of the Gun Club or the
Hurlingham Club in England were accepted automatically, but
others needed the support of at least two members of the
appropriate committee.

There was one sport in which the British did not enjoy special
pre-eminence on the Riviera, and their standing in this was to
some extent a reflexion of new challenges which were being
made to British technology and British industry. In the invention
and early development of the motor-car Britain had been
forestalled by Germany and effectively rivalled by France and
Italy. Similarly in the early motor-racing and motor-rally
contests on the Riviera the British competed sometimes with
success, but frequently without. In her diary for 1904 Princess
Daisy of Pless, after describing a visit to Nice, wrote:

> We did not stay to see the motor race, but the record of the
> world was beaten today by Rigolly, driving a Gobron-Brillie
> car in the third Henri de Rothschild Cup race; he attained a
> speed of over one hundred kilometres an hour – a world's
> record – quite extraordinary.

The first of the famous Monte Carlo rallies was held in 1911.
Thirteen years earlier a new kind of motoring event had been
staged in Monaco for the first time. It was a *concours d'élégance*, a
kind of contest not particularly well suited to the British genius.

V

Almost exactly a hundred years after Smollett had deplored the lack of any libraries in Nice his fellow-countrymen established a library of their own there. This was opened on 23 December 1863 and was originally called the Nice Book Club. It later became known as the Nice Library and then as the English-American Library. It was financially self-supporting. To many of the British on the Riviera in the last century the three-decker novel was an important ingredient of their lives. These were sent to them from Smith's or Mudie's or whatever other subscription library they patronized in England, but a local library was important not only as a source of immediately available reading matter but as a social centre. Menton also had a circulating library which developed from a book-club. This may have been part of the establishment of which Dr Bennet wrote:

An elegant Cercle or club has been built in the centre of the town, which is well supplied with newspapers. It is open to visitors by subscription, and contains billiard, card and conversation rooms, and a good-sized theatre and ball-room.

The first newspaper published on the Riviera primarily for visitors was produced by John Taylor in the 1860s. It was distributed three times a day to the main hotels in Cannes at 7 a.m., 3 p.m. and 6.30 p.m. and contained lists of visitors who had arrived recently, names of doctors and meteorological notes. The *Cannes Gazette*, which first appeared in December 1889 and was edited by an English tailor named H.M. Lumbert, was similar in content. Various other English newspapers sprang up from time to time on the Riviera, but by far the most successful was the *Menton and Monte Carlo News*, whose first number was issued on 6 November 1897. From a modest four-page sheet costing 20 centimes it developed into the main source of information for British residents and visitors on social life, sport and entertainment on the Riviera. As it grew in size more and more new features were introduced, but even in the 1930s the editor still maintained the practice of regularly listing new arrivals with the names of the hotels in which they were staying.

The *Menton and Monte Carlo News* was published for six or seven months of the year, closing down as the summer approached. It appeared weekly and sometimes ran to 28 pages, or 36 when there was a Christmas or other supplement. Its success was evidence not only of the purchasing power of the British visitors and residents, for the paper was well supported by advertising, but of the extent to which English had become the Riviera's unofficial second language and, in certain areas, its first. But the ultimate proof of the prevalence of English was not afforded until 1923. Then it was found an acceptable commercial risk to send an English theatre company to perform plays in English for a six-week Riviera season. The company, which was brought out by Anmer Hall, gave alternate performances of two plays, of which one was the farce called *French Leave*. The title must have been puzzling to French members of the audience, if indeed there were any.

The English penetration of the French language, which has come to be known as *franglais*, became common practice on the Riviera earlier than in most areas of France, largely because of the important part played in Riviera social life by sport. The correct French golfing term to denote that a match is level is 'all square'. A Frenchman takes 'son putter sur le green', and only an Englishman trying to be helpful would use such an expression as 'sur le vert'. The *Cannes Gazette* was published in a house in the rue d'Antibes, which now shows no sign of having once been a newspaper office. But traces of the language in which the paper was printed are to be found in the dry-cleaning establishment which today occupies part of the building. Among the garments accepted for cleaning, a notice states, is 'le pull-cardigan'.

Franglais has become widespread, but there was one kind of anglicization of the French language which seems to have been peculiar to the Riviera. Among the British residents of long standing there grew up a body of people who spoke French with some fluency but with little regard for the niceties of grammar, particularly genders. After a time a number of the French who depended on British custom for their living began to imitate their modes of speech. In Hyères, for instance, there was a French hotelier who regularly used such expressions as 'mon maison' and 'mon femme'. It was one of the stranger corruptions of the language of Racine.

VI

In 1891 the authors of *Monte Carlo and How to do It* offered some advice to Americans who were in difficulties of any kind on the Riviera. This was to 'inflict themselves' on the British Vice-Consul in Monaco, a banker named Edward Smith, who could 'gauge in a moment the calibre' of any Englishman or Englishwoman to whom he spoke.

At the time when it was offered this advice may well have been considered reasonable by many Americans on the Riviera. A dozen years later, in his treatise on roulette systems, *Monte Carlo. Facts and Fallacies*, Hiram S. Maxim wrote: 'There is an old saying that "When you are in Rome you should do as the Romans do", but the Americans have improved upon this. According to their version, "When you are in Rome you should do as Englishmen do."' He went on to describe an incident he had witnessed in which an Englishman, whose winnings at a crowded table in Monte Carlo had been seized by 'an evil-looking individual', had kicked the thief across the gaming-room, out of the casino and down the steps, 'all this in the face of the attendants, none of whom interfered in the least.'

That an individual Englishman should use force to defend his rights on the Riviera was, as Maxim pointed out, hardly to be questioned, and there was even a time when the armed forces of the British crown were nearly called upon to uphold the established order.

In 1910 there was a threat of a popular rising in Monaco in favour of a more democratic form of government. At the request of Prince Albert I a detachment from the Royal Navy stationed at Villefranche was ostensibly given leave and instructed to converge on Monte Carlo. It was agreed that if the sailors' help was needed they were to be notified by the hoisting of a flag on the roof of the Hôtel de Paris. On receipt of this signal they were to open a number of cases supposed to contain wine, which in fact concealed rifles and ammunition, and be prepared to defend British property. The crisis passed, the presence of the Royal Navy was not needed, and a new constitution was promulgated the next year providing for an elected council of Monégasque citizens. Thirty-four years after the threat of the rising in Monaco British forces did participate in landings on the Riviera. They were then greatly outnumbered by Americans.

4 Royal Presences

'Drove to Beaulieu', Queen Victoria wrote in her journal on 1 May 1899, adding: 'Alas! my last charming drive in this paradise of nature, which I grieve to leave, as I get more attached to it every year.' She was not to see the Riviera again. The following year she was advised not to visit France because of the strength of the anti-British feeling which the South African war had aroused, and in January 1901 she died.

For a long time the Queen had regarded the Riviera with misgivings. Cannes she associated with her eldest son's notions of pleasure, and she never overcame her aversion to Monte Carlo. On her first visit to the Riviera she passed through Monaco in the manner of an ordinary tourist, ignoring the Prince, who was then in residence, and returning unopened a bouquet which the Monégasque administration had sent to her. As alternative holiday resorts to the Riviera she tried both Florence and Aix-les-Bains, but in the last ten years of her life she succumbed to the prevailing fashion, travelling to the Riviera no fewer than seven times. She spent one holiday in Grasse, one in Hyères and five in Cimiez.

The Queen's first visit to the Riviera, like that of many of her subjects, was a direct consequence of illness. Her son Prince Leopold, who was created Duke of Albany, suffered from haemophilia. He had been advised to visit Menton, and in 1882 the Queen spent some time with him there.

In this journey to Menton the Queen was accompanied abroad for the last time by her Scottish attendant John Brown. She stayed in a villa on the outskirts of Menton, making excursions by carriage, though her pleasure in these was restricted by Brown's fear of Fenian assassins and his determined refusal in consequence to stop the carriage in the streets. Brown, the Queen wrote, had 'an increasing *hatred* of being "abroad". He can communicate with *no* one when out, nor keep anyone off the carriage.' After a time Dr James Henry Bennet put his eight-acre garden at the Queen's disposal, and there she and Princess Beatrice, who, as so often, had accompanied her mother abroad, could stroll and sketch in privacy. To mark the Queen's visit the chief of the Menton municipal band composed a cantata in her honour, and the Queen in turn presented him with a diamond breast-pin.

With her visit to Grasse in 1891, for which she chose hotel rather than villa accommodation, Queen Victoria began to set the pattern for her future Riviera holidays. She would leave England early in March, resolutely refusing to cross the Channel on a Friday, and travel through France in the royal train, calling herself the Comtesse de Balmoral.

The royal train consisted of seven coaches, two of which were the Queen's personal property. The walls of the drawing-room coach were hung with silk. There was a dark Indian carpet, a beechwood table stood between the windows, and there were two armchairs, a sofa and footstools in Louis XVI style, all covered in blue silk. The train's speed was restricted to 35 miles per hour by day and 25 by night. Between eight and nine o'clock in the morning it was halted to allow the Queen to dress, and hot water was taken on board at the appropriate time to enable the male members of the travelling party to shave in relative comfort. The food brought from England included Irish stew, which was kept lukewarm in red flannel cushions. Marie Mallet, who had been appointed a maid of honour to the Queen and travelled with her frequently, commented plaintively that the stew 'could not be compared with the excellent dinner provided in the train that goes round Paris'.

The Queen brought large quantities of china, glass and linen to the hotels in which she stayed, and half-an-hour had to be allowed for the unloading of the train when it reached the

Riviera. A large domestic staff was also transported, including a number of Indians, whom the Aga Khan described as 'distinctly second-class'. They were, he wrote, 'the kind that the newly-arrived or transient European is apt to acquire in the first hotel in which he stays', and were altogether different from the 'admirable and trustworthy' servants to be found in the Viceregal Lodge in India.

The question whether a particular Indian should accompany the Queen to Cimiez was the cause of one of the comparatively rare differences which she had with Lord Salisbury. The Indian was Abdul Karim, a lawyer known as the Munshi, whom the Queen described as her Indian secretary and who gave her lessons in Hindustani. Salisbury's assessment of the Munshi's merits differed somewhat from the Queen's. When the Queen suggested that the Munshi should be appointed to a diplomatic post, advancing the interesting argument that she had more Moslem subjects than the Sultan of Turkey, Salisbury induced her to drop the proposal. But when Salisbury advised against the inclusion of the Munshi in the Queen's travelling party to Cimiez she flew into such a rage that she swept everything on her desk on to the floor. The outcome was a drawn battle. The Munshi did not travel with the Queen, but he arrived in Cimiez shortly after she did.

The central event of the Queen's day on the Riviera was her carriage outing, which took place even when the mistral was blowing at its most penetrating. She had a predilection for cemeteries and spent much of one day looking at the graves of friends in Cannes. About a week later Marie Mallet recorded: 'We went to another funeral this afternoon. The Queen really enjoys these melancholy entertainments.' But there were also less lugubrious outings. On one occasion the Queen visited a private zoo and was presented with an ostrich egg, from which an omelette was made for her. She was also given the shell, on which the owner of the zoo, a countess described as '*ci-devant cocotte*', had written her name. 'Just as if she had laid it herself', the Queen commented. On another occasion the Queen, stopping outside the Cercle Nautique in Cannes, sent in for a glass of port.

Queen Victoria took an active part in Nice's battle of the flowers, and she particularly enjoyed pelting French officers. To the beggars and itinerant musicians of Nice she acted as a magnet, and day after day she would put her head out of a window of the Grand Hotel or the Hôtel Excelsior Regina in Cimiez and hear the strains of *Funiculi, funicula* coming from the garden. She unfailingly dispensed largesse, and one lame beggar went so far as to inscribe on his go-cart 'by appointment to Her Majesty'.

Meals were gargantuan, a typical luncheon menu consisting of risotto, grilled mutton chops, chicken with noodles, asparagus, tapioca pudding and meringues with strawberries. On Sundays there were church services to attend. At one of these, Marie Mallet recorded, the Bishop of Ripon preached the sermon, Princess Beatrice played the organ, and among the more vociferous of the singers was the fat Highlander Rankin, a former gillie. Princess Beatrice's musical accomplishments also helped to provide entertainment in the evenings, when the Queen herself would sometimes conduct with a knitting needle. Evenings ended with extracts from newspapers being read to the Queen by one of her daughters or attendant ladies. The readers were instructed to choose only agreeable or humorous items.

While in residence on the Riviera Queen Victoria received a number of other heads of state. In March 1896 the Emperor Francis Joseph and his Empress called on her, and she recorded in her journal her satisfaction at seeing 'how pleased the Emperor of Austria is by the gift of the Colonelcy-in-Chief of the First King's Dragoon Guards.' A year later the Emperor again visited the Queen at Cimiez, and she asked him to address her as 'du'. This too, she recorded, 'seemed to please him'. When the Empress-Mother of Russia visited her at Cimiez the Queen complained that the Russian Government's attitude to Britain had become less friendly and 'begged her to mention this to Nicky. She said she would do so.'

Queen Victoria's first meeting with President Félix Faure of France took place on 11 March 1897 in her train while it was stopped on the *ceinture* outside the centre of Paris. 'I asked him to sit down,' the Queen recorded, a concession which, as he was Head of State of the country she was visiting, seems in retrospect to have been not unreasonable. A year later the President himself came south to recuperate after influenza. The Prince of Wales received him on the ground floor of the Hôtel Excelsior

Regina in Cimiez, three of the princesses met him at the top of the stairs, and the Queen stood at the door of the drawing-room to welcome him. President Faure made a favourable impression, the Queen describing him in her journal as 'very courteous, amiable and not at all *parvenu*'.

Among the Queen's other visitors were Sarah Bernhardt, who gave a private performance which pleased the Queen greatly, and Ruggiero Leoncavallo, who played extracts from his newest opera to her, an event which Marie Mallet described as 'a relief to our otherwise sombre evenings'. It was in her Riviera hotel too that Queen Victoria had her last meeting with William Ewart Gladstone. The invitation to call on the Queen was issued to Gladstone by Princess Louise, but Gladstone felt he could not accept it unless it was a royal command. Princess Louise overcame the difficulty by herself inviting Mr and Mrs Gladstone to tea in the hotel. There they met the Queen, who described them as 'both looking much aged'. The meeting took place in March 1897, a little more than a year before Gladstone died.

Though recognized as being on holiday while she was on the Riviera, the Queen received daily consignments of state papers, and when Lord Salisbury was in residence at Beaulieu issues of policy could be, and were, discussed without inconvenience to either. But whether her prime minister was at hand on the Riviera or in England the Queen continued to bombard him from her hotel in Cimiez with her opinions on ecclesiastical appointments, army administration or foreign affairs. Even while travelling she insisted on being kept informed of matters which concerned her. Towards the end of April 1896, as she was about to begin her journey home, the Queen learnt that sentences of death had been imposed on the ringleaders of the Jameson raid. She despatched a cipher telegram to Joseph Chamberlain, stating: 'We leave in less than an hour. Pray send news on to the principal stations, as I am most anxious to hear.'

The political importance of Queen Victoria's annual visits to the Riviera and their effect on Franco-British relations came to be increasingly appreciated in both countries. After the clash between the two countries' interests on the upper reaches of the Nile known as the Fashoda incident, which was both an exercise of British power and a humiliation for the French, anti-British feeling in France ran high enough for the advisability of a visit by the Queen to Cimiez to be called into question. The respective ambassadors in London and Paris advised in favour of it, and Lord Salisbury was of the same opinion. 'If she were nervous', he wrote in a confidential letter to the Queen's Private Secretary, Sir Arthur Bigge, 'she could always, with her horses, find herself on the other side of the frontier in two hours. I can suggest no precautions except perhaps taking a suite of rooms at Bordighera in the name of one of the Ladies-in-Waiting.'

The visit took place, and shortly after the Queen's departure Sir Edmund Monson, the British Ambassador in Paris, wrote to Salisbury: 'The annual visit of the Queen to the Riviera has come to be regarded in France as an outward and visible sign of the friendly sentiments entertained by her Majesty for the French people.' Even when it was decided that because of the South African war the Queen should not make her usual visit the *Menton and Monte Carlo News* reassured the Queen's subjects by offering another explanation of the decision. The real reason, the newspaper stated, was the combined effect of the noise caused during the Queen's last visit by the laying of tramways and the 'horrible smell of petroleum' which hung about the roads 'following the passage of automobiles'.

The memory of Queen Victoria's presence on the Riviera and of the importance of the part-she played in its life lasted long after she died, so much so that in April 1939, forty years after her last visit and more than thirty-eight years after her death, a statue of her was unveiled at a ceremony in Menton.

II

When Queen Victoria, in one of her letters of admonition to her eldest son, reminded him in 1886 that he had already passed his forty-fifth birthday, he replied that this was something he had 'not forgotten'. He added: 'You are, I think, rather hard upon me when you talk of the round of gaieties I indulge in at Cannes, London, Homburg and Cowes. I like Cannes excessively, especially for its climate and scenery, just as you do Aix. To be away from England in the South for three weeks is a very beneficial change to me.'

Cannes was as decidedly the future King Edward VII's

preferred place of residence on the Riviera as Cimiez was to become his mother's. After experimenting with different kinds of hotel and villa accommodation he found the most satisfactory arrangement was to stay as the guest of the Cercle Nautique, where he was given the central apartment.

Unlike his mother, Edward, when Prince of Wales, liked to break his journeys either to or from the Riviera with a week or more in Paris, where he became such a familiar figure in certain quarters that on entering a music-hall he was liable to be greeted with the cry of ''Ullo Wales'. He was preceded on his journey south by a Swiss named Fehr, who did a good deal of expert haggling with various tradesmen, the Prince himself following with enough suitcases of clothes to keep the two valets who accompanied him fully occupied.

For some years the Prince arranged for his yacht *Britannia* to be sent to the Mediterranean to await his arrival. This enabled him to entertain in some degree of privacy as well as to take part in regattas and make excursions to Villefranche, Monaco and Menton. In the 1890s the Prince's enthusiasm for yachting began to decline, largely because his nephew, the German Emperor William II, persisted in using Cowes week to advance his own and his country's prestige, and in 1897 he sold *Britannia* to the inventor of Bovril. Golf served for a time as a substitute for yachting, but the Prince's ventures on to the tennis courts, which in the 1880s had increased popular interest in the game, did not give rise to any lasting enthusiasm on his part.

In addition to these intermittent sporting activities the Prince of Wales sought his pleasure on the Riviera largely in gambling, tobacco, food and sex, though not necessarily in that order of preference. It was on the Riviera that he developed his taste for baccarat, an indulgence which shocked large numbers of British newspaper readers when the details were revealed of a country-house week-end in England, which the Prince attended as a guest and at which, in the course of a game of baccarat, another of the guests was found to be cheating. But it was not only the middle-class, newspaper-reading public whom the Prince succeeded in shocking by his gambling habits. On meeting Lady Brougham, the wife of the nephew of the former Lord Chancellor, in the Monte Carlo casino, he suggested bringing a party to her villa in Cannes the following Sunday to play baccarat. Her husband, the third Baron Brougham, announced that it was against his principles to allow gambling in his house on a Sunday and refused to give way. According to Frank Harris, the narrator of the incident, the Prince never forgave the slight to his dignity and never dined in the Villa Eléonore again.

The Prince of Wales was not a heavy drinker, preferring champagne to port, but he smoked excessively, finding it required self-discipline to limit himself to one cigar and two cigarettes before breakfast, and he ate hugely. After disposing of the other meals of the day he frequently chose for his supper a dish of grilled oysters.

The Prince was not of course alone in continuing, while on the Riviera, to indulge the enormous appetite which he had developed at home. Among the young women whom he pursued in Cannes was a Miss Chamberlayne from Cleveland, Ohio, whom he had first encountered in Homburg. Miss Chamberlayne, whom the normally indulgent Princess Alexandra always referred to as 'Chamberpots', was so well protected by her parents that the Prince was unable to see her alone, but his pursuit of her aroused sufficient public interest for an American newspaper reporter to seek an interview with her in Cannes. In this she divulged that for her a satisfactory breakfast consisted of two eggs, a fried sole, a beefsteak and plenty of potatoes.

When taking part in the Cannes battle of flowers in 1889 the Prince of Wales made his general intentions clear by dressing as the Devil in a scarlet costume and with horns on his head. In Monte Carlo the story is still told of an incident which occurred in the Café de Paris when the Prince was entertaining a young companion. In the preparation of a pancake for the Prince some *fine champagne*, which had been spilt, caught fire and the waiter, skilfully covering up the mistake, offered the Prince a new dish to be called *crêpes Prince des Galles*. The Prince, who liked the taste, indicated his companion and suggested it should be called *crêpes Suzette*. The story has been given other settings at other times, but the Café de Paris in Monte Carlo seems as likely a setting as any other. The identity of Suzette has not been established.

Sex could also be enjoyed vicariously. Mrs Ogden Goelet, an ambitious American hostess, once persuaded the Prince of Wales to visit her Riviera home by promising to produce the singer of his choice. The Prince chose Yvette Guilbert, whom Mrs Goelet induced to break a contract by offering her an enormous fee. At first Yvette Guilbert followed Mrs Goelet's instructions and sang some harmless little ditties, but seeing how bored the Prince obviously was, she decided to launch into the richest songs of her extremely rich repertoire, thereby, it seems, delighting the Prince as much as she dismayed Mrs Ogden Goelet.

Frank Harris, who has long been discredited as a reliable witness, but whose memoirs may well outlive those of all but a few of his more truthful contemporaries, claimed that the Prince of Wales sought him out on the Riviera because the Prince's uncle, the Duke of Cambridge, had described Harris as the best story-teller he had ever met. The first encounter between Harris and the Prince of Wales took place in the Monte Carlo casino. The Prince asked Harris whose luck was in, to put some money for him on the tables. Harris returned with the winnings and told the Prince what he described as 'a naughty rhyme'.

' "Tell me another, tell me another," the Prince cried' – according to Harris's version – in the guttural voice which, Harris wrote, was like that of a German Jew. The recital was said to have continued for half-an-hour, the Prince, with his arm on Harris's shoulder, shaking with laughter.

> 'Of course,' I went on, 'that's not what Caesar really said; what he really said was, 'I saw, I conquered, and – I came.'
> The Prince laughed heartily.
> 'You are incorrigible,' he said.

Far from sharing his mother's pleasure in meeting members of the various royal families of Europe to whom they were related by blood, the Prince of Wales found the presence of such people on the Riviera irksome, and he tried, though with only limited success, to avoid them. He could hardly share his mother's moral objections to the way in which the economy of the principality of Monaco was managed, but he found the Prince, Albert I, too serious-minded for his liking. *The Times* was perhaps blurring the issue somewhat when it complained in 1888 of 'the unfortunate weakness which has led him to patronize American cattle-drovers and prize-fighters', but during his holidays on the Riviera the Prince, travelling as Baron Renfrew and thereby enjoying all the privileges and escaping nearly all the obligations of royalty, was able to choose the company he wanted. That this should have included what was then known, rather charmingly, as the *demi-monde*, as well as men who were prepared to advance him money on terms which he considered favourable, is hardly surprising, his appetites being what they were.

The question whether the Prince of Wales could have played both an important and a useful part in British diplomacy in his mother's lifetime, had he been given the opportunity, has often been argued, and there are differing opinions on the extent to which his personal charm, his genuine liking for French life and his excellent command of the French language did help in forging the *entente cordiale*. But of his contribution to what was already a fairly important part of the French economy, its tourist trade, there can be no dispute.

His appearance on the Riviera together with Princess Alexandra shortly after the conclusion of the Franco-Prussian war immediately stimulated trade. After being hissed in Paris at the time of the Fashoda incident he insisted on taking his Riviera holiday in the usual manner, and the French authorities showed sound judgment in inviting him to lay the foundation stone of the new jetty in Cannes in 1898, when he made a forthright appeal for a better British understanding of France. But it was in his unique role as a setter of fashion, particularly in the pursuit of pleasure, that his impact was greatest.

Princess Daisy of Pless wrote of him after he had come to the throne:

> The King knew that without the slightest effort or insistence on his part he was the first personage in any assembly anywhere he chose to go. He needed neither crowns, nor clanking swords, nor Horse or Foot Guards to remind people that he not only occupied the greatest throne in the world – ruling over one-fifth of the whole earth – but that, by virtue of his own personality, he was the first gentleman in Europe – or anywhere.

Had there been any doubt that during a certain period of the year the French Riviera was the centre of the fashionable world, the continued presence of Edward Prince of Wales would have served to eliminate it.

III

Nearly all Queen Victoria's daughters suffered, as did their mother, from rheumatism. This gave them an inducement to visit the Riviera, where several of them made an appreciable impact on its social life. So indeed did their brothers.

In 1869, more than a dozen years before the Queen's first Riviera visit, her eldest daughter, Princess Victoria, who was by then the mother of the heir to the Prussian throne, spent a two-month holiday in the Grand Hotel in Cannes in the company of her sister Princess Alice, Grand-Duchess of Hesse-Darmstadt. Princess Victoria was accompanied by twenty-five attendants, Princess Alice by four. This was a fairly accurate reflexion of the social status which each could claim. Princess Victoria was also honoured by the Cannes municipal band, which lined up outside her hotel to serenade her on her birthday. As this fell on a Sunday she sent the band away, pointing out that the playing of dance music on a Sunday was contrary to English principles. She asked the band to return at eight o'clock the next morning, explaining to those around her that she had never lost the good habit of early rising instilled into her at Windsor. The musicians seem to have taken it all in good part and, rather remarkably perhaps, turned up the following morning on time.

Princess Beatrice, who for long seemed cast for the role of permanent companion to her mother, found new opportunities for social life when ships of the Royal Navy visited Villefranche, though she eventually married 'a soldier. This was Henry of Battenberg, who was killed while campaigning in West Africa, his body, preserved in Navy rum, being brought home in a British cruiser. To console her in her grief the Emperor Napoleon's widow, the Empress Eugénie, with characteristic thoughtfulness, offered Princess Beatrice the use of her villa at Cap Martin, an offer she made again immediately after Queen Victoria's death.

Princess Helena, known in the family as Lenchen, also attended her mother on a number of the Riviera visits. After the death of her husband, Prince Christian of Schleswig-Holstein, who seems to have been a man of abnormal dullness, she did much charitable work in England in the interests of nurses. One consequence of this was that among British and other families resident on the Riviera, who were looking for an English nanny, it came to be widely recognized that there was no better qualification than the title of Princess Christian nurse. One such family was that of the Grimaldis, a Princess Christian nurse named Kathleen Churchill-Wanstall playing a major part in the upbringing of the future Prince Rainier III.

Queen Victoria's second son, the Duke of Edinburgh ('Affie'), who would probably have become King of Greece but for the advice of Palmerston and Lord John Russell and who did become Duke of Saxe-Coburg, repeatedly visited the Riviera in his capacity of Commander-in-Chief of the Mediterranean fleet. So too for different reasons did Prince Leopold, the sufferer from haemophilia, who had the unusual distinction in his family of speaking English without a foreign accent and who, partly for that reason no doubt, had acquired a certain reputation as a public speaker. On one of his visits the Prince, who was staying at the Cercle Nautique in Cannes, fell heavily on the stairs. To one with his affliction the accident was fatal, and he died the next morning. Two days earlier he had been heard to say that he hoped, when he died, he would be accorded a military funeral. His wish was granted, his eldest brother, stricken with grief, escorting his body home.

Of all Queen Victoria's children the one who had the longest personal association with the Riviera was Arthur, Duke of Connaught, for Edward VII, after he came to the throne, ceased to visit the Riviera. The Duke of Connaught was Queen Victoria's youngest son and by common consent was the most likeable member of the family. Marie Mallet, who described herself as a republican 'except as regards the Queen whom I really *love* and respect', also made an exception in favour of the Duke of Connaught. 'My "culte" for the Duke of Connaught', she wrote, 'increases as time goes on, he is such a gentleman, so courteous and kind.' Princess Daisy of Pless, who spent the First World War in Germany and afterwards had to live in much more modest circumstances than she had been accustomed to, wrote of the Duke: 'He was the first British Royalty I had spoken to after the war, and, needless to say, he was the friendly, charming, gallant gentleman he has ever been.' Consuelo Vanderbilt, who became Duchess of Marlborough and later Madame Jacques Balsan, described the Duke as 'by far the most popular royalty on the Côte. The French', she wrote, 'more especially appreciated the part he took in the life of the community, for he never failed to be present at a local ceremony.'

The Duke had soldiered with distinction at Tel-el-Kebir, where Sir Garnet Wolseley had described him as taking more care of his men than any of the other general officers. In the 1920s he spent a part of every year on the Riviera, first at Beaulieu, then at his villa at Cap Ferrat, where his garden was thrown open to all ranks whenever the Royal Navy visited Villefranche. During those years, with his punctiliousness, his courtesy and his readiness to undertake ceremonial duties, the Duke's conduct was not unlike that of the best type of governor-general of a former colonial dependency which has graduated to self-rule.

To the next generation of the British royal family the Riviera appealed less strongly. The future King George V paid a few visits there as a young man, spending much of his time in the company of his father or his grandmother. But gambling in the casino did not attract him, and he shared neither the zest for pursuing women nor the enjoyment of the French way of life which had served to shape the pattern of so many of his father's holidays. When relaxing he was happiest in the role of sailor turned Norfolk squire, with plenty of birds to kill and plenty of stamps to stick into albums.

To the British residents on the Riviera, as well as to the hoteliers and others engaged in the tourist trade, a new era of royal patronage did however seem to lie ahead when the future Edward VIII, as Prince of Wales, began to evince an interest in the pleasures of Riviera life.

IV

In the summer of 1928 Mrs Wallis Spencer of Baltimore, whose maiden name was Warfield, spent some time in Cannes with her friends Herman and Katherine Rogers before leaving to marry her second husband, Ernest Simpson. Six years later she returned

to Cannes in somewhat different circumstances, when she and
her aunt, Bessie Merryman, were among a small number of
guests whom the Prince of Wales invited to stay at the villa he
had taken in Biarritz. From Biarritz the party went by yacht to
Cannes and then to Genoa. In Cannes, after they had dined with
Herman and Katherine Rogers, the Prince of Wales presented
Mrs Simpson with a diamond and emerald charm, a first clear
indication, it seems, of his future intentions.

The next year the Prince of Wales took a villa in Cannes for his
summer holiday. There was another cruise, this time to Corsica
on board the Duke of Westminster's yacht *Cutty Sark*, and again
Mrs Simpson was a member of the party. In July of the following
year, 1936, people on the Riviera were expecting to greet the
former Prince of Wales for the first time as King, but his holiday
plans were changed, largely because of fears of social unrest in
France. Instead he had the use of Lady Yule's yacht *Nahlin* for the
cruise in the Adriatic which first brought the name of Mrs
Simpson to the front pages of newspapers, though not the
newspapers of Britain, where a voluntary press censorship was
still being maintained.

When it was realized that, rather than abandon his plan to
marry Mrs Simpson, the King was prepared to abdicate there
was general agreement among those most intimately concerned
that Mrs Simpson ought to leave Britain. For her there was, she
wrote later, 'only one sanctuary within immediate reach – Villa
Lou Viei, the house of Katherine and Herman Rogers at
Cannes.' Lord Brownlow, a former Guards officer, known to his
friends as Perry, was deputed to escort her, together with a
chauffeur and a detective, the aim being to avoid, if possible, the
attentions of the press.

Unfortunately Lord Brownlow lacked two at least of the more
important qualifications for organizing a secret journey through
France. He spoke very little French and in spite of his service in
the Grenadier Guards he seems to have had some difficulty in
reading a map. Trouble began at Dieppe, where it was
discovered that although Mrs Simpson had assumed the name of
Harris for the journey her car registration papers were in the
name of Simpson. Further leakages were encouraged by Mrs
Simpson's insistence on ringing local telephone exchanges and
asking to be connected to Buckingham Palace. Nevertheless the

1 King Edward VII in the south of France: a caricature, 1901

2 James Gordon Bennett

3 Cora Pearl: the most celebrated courtesan of the Second Empire

4 Duke of Connaught and the King of Sweden

5 Winston Churchill with Somerset Maugham, at Villa Mauresque, Cap
Ferrat, April 1959

6 Marie Bashkirtseff

7 Renoir's house, Bas-de-Cagnes

8 Mrs Frank Jay Gould

party reached Rouen relatively unmolested, but the next day, as they began to approach Deauville, it was realized rather belatedly that they were heading in the wrong direction. Not surprisingly, by the time they arrived at the Rogers' villa they were accompanied by a sizeable press convoy.

Among the early outings Mrs Simpson made from Cannes was to a villa near Monte Carlo belonging to Esmond Harmsworth's mother. The King was still on the throne, and Mrs Simpson now learnt of a plan to appoint a council of state in Britain, with the King going abroad until, as she put it, 'the crisis simmered down'. Nothing of course came of the plan. Mrs Simpson remained at the Villa Lou Viei, waiting for the day when her divorce would be made absolute. Aunt Bessie was installed in the Carlton Hotel in Cannes, and the Duke of Windsor, as he had become, stayed at Schloss Enzesfeld in Austria, the home of Baron Eugène de Rothschild, where he had been joined by his loyal friend Edward Dudley Metcalfe, another former Army officer, who was known to his intimates as Fruity.

From Schloss Enzesfeid the Duke of Windsor telephoned Mrs Simpson in Cannes every evening. The calls produced such tensions in her that she broke more than one of the Rogers' coral-handled soup-spoons which she clutched as she talked. Of the effect of these talks on the Duke of Windsor Fruity Metcalfe wrote to his wife: 'He's on the line for hours and hours every day to Cannes. I sometimes don't think these talks go so well. She seems to be always picking on him and complaining.' When the time came for him to leave, the Duke failed either to speak to or tip the servants who had looked after him during his prolonged stay, an omission attributed by Fruity Metcalfe to 'more d-n talking to Cannes'.

The Duke of Windsor and Mrs Simpson planned to be married on the Riviera, but, according to her account, the wishes of King George VI, who was disturbed by the Riviera's 'reputation as a playground', prevailed, and a sad little ceremony took place in a somewhat unsuitable French château, at which only seven British guests were present.

For some time the Windsors hesitated over acquiring a property on the Riviera, the Duchess explaining to Harold Nicolson: 'One never knows what may happen. I don't want to spend all my life in exile.' But in the spring of 1938 they took a ten-year lease on a villa outside Cannes, where they were staying when Poland was invaded and Britain declared war on Germany.

Three days after the declaration of war Sir Walter Monckton, who throughout the abdication crisis had given the King legal and other advice, appeared at the Windsors' home on the Riviera and informed them that they were expected to return to England. The Duchess refused to fly, and when it became apparent that the major obstacles in the way of their departure were to be the quantity of the Duchess's luggage and the question of her status in Britain even the loyal Fruity Metcalfe was driven to an outburst of anger. Eventually the Windsors reached a French channel port, the Duchess bringing so many cardboard boxes with her that a man as resourceful as Captain Lord Louis Mountbatten was seen to quail at the prospect of stowing them all on board a naval vessel.

The Duke of Windsor, as a British Army officer, carried out certain liaison duties in Paris, but after the French military collapse in 1940 he and the Duchess found themselves again for a time in their Riviera villa. Here in the company of Maurice Chevalier, whom they had invited, as the Duchess wrote, 'in the perhaps forlorn hope that he might be inspired to supply a last flash of lightheartedness in that dismal atmosphere', they heard on the radio that Italy had entered the war.

At this point, though neither of them seems to have shown much appreciation of the fact, the Windsors became a new source of concern to the British Government, for the prospect of their being taken into custody by the enemy was a disturbing one. There was therefore some relief when it was learnt in London that they had crossed the Spanish frontier in a convoy organized by the British consul in Nice, so beginning a journey which in the course of time was to take them to the Bahamas.

After the war the Duke and Duchess of Windsor returned temporarily to the Riviera. In July 1947 they gave a press conference there, at which it was revealed that the Duchess was studying the French language. In 1949 the *Riviera News* announced: 'The decision of the Duke and Duchess of Windsor and Mr and Mrs Winston Churchill to see the New Year in at the Monte Carlo Sporting Club launched the Winter Season more successfully than any other publicity could have done.' But the Windsors' new association with the Riviera was to be short-lived.

They found it changed, and they soon developed a new style of life which was centred on Paris. In this the Duke, finally relieved of all responsibility, may well have found much quiet satisfaction. The Duchess for her part came to earn the accolade of the indefatigable hostess Elsa Maxwell, who described her as 'my favourite among all pace-setters in France'.

V

In the last decade or two before the First World War half-a-dozen or more sovereign rulers might have been found on the Riviera at any one moment during the winter season. In an entry which she made in her journal in Cimiez in April 1898 Queen Victoria, describing a carriage drive, recorded laconically: 'On our way down to Villefranche we met Leopold of Belgium walking.' A chance encounter on the road between two reigning monarchs was not an unusual enough event to excite more than passing comment. The flow of royal visitors continued during the inter-war years, but although it was to French resorts that the members of European and other royal families came, it was largely a British way of life that many of them adopted once they were there. The Russian Grand Duke Michael, for instance, who as a layer of foundation stones fulfilled a role similar to that assumed later by the Duke of Connaught, formally opened the new golf course at Valescure at a time when golf can barely have been known in Russia. Prince Albert of Prussia regularly attended Anglican services at Christ Church in Cannes, where he made it known that he hoped the hymns would include *The Son of God goes forth to war*.

It was in Cannes that King Gustav V of Sweden first saw tennis being played. He asked an English visitor to instruct him in the game and so conceived an interest which was to bring his name before the general public outside Sweden as no fulfilment of his monarchical duties ever did. For many years the King's tall figure dominated the Riviera tournaments, where he would dribble and splutter so persistently that Elsa Maxwell advised her other guests to wear raincoats whenever they were invited to meet the King. The King would leave his more skilful partners to occupy two-thirds of their side of the net, an arrangement which enabled him to say, whenever his partner missed, 'pity you didn't leave that to me', and with the passage of time his judgment of whether balls struck by his opponents were in or out became increasingly eccentric. But he was still playing at the age of eighty, partnered by pretty girls on the tennis courts and by pretty boys elsewhere.

Charles Graves described how the Paramount Pasha of Marrakesh, accompanied by his Grand Vizier, played golf at Mont-Agel. E. Phillips Oppenheim described how the Queen of Siam, as the country was then generally called, played tennis partnered by H.W. (Bunny) Austin. Once she had taken her position on the court the Queen resolutely refused to move, a practice which Austin, one of only two Englishmen to reach a Wimbledon singles final in the last half-century, found so disconcerting that he could do little except serve a string of double faults.

King Manoel of Portugal suffered an unfortunate experience as a result of one or two meetings on the Riviera with the actress Gaby Deslys. Through her press agent she announced that the King had given her a costly string of pearls, later admitting that she had done so for publicity purposes, the pearls having been the gift of a rich Argentinian. But the original story gained enough credence to do the King a good deal of damage, and Mlle Deslys only narrowly escaped physical violence when she visited Lisbon. After being deposed the former King was heard to say that he preferred the life of an English gentleman to the turmoil of statecraft, an opinion shared, in part at least, by another well-known figure on the Riviera, ex-King Alfonso of Spain. He indeed played polo for the 165th Lancers, of which he was colonel-in-chief, and said to the commanding officer after the game, according to Charles Graves: 'Thank God I didn't let the regiment down, old boy.'

Leopold II, King of the Belgians, who was largely responsible for bringing a vast area of Africa under Belgian control, became in his later years an addict of Riviera life. Unlike Queen Victoria, who timed her visits judiciously, King Leopold offended many of his subjects by spending as much time as he did in what they regarded as a playground, though any criticisms they expressed left him largely unconcerned. 'I do not seek the applause of the masses,' he once declared.

Princess Daisy of Pless gave a vivid picture of King Leopold on the Riviera peeling grapes with his long finger-nails, 'a look of cruelty on his face as if he were skinning alive the President and all the members of the Aborigines Protection Society.' She added that she had not seen his toe-nails, though she understood plenty of other women had done so. At an advanced age he was still strenuously pursuing young women in spite of a white beard which was of such inordinate length that in photographs it has all the appearance of a comic stage-prop. One of his girls, Blanche-Caroline Delacroix, he first met when he was sixty-five and she was eighteen. For a time they occupied adjoining suites in hotels when travelling, but eventually he gave her a house in Belgium and created her Baroness de Vaughan, largely, it seems, in order to annoy the cardinal of the same name. Apart from the pursuit of young girls King Leopold's principal interest in his Riviera days was his cult of physical fitness through exercise. His preferred daily reading was the London *Times*.

King Leopold, whom Princess Daisy described as 'a true Coburg', may well be regarded as the least attractive of all the royal personages who made a major impact on the social life of the Riviera. The most charming was, in the opinion of many, the Empress Eugénie.

During much of the Second Empire a summer court was held in Biarritz, near the frontier with the Empress's native country, Spain. Later she made a home for herself on the Riviera, largely under the influence of Prosper Mérimée, who had been a kind of unofficial tutor to her as a girl and who became one of her principal confidants when she felt the need to discuss such subjects as the Emperor's infidelities. Mérimée himself, who consciously adopted the manner known as *flegme britannique*, lived, when he was in Cannes, more in the style of an Englishman than of a Frenchman. Among the offices he held was that of President of the Archery Club. Here his arrows were regularly picked up by the two English sisters who accompanied him whenever he went out, and whom the ex-Lord Chancellor Brougham described as 'scarcely appropriate Psyches for such a large Cupid'.

The Empress had attended an English school at Clifton, where in spite of being called Carrots, she seems to have taken a liking to English ways. After the fall of the Empire she left for England from Deauville aboard an English yacht. She made new homes for herself in Chislehurst and later Farnborough. Her son, the Prince Imperial, became a British officer and was killed, fighting with almost foolhardy gallantry, in the Zulu war. She herself, in spite of being the wife of a Bonaparte, charmed Queen Victoria.

When she returned to France to stay in the villa she had built at Cap Martin it was in the role of an exiled monarch, whose roots were now mainly in England. In time she came to be described as the *doyenne* of royalty on the Riviera, still exercising in her nineties the charm which had distinguished her all her life.

Of all the hereditary rulers who spent much of their time on the Riviera none was more influenced by certain aspects of British life than the Aga Sultan, Sir Mohammed Shah, known as Aga Khan III, the acknowledged leader of millions of Moslems who were subject to British rule.

The Aga Khan first visited the Riviera in 1898 by steamer from Bombay. He was then aged twenty and, in his own words, 'a solemn young man, very serious about scientific and cultural interests'. Queen Victoria was at Cimiez, the Emperor Francis Joseph was at Cap Martin, and there were, he wrote,

> a score or so Russian Grand Dukes and Austrian Archdukes in their villas and palaces, half the English peerage with a generous sprinkling of millionaires from industry and finance; and most of the Almanac de Gotha from Germany, the Austro-Hungarian Empire, the Balkan countries lately 'emancipated' from Ottoman rule, and Tsarist Russia.

As he himself put it, 'the young man from Bombay was dazzled and awed.'

Ten years after his first visit the Aga Khan made the acquaintance of a young Italian dancer of the Monte Carlo ballet, Theresa Magliano, whom he married according to Moslem law in Cairo. She gave birth to a son in Turin, and later the Aga Khan installed mother and son in a villa above Monte Carlo. He continued to pay them regular visits, and in time the sight of the Aga Khan, dressed according to the English custom in blue blazer and white flannel trousers, became one of the most familiar among Riviera promenaders.

The Aga Khan's sympathies with British customs and British policy were to have important consequences in the First World War, for immediately after its outbreak he informed his followers in India, East Africa and elsewhere that he expected them to support the British authorities, guidance which was readily accepted in spite of the fact that the principal Moslem power engaged in the war, Turkey, was ranged on the other side.

In the inter-war years the Aga Khan enjoyed during his Riviera visits a privileged political and social status. At a luncheon given at the Hôtel Metropole in Monte Carlo by the British Ambassador in Berlin, Lord D'Abernon, for instance, there were only two guests present, the Aga Khan and Gustav Stresemann, the German Foreign Minister. The main topic of discussion was whether people of the same European race should be allowed to unite by peaceful means, a process then known as 'rectification'.

The son whom Theresa Magliano bore to the Aga Khan, although educated largely in England, felt himself more at home on the Riviera than anywhere else. As Major Aly Khan he served in the Second World War in the Free French forces and in 1944 landed with them at St Tropez. In the same year his father took another wife, a young Frenchwoman from Cannes who in 1930 had won the title 'Miss France' in a beauty contest.

In the years following the Second World War Aly Khan was to become perhaps the best known of all Riviera playboys of his generation, the highlight of his activities there being his marriage to the Hollywood star, Rita Hayworth.

To mark the occasion the communist mayor of Vallauris proclaimed a public holiday. The presence of British Royalty on the Riviera was by then little more than a memory.

5 Political Leaders

I

In 1859 Richard Cobden, after declining Lord Palmerston's invitation to become President of the Board of Trade, offered his services instead as a special negotiator with the French Government. The outcome was the Anglo-French commercial treaty of 1860. Cobden spent more than a year in France before he had completed his task, and in March 1860 he visited Cannes.

Cobden was no *grand seigneur*. He was the son of a small farmer and began work as a clerk in a warehouse. The calico-printing business which he had created was in ruins, largely because he had neglected it to campaign for the repeal of the corn laws, and for the greater part of his time in France he enjoyed no official standing. Yet while he was on the Riviera he was approached by three of the leading citizens of Grasse, who asked him to intercede with the French Government to have a railway built from Grasse to Cannes.

> I remarked [he wrote later] that in England a rich and industrious community like theirs would have a meeting and form a company to make a line for themselves, seeing that it would pay a good interest for their investment. They replied that it was not their way of doing things in France; they were accustomed to look to the Government to take the initiative.

An incident such as this helps to explain the ambivalence of the attitude adopted by a number of leading British statesmen who came to know the Riviera. In diplomatic negotiations with the French they acted as representatives of one major power dealing with those of another major power, whose arts and sciences and traditions they generally respected. When holidaying on the Riviera, by contrast, they thought and acted for the most part as inherently superior beings, an attitude which the economy of the Riviera did nothing to discourage and much to promote.

The first British Prime Minister to establish a home for himself on the Riviera was Robert Gascoyne-Cecil, third Marquess of Salisbury. Creating this home appealed to him at first mainly as a means of escaping from the pressure of people while recovering from the effects of the English winter.

Lord Salisbury was not a gregarious man. At Eton he had been so badly bullied that during the school holidays he would avoid the main streets of London for fear of meeting some of his schoolfellows. Even before going to Eton he had begun to develop his lifelong interest in a subject which readily appeals to solitary people, the study of botany. 'Solitude', his biographer A.L. Kennedy wrote, 'was as much a necessity to him as it had been to his hero the younger Pitt.'

In his earlier years in office Lord Salisbury was not much attracted by the prospect of foreign travel. On being chosen to represent Britain at the conference of great powers in Constantinople in 1876, he wrote to his wife: 'An awful nuisance – not at all in my line – involving seasickness, much French, and failure.' But while out of office between 1880 and 1885 he developed the habit of taking an annual holiday in France. Sometimes he chose Dieppe, sometimes Biarritz and sometimes the Riviera, and on his return to office he was reluctant to discontinue his visits. He could, he pointed out to his Foreign Office staff, be reached just as easily in Dieppe as in Scotland.

For a number of years Salisbury succumbed to attacks of influenza at the end of the winter, and it was the recurrence of these which decided him to choose the Riviera in preference to any other part of France as the site of his holiday home.

Lord and Lady Salisbury, unlike a number of their distinguished contemporaries, did not care for hotel life, and during a month spent in a Monte Carlo hotel in 1886 they decided to buy a plot of land in the hills above Beaulieu, which was then little more than a village with one street. Building began some four years later.

During the greater part of the 1890s Salisbury held the posts of both prime minister and foreign secretary. Year after year he was obliged to spend several weeks on the Riviera convalescing, not during the summer parliamentary recess, but in the spring. From time to time his nephew Arthur Balfour took temporary charge of the Foreign Office, but it was not until late in 1900, less than three years before his death, that Salisbury, who was already over seventy, decided he would no longer try to combine the two offices in one person.

In his last dozen years Salisbury, while on the Riviera, found continual pleasure in his garden. 'A glorious garden,' Marie Mallet wrote, 'where tulips, anemones, irises and forget-me-nots grow wild and in great masses.' His social life was quiet and his contact with the Monte Carlo casino limited. According to his daughter Lady Gwendolen Cecil, he was once refused entry to the casino because of his unconventional style of dress. The version of the story given by General Pierre Polovtsoff, who in the inter-war years became President of the International Sporting Club, is that Salisbury, having arrived at the casino without a passport, explained: 'You see, I'm the man who issues them.' But the two versions agree on one point. This is that he was not allowed in.

By the time Salisbury was refused admission the casino authorities already took pride in the fact that there were certain rules which could be waived for no one – not even Lord Salisbury, whose standing on the Riviera was such that in 1897, when he had one of his more serious attacks of influenza, bulletins of his progress, as they were received from London, were prominently displayed on the casino premises.

II

Like Salisbury, Gladstone discovered the attractions of the Riviera only in his later years. In 1883, when he was seventy-three, he had a six weeks' holiday in Cannes. Towards the end of it he learnt that Queen Victoria had offered to confer a peerage on him, but he was so refreshed by his holiday that not only did he refuse the peerage, thereby making it clear to the Queen that he had no intention of retiring, but he returned to England believing, in the words of one of the best of his biographers, Sir Philip Magnus, that he was 'tied to politics by a divine summons to make a Christian response to a series of political challenges.'

Four years later Gladstone and his wife stayed in the Château Scott in Cannes as guests of Lord Wolverton. Of this experience he wrote:

Here we fell in with the foreign hours, the snack early, déjeuner at noon, dinner at seven, break-up at ten. I am stunned at this wonderful place, and so vast a change at a moment's notice in the conditions of life.

Among those whom Gladstone met during this visit to Cannes was Georges Clemenceau, whom he described as 'decidedly pleasing'.

In 1897 came the final meeting with Queen Victoria. The Queen on this occasion shook hands with Gladstone, 'a thing', he noted, 'which had never happened to me during all my life.' He also noted that the Queen's room was 'populated by a copious supply of Hanoverian royalties'.

About a fortnight before this meeting Gladstone, who was then eighty-seven and on holiday, wrote an open letter from Cannes to the Duke of Westminster, in which he pleaded for a policy of liberty, humanity and Christianity in dealing with the problems of the Near East. In this he described Turkey and Germany as two powers ruled by young men, the one 'a pure and perfect despotism', the other 'equivalent to it in matters of foreign policy'. Of the English he wrote: 'The air of freedom is the very breath of their nostrils.'

Gladstone spent his eighty-eighth birthday in Cannes, ravaged by cancer and suffering from what he described as 'roaring pains'. He stayed with Lord Riddell, whose daughter had married Gladstone's son, and when he left the house for the last time in February 1898, 'the eagle eye', according to another of his biographers, Sir Wemyss Reid, 'lighted up once more as it swept the faces of his friends.' Gladstone then 'reverently uncovered his head, and in a low, solemn voice prayed to God that the house and all in it would be blessed by Him.' Sir Wemyss concluded: ' "He did not forget anyone, not even the servants," said to me one who watched the pathetic scene with eyes brimming over with tears.'

III

The period when leading British political figures were most numerous and prominent on the Riviera was shortly after the First World War, the central figure among them being the Prime Minister, David Lloyd George. Lloyd George had spent some time on the Riviera in 1911, when he was aged forty-eight, convalescing and, according to a variety of ill-founded rumours, suffering from cancer of the throat, certain to resign and likely to die soon. He planned to visit Nice in 1920, but the visit was cancelled, the *Menton and Monte Carlo News*, in a remarkable inversion of cause and effect, offering as the reason for the canellation 'the economical difficulties which have arisen in England in consequence of the great amount of unemployment.' Two winters later Lloyd George did come to the Riviera, his visit this time being perhaps as memorable as any made by a British statesman to the area.

After the First World War leaders of the principal European powers held their conferences by preference in holiday resorts either on the shores of the Mediterranean or on those of the Swiss or Italian lakes, a practice started during the war itself with the meeting at Rapallo, whose main purpose had been to persuade the Italian Government to continue to wage war. When the Supreme Council of the Allies decided to hold a major conference to settle, among other issues, the question of German reparations, it was in accordance with current procedure therefore that the site chosen should be Cannes.

Lloyd George arrived in Cannes several days before the opening of the conference, which had been fixed for 6 January 1922. For part of the time he was able to relax with excursions into the mountains, picnics beside the Grande Corniche and golf. But he was not allowed to escape entirely from the kind of political intrigue which characterized British politics of the time, nor perhaps would he have wished to. While in Cannes he received a letter from the Liberal Chief Whip advocating an early dissolution of Parliament. This was followed by a letter from Austen Chamberlain, who was then the effective leader of the Conservative Party within the Coalition Government, bitterly opposing the suggestion. Lloyd George instructed his secretary, J.T. Davies, to take soundings in London, and in particular to consult Lord Birkenhead and Winston Churchill. Birkenhead's advice was that if the support of Andrew Bonar Law could be obtained for the dissolution plan the Chamberlain faction would be routed.

Bonar Law was in Cannes at the time. So was his friend Lord Beaverbrook, who was staying at the Carlton Hotel. So was the Foreign Secretary, Lord Curzon, who was at the Grand Hotel. According to the account given by one of Lloyd George's biographers, Frank Owen, who obtained much of his information from Lord Beaverbrook himself and from the Beaverbrook papers, Lloyd George followed Birkenhead's advice and offered Bonar Law the post of Foreign Secretary without, of course, consulting the holder of the office at his hotel round the corner. Bonar Law refused the offer because of the state of his health, there was no immediate dissolution, and some nine months later the famous 1922 meeting took place at the Carlton Club in London, at which Bonar Law became leader of the Conservative Party.

To the bulk of the British on the Riviera, who were spared any knowledge of these manoeuvres, the presence of Lloyd George accompanied by an impressive delegation was an encouraging manifestation of British authority.

Let us hope [the *Menton and Monte Carlo News* wrote] that Cannes is duly grateful and that the town which Lord Brougham discovered as a simple little fishing village will realise that it has now taken its undying place in the history of the world thanks to another Englishman – beg pardon, Welshman.

The leader of the French delegation to the conference, which was held in the Cercle Nautique, was Aristide Briand, with whom Lloyd George had established excellent relations during the war, the *rapport* between them being attributed by Lloyd George largely to the fact that they were both Celts. During the conference, in spite of political difficulties, the two men remained in close personal harmony. In the villa in which Lloyd George was staying there was a parrot, whose vocabulary was limited to three words. These it produced with exquisite timing when a member of the British delegation, Sir Laming Worthington-Evans, the Secretary of State for War, was treating the other guests to a discourse. The three words the parrot knew were 'you bloody fool'. The story spread around Cannes, and it was typical of the Briand–Lloyd George relationship that when the German delegate Walther Rathenau was addressing the conference Briand asked Lloyd George if he could borrow the parrot.

Briand was the target for a good deal of criticism in the French press once the conference had begun. On the two main subjects which it had been convened to settle, German reparations and the future military commitments of the victorious allies to each other, popular opinion in France ran high, and there was a widespread belief that in his dealings with Lloyd George Briand was willing to concede too much. Progress in the Cercle Nautique was slow, and Lloyd George came to the conclusion that an informal lunch might help to break down barriers. The venue chosen was the clubhouse at the Cannes golf course, and the guests included Briand, Curzon, Bonar Law and the Italian Prime Minister, Ivanoe Bonomi, who was to have a brief return to office more than twenty years later after the Allied occupation of Rome in 1944.

After lunch a journalist representing the Central Press Agency in London suggested that the Prime Ministers should have a round of golf. Lloyd George had played a good deal of golf, much of it at Walton Heath, where the proprietor of the *News of the World* had presented him with a house near the course. Briand and Bonomi had never played, but this did not deter them. Nor did it deter the press photographers. Off the first tee Briand and Bonomi both hit surprisingly good drives. After that their troubles started, Briand cutting up so much turf and throwing up so many clouds of sand that Lloyd George seemed to be collapsing with laughter. Whenever either Briand or Bonomi did eventually hole out it was the signal for vociferous congratulations.

The golf outing took place on 9 January. On the 11th the messages Briand received in Cannes convinced him he must return to Paris at once. Not only was he accused of betraying France's interests, but he had been shown in press photographs to be neglecting his duties and making himself ridiculous by his antics on the golf course. He left from Cannes railway station, promising to return within thirty-six hours. It was a promise he could not keep. Within hours of his return his government was overthrown, his Foreign Secretary, Jean Barthou, having chosen to side with Briand's adversary, Raymond Poincaré. Briand asked Barthou what the current equivalent was of thirty pieces of silver.

With the fall of Briand the Cannes conference was dissolved, and the delegates returned home, having achieved virtually nothing. How far the golf episode was responsible for the failure must be a matter of opinion. Contemporary English newspaper comment suggested that it was of little account. The only reference to golf in the lengthy reports and analyses of the conference which appeared in *The Times*, for instance, was: 'M. Briand went on with his work, taking his golf lesson from Mr Lloyd George and giving smiling assurances to the world that all was going well.' With hindsight it may be thought that the decision to include two such contentious and large unrelated issues as German reparations and military security in the agenda jeopardized the chances of success from the start. But the belief has grown up and has been supported by thoughtful historians that it was the comic golf match which killed the Cannes conference. What is certain is that with the replacement of Briand by Poincaré a deterioration began in Anglo-French political relations, a deterioration which, it may be thought, was not effectively arrested for more than half a century.

The following year Lloyd George came back to Cannes again. He chartered a yacht and lunched with Sir Basil Zaharoff, the armaments king, who then controlled the Monte Carlo casino. Subsequently his Riviera visits became less frequent, but in 1938 he celebrated his golden wedding in Antibes. It was during this visit that he wrote a letter from Antibes to a Welsh professor at Heidelberg University, T.P. Cornwell-Evans, which revealed with frightening clarity the deterioration which had taken place in his judgment. 'I have never doubted', Lloyd George wrote, 'the fundamental greatness of Herr Hitler as a man.' He went on to state: 'I only wish we had a man of his supreme quality at the head of affairs in our country today. Mussolini is temperamentally an aggressor. I have never thought that Herr Hitler was, and I do not believe it now.'

In February 1939 Lloyd George visited the Riviera for the last time, staying in Monte Carlo as the guest of Lord Beaverbrook. Beaverbrook was still confident that war could be avoided, but in mid-March, on learning of the German occupation of Czechoslovakia, Lloyd George shed what remained of his belief in Hitler's pacific intentions and returned sorrowfully to England and to what he now believed to be the certain prospect of war.

IV

At the age of seventy-eight Winston Churchill said to his physician, Lord Moran: 'They talk of my taking a holiday in France. It is absurd. I don't take holidays, coconut shies and that sort of thing. I shall work all morning and paint all afternoon.'

It was a regime with which he had become familiar on the Riviera more than thirty years earlier. In January 1920, when he was staying at the Hôtel Regina in Nice, a newspaper report stated: 'Every afternoon he motors out to the Pont du Var, and, choosing a picturesque spot, gets to work with palette and brush.' He learnt to develop his landscape style largely as a result of a chance encounter in the south of France with some disciples of Cézanne, and during his fairly frequent visits to the Riviera in the inter-war years he painted at times with such zest that he was dissatisfied when he did not complete two pictures in a day.

Painting for Churchill was a recreation. The work he spoke of when telling Lord Moran how he intended to spend his time in France was writing, and into this too he threw himself vigorously during a number of his visits to the Riviera between the wars. In December 1922, for instance, after being defeated in the parliamentary election for Dundee East – 'if you ever saw the kind of lives the Dundee folk have to live', he wrote, 'you would admit they have many excuses' – he set off for France where he rented a villa in Cannes. Here he spent most of the spring of 1923 working on the second volume of *The World Crisis*.

It was not Churchill's normal practice to rent a villa. Usually he stayed as a guest in someone else's home, more often than not with Americans or Canadians. Among his hostesses were Madame Jacques Balsan, formerly Consuelo Vanderbilt, who had a villa in the hills above Eze, and the American actress Maxine Elliott, owner of the much admired Villa l'Horizon, which overlooked the bay of Cannes from the Cap d'Antibes.

By the time he acquired his taste for Riviera life Churchill, who at one time had played golf fairly frequently with Lloyd George, had lost interest in the game, for which he was temperamentally too impatient. Gambling in the casino on the other hand continued to attract him. Of the various eye-witness accounts of Churchill in the Monte Carlo casino one describes an occasion when he arrived there with Maxine Elliott. Lord Beaverbrook was also of the party. So too was a red-haired young man, whose identity was not then generally known, a failed schoolmaster and something of a political and financial adventurer, who was to become a remarkable good Minister of Information in the Second World War, Brendan Bracken. Maxine Elliott was extremely fat in her later years and spent much of her time sitting beside her swimming-pool in the Villa l'Horizon playing backgammon. But when the dance-band struck up *Under the Spreading Chestnut Tree* she and Churchill joined in enthusiastically with all the appropriate gestures. Of the numerous legends which have attached themselves to Churchill's forays into the gaming-rooms one relates how he lost, presumably at baccarat, to the German arms manufacturer Gustav Krupp von Bohlen. Churchill, the story goes, swore he would have his revenge, but was prevented from meeting Krupp in the casino again by the outbreak of war in 1939. Like the story of the *crêpes Suzette* it is at least *ben trovato*.

Writing, painting and gambling occupied much of Churchill's time when he visited the Riviera in the 1930s, but it was on the Riviera too that he spent an appreciable part of that period of brooding in the wilderness which not uncommonly precedes the return to power of men whose decisions shape the lives of millions. In the summer of 1934 the information which had reached him of the speed at which Germany was rearming caused him so much concern that with his son Randolph he set off by car from Cannes to see the Prime Minister, Stanley

Baldwin, at Aix-les-Bains. Baldwin does not seem to have welcomed this interruption of his holiday.

In 1938 Churchill invited two men who happened to be on holiday on the Riviera to lunch with him and to discuss the gravity of the threat facing their country. One of them, Lloyd George, had been his closest colleague when confronted with some of the most contentious issues of the First World War. The other, Anthony Eden, was to share with him the formulation of British foreign policy in the Second.

Churchill was at Antibes early in 1939. During the Second World War he did not set foot on the Riviera, though there was one occasion when he came near to doing so. The decision to invade the south of France in the summer of 1944 was an American one with which Churchill disagreed. He considered it would be a wasteful employment of a powerful striking force and, in his own words, he did his best 'to constrain or divert' the whole operation. The Roosevelt-Eisenhower judgment prevailed, and, accepting the decision in good part, Churchill decided to watch the landings from the destroyer *Kimberley*, which conveyed him from Corsica.

Somewhat to his annoyance Churchill learnt that the destroyer's orders were to approach no nearer than a few miles from the coast, largely because of the danger of mines. Had he known this, he commented a little peevishly later, he could have 'asked for a picket boat and gone ashore'. He did not see or hear any shots fired at the landing forces, and on the return journey to Corsica he occupied himself by reading Vicki Baum's *Grand Hotel*, a copy of which he had found on board the destroyer. He was to return to the Riviera later.

V

Salisbury, Gladstone, Lloyd George, Churchill, were not the only British Prime Ministers, present, past and future, who visited the Riviera repeatedly. Arthur Balfour came there a number of times, both before the First World War and in the 1920s after his withdrawal from the political scene. In 1912 he represented Cannes against Nice at golf, and in the same year he informed his sister in a letter from Cannes that he had 'won two prizes at lawn tennis', adding 'both of course under handicaps'. As even in country house tennis he made a practice of asking for new balls, not because they were easier to control but because they made his shortsightedness less of an impediment, this was evidently a triumph of determination or of the handicapper.

The arrival of Anthony Eden at Monte Carlo in February 1937 'aroused', the *Menton and Monte Carlo News* reported, 'a great deal of interest, perhaps more than was to the gentleman's liking.' Of his discussions the next year with Churchill and others Eden, with his unwavering talent for describing the most momentous events in words of almost total banality, wrote: 'We discussed the state of Europe and the threats of the two dictators.' Of the rest of his visit he added in equally scintillating prose: 'I played tennis and the days rolled uneventfully by.'

Eden's holiday in 1938 was interrupted by a telephone call from Sir Alexander Cadogan, the Foreign Office's Permanent Under-Secretary, who advised him to return to London. An important despatch would, Cadogan explained, be awaiting him at the British Consulate-General in Marseilles. Accompanied by his private secretary Harold Caccia, who was himself later to become Permanent Under-Secretary, Eden promptly set off by train from Cannes. When he reached the consulate there was no despatch. It was then discovered that the train from Paris which was supposed to be bringing it had been divided into two parts. One part had gone to Marseilles and the despatch had been put in the other. It was not until he reached England, after an exceptionally disagreeable channel crossing, that Eden learnt of the personal message sent by President Roosevelt to the Prime Minister, Neville Chamberlain, expressing his concern about the deterioration in the international scene. It was a message whose significance Eden was better equipped to appreciate than its recipient.

Neville Chamberlain himself was unusual among British Prime Ministers in the first half of the twentieth century in not being a devotee of the Riviera. But he had a symbolic presence there in January 1939, when it was announced, in recognition of his achievements in preserving peace, that the Place des Iles in Cannes was to be renamed Square Neville Chamberlain.

British political figures of the second rank were to be found on the Riviera in such numbers in the inter-war years that the presence of all but the most colourful was liable to be barely noticed. One who did arouse the indignation of the *Menton and Monte Carlo News* was described as 'the young Socialist M.P. Mr Oswald Mosley', who in April 1926 was staying at the Grand Hotel on the Cap d'Antibes with 'his equally Socialist wife, Lady Cynthia Mosley'. The Mosleys, the report stated, appeared 'to be doing themselves rather well, and in a way which might possibly arouse the envy of their Socialist "comrades".' The report concluded: 'Perhaps there are degrees of Socialism, as of other things.'

The arrival rather more than five years later of Arthur Henderson, the former Labour Foreign Secretary, to recuperate after influenza in the Hôtel des Anglais in Cannes as the guest of the Hon. Mrs Phillimore aroused no such editorial indignation. But by then the Labour Party had suffered such a massive electoral disaster, with Henderson himself losing his seat, that a more charitable judgment was no doubt deemed appropriate.

In the different British political dramas enacted on the Riviera one character who seemed to be perpetually on stage was Lord Beaverbrook, entertaining and manoeuvring, feuding and distributing largesse. The manner in which he indulged his personal tastes varied widely. Sometimes he would be under the joint influence of his calvinist inheritance and incipient hypochondria. The actress Ruby Miller, who met him in Monte Carlo when he was eating 'only some nasty-looking gooseberries', drinking mineral water and announcing he had only a few days to live, cured him by taking him to a party, where she insisted on his drinking champagne, dancing and eating a good dinner.

At other times Beaverbrook set out to enjoy himself, most noticeably when he was in the company of Lord Castlerosse, the huge Irish peer with the sharp wit and enormous appetites, whom Beaverbrook employed partly as social columnist and partly as buffoon. Lady Astor called him 'Lord Beaverbrook's Buttons'. The first meeting between Beaverbrook and Castlerosse had taken place in Monte Carlo, when Castlerosse had complained of the quality of an article written by Beaverbrook for the *Daily Express* and Beaverbrook had challenged him to do better. The subject of other meetings was the size of the gambling debts which Castlerosse had incurred and which

Beaverbrook settled.

Neither amusements nor politics prevented Beaverbrook from maintaining the rigid control of his newspapers, of which his daily telephone call to Fleet Street was both the symbol and the expression. From the Riviera as successfully as from anywhere else he was able to ensure that his highly individual policies were expressed in that distinctive prose style, an amalgam of tele-graphese and the Authorized Version of the Bible, which in prac-tice raised appreciably the general standard of English journal-ism in the 1930s.

Like Churchill, Beaverbrook was to return to the Riviera after the Second World War, both of them by then old men who had fought all their great battles and won the preponderance of them.

VI

In May 1948 Mrs Attlee, wife of the Prime Minister, arrived in Nice by air to play a role in the tradition of Lady Bountiful. A new convalescent home for French children had been built at Cap d'Antibes. All the money needed for it had been raised by voluntary contributions in Britain, and Mrs Attlee had come to perform the opening ceremony. The first two or three times Winston Churchill entered the Monte Carlo casino the following winter he was loudly applauded. Casino employees who witnessed the scene could remember a similar reception being given to Charles Chaplin in 1930. They could recall no other.

Anyone who may have thought that such incidents presaged a revival of the status which leading British political figures had enjoyed on the Riviera in the past must soon have been disillusioned. Circumstances had changed, foreign holdings had been mortgaged, and though, politically, Britain did accept the obligations and did try to assume the status of one of the world's two or three major powers, private spending abroad was limited by law to what those who had been able to afford foreign holidays in the past considered a derisory sum. As late as 1952 Churchill complained that he was unable to gamble when he was on the Riviera because he had no money to spend.

As the restrictions were gradually eased new holiday habits

were formed, and the British political figures of distinction who did come to the Riviera tended to be those whose greatness was in their past. Lord Beaverbrook, for instance, bought the villa once owned by Captain Edward Molyneux, the dress designer, at Cap d'Ail. Here he spent much of his time in the swimming-pool, only his straw hat showing above the surface as a male secretary read to him the day's leading articles in *The Times*. Whenever helicopters passed overhead the readings had to be repeated.

Churchill, who was made honorary mayor of Cap d'Ail, stayed there with Beaverbrook a number of times. On one of his visits at two o'clock in the morning, while playing gin-rummy, he suffered a stroke. He was then seventy-five. 'The dagger struck', he wrote, 'but this time it was not plunged in to the hilt.' He also described the experience as 'like being balanced between the Treasury bench and death'. Three days later he lunched at the Hôtel de Paris in Monte Carlo. The other hotel guests rose to their feet, nobody appeared to notice anything amiss, and Churchill's confidence immediately revived.

Churchill's last visits to the Riviera were as the guest of Aristotle Onassis, and on one occasion the three people present at a dinner in Nice were Onassis, Churchill and Greta Garbo. The Churchill–Onassis relationship puzzled Lord Moran, who described the two men as both assuming 'a kind of ruthless juggernaut pose'. But he added: 'I believe Ari to be a kindly man, a lonely soul for all his great wealth.' Churchill clearly found contentment on board Onassis's yacht in his final enfeebled state, and when Onassis was seen to be feeding him on one occasion with caviare from a spoon the gesture might have been interpreted as a tribute from the new power on the Riviera to the most famous representative of the grandeurs of the past.

6 The Rich and the Pleasure-loving

I

'Oh God, have pity on me! Out of charity – give me the Duke of Hamilton,' Marie Bashkirtseff wrote in her journal in Nice. 'Whose yacht is that?' Amanda asks in the first act of Noël Coward's *Private Lives*. Elyot replies: 'The Duke of Westminster's I expect. It always is.'

The Duke of Hamilton for whom Marie Bashkirtseff pined was the twelfth duke and a frequent visitor to Nice in the 1860s and 1870s. In himself he was a man of no great distinction, but he was Knight Marischal of Scotland, his mother, Princess Mary of Baden, was related to the Emperor Napoleon III through the Beauharnais connexion, and his sister married Prince Albert of Monaco. He was also immensely rich. To the adolescent Russian girl belonging to a slightly disreputable provincial family, whom the Russian nobility in Nice would not even receive, he represented perfection.

'A man of thirty,' she wrote of him, 'a man who lives only for racing, horses, shooting, hunting, and who adores good wine and bad women, who goes to see his mistress, lights his cigar with a calm and contented air.' On another occasion she commented: 'To have a woman since it's necessary for *le chic*; horses, a woman, pigeon-shooting, all those are the attributes of a young English nobleman who has fallen early into bad company.'

Two of the more impressive manifestations of the Duke of

Hamilton's wealth and of his standing on the Riviera were his yacht, the 480-ton steam yacht *Thistle*, and his mistress, a beautiful Italian named Gioia, whom he kept in a villa in Nice. Marie Bashkirtseff took a vicarious pleasure in watching Gioia drive through Nice in her carriage, sometimes in the company of the famous courtesan Cora Pearl, for her opportunities of seeing the Duke himself were limited. 'He's too rich and fashionable', she wrote, 'to stay at Nice in April.' For herself by contrast there was the prospect of a summer in Nice seeing only a few foreigners detained on business, gamblers, prostitutes and the Niçois whom she affected to despise.

Marie Bashkirtseff's prayer to be given the Duke of Hamilton was not of course granted. She never spoke to him, and less than a year after the first entry in her journal he was married to the eldest daughter of the seventh Duke of Manchester. Yet it was largely to give herself a means of expressing what she felt for the duke that she began the journal which, she rightly declared, would be 'interesting even in a hundred years'.

Marie Bashkirtseff's journal was begun in 1873. Gertrude Lawrence, for whom the part of Amanda was written, and Noël Coward began rehearsing *Private Lives* in Edward Molyneux's villa at Cap d'Ail in 1930. The Duke of Westminster whose yacht Amanda spotted was the second duke. In the years between the two world wars he enjoyed a standing on the Riviera comparable with that of the Duke of Hamilton half a century earlier, and he too was enormously rich.

The Duke of Westminster, known to his intimates as Bendor, a name he shared with a racehorse of which his family were inordinately proud, owned two superb yachts. One of these, *Flying Cloud*, remained for the most part in the Mediterranean, the other, *Cutty Sark*, being used for voyages elsewhere. *Flying Cloud* was a four-masted schooner more than two hundred feet in length with an auxiliary twin-screw engine. Her upper cabins were reached through an ornamental doorway and furnished with small-scale Queen Anne furniture. The yacht was also unusual in being fitted with a refrigerator.

Like those of the Duke of Hamilton, the Duke of Westminster's descents on the Riviera did not last long. His third wife Loelia, who remained married to him for five years before deciding on a separation, wrote: 'During the whole time that

Benny and I were together we were only once three weeks in the same place.' It was rare for the Duke to spend more than two or three days at a time on the Riviera, but this was long enough to allow him to hazard huge sums in the Monte Carlo casino. Not only did he play roulette for the maximum stake permitted, but he preferred to do so at three or four tables simultaneously. His slightly longer sojourns in France tended to be in Normandy, where he had a château. This he used mainly as a base for boar-hunting, an occupation for which he dressed in the traditional garb of an English master of foxhounds. An appreciable proportion of the expenditure he incurred through boar-hunting arose from the claims for compensation for damage which the local peasantry regularly submitted.

That the titled British and their friends should spend money freely was expected by the native inhabitants of the Riviera, and many British visitors enjoyed a reflected glory from their activities. Cousin Bette, the name under which the social gossip columnist of the *Menton and Monte Carlo News* wrote, could be relied on, for instance, to treat her readers regularly to such morsels as: 'Lady Kekewich, whose husband, Sir Trehawke, is of old Devonshire stock, is one of the very pretty women .... Lady Essex comes over from Beaulieu pretty often; her hair is a regular "Frimousse." ... The Duchess Sforza is interesting and exotic.'

Name-dropping of this kind could have been continued almost indefinitely, but increasingly in the twentieth century the hereditary aristocracy were outshone as big spenders among the British on the Riviera by men who had acquired their wealth more recently. Of the new rich few if any were more colourful than the progeny of Isaac Isaacs, who had earned a hard and meagre living in an overcrowded quarter of the east end of London.

II

Harry and Barney, the sons of Isaac Isaacs, took the name Barnato for a music-hall act which they performed as boys. It was not very successful, and Harry set off for South Africa to seek his fortune, followed before long by Barney. The going to begin with was hard. Barney got his first job as boxer-cum-clown in a travelling circus by first knocking out a man billed as the champion of Angola and then reciting Hamlet's 'to be or not to be' monologue while standing on his head. But with a capital of £200 they put up a sign which read 'Barnato Brothers, Dealers in Diamonds and Brokers in Mining Property', and with a speed which was astonishing even by the standards prevailing in South Africa in the late nineteenth century both brothers made fortunes.

Harry Barnato decided to enjoy his fortune in Europe and bought a villa on the Riviera, where he spent much of his time. When he died in 1908 he was worth £3 million. Barney found it less easy to divorce himself from commerce, and when asked whether it was true that he had £20 million he replied that he would need another £5 million to feel safe. He never did feel safe, he drank excessively, he was diagnosed as a manic-depressive, and it is more than likely that he deliberately took his own life when he went overboard from a ship.

As Harry Barnato was increasingly lured by the prospect of retirement to Europe his eldest nephew began to take on the role of Barney's deputy. This was Woolf Joel, son of Kate, the sister of Harry and Barney, who had married a man named Joel Joel. Woolf Joel soon followed his uncle Harry to the Riviera, where he acquired considerable prestige through a bet he made with an Australian financier named Frank Gardner. The bet was for £100 and the contest a walking race from La Turbie to Nice. Woolf Joel won the race, placed his £100 on red in the Monte Carlo casino, was paid out ten consecutive times, and made £16,000 in half an hour. Like that of his uncle Barney, Woolf Joel's death was sudden and has never been fully explained. He was shot by a German adventurer and blackmailer named Karl Kurtze, who called himself the Baron von Veltheim and who was certainly fortunate to have his plea of self-defence accepted.

Of the children of Joel and Kate Joel the one who appealed most to Barney Barnato was the third son, Solly. When he learnt that as a boy Solly Joel had sold pigeons to the local fanciers which had been trained to home on the Joels' loft, and had then resold them several times to the same buyers, he felt he had discovered someone with a future.

Solly Joel became one of the best known figures of his time on racecourses, in the world of musical comedy and on the Riviera. As an owner of winners of big races he was a rival to Lord Derby and the Aga Khan. He had a controlling interest in the Drury Lane theatre when shows as famous as *Rose Marie* and *Showboat* were staged there; he gave parties at which chorus girls were supplied with swimsuits which disintegrated when they came into contact with water; and on one occasion when he entered his theatre Clarice Mayne varied the routine by singing, 'Here comes Mr Solly Joel. Isn't he a jolly soul?' On the Riviera he liked to dress in white ducks and to smoke gold-tipped cigarettes in a holder encrusted with diamonds. (His uncle Barney, by contrast, had been known to attend important business conferences with his braces dangling from his trousers and with a parrot on his shoulder.)

Solly Joel was offered the casino concession at Monte Carlo but refused it. He sometimes gambled for huge stakes, but on one occasion, according to the biographer of the Barnatos and Joels, Stanley Jackson, sitting on the terrace of the Hôtel de Paris he was challenged to a game of *chemin-de-fer* by a young man and replied: 'What's the good? If I win a thousand pounds it makes no difference. If I lose it I'm miserable for the rest of the day.' In his later years Solly Joel gave the impression of being a lonely figure. He had quarrelled with his elder daughter Doris because he disapproved of her choice of a husband, and in a somewhat impotent expression of petulance he changed the name of his magnificent yacht, which was frequently to be seen in Cannes harbour, from *Doris* to that of her younger sister *Eileen*.

The last of the descendants of Isaac Isaacs to be acclaimed as a celebrity on the Riviera was the famous racing driver Woolf Barnato, son of Barney. Woolf Barnato won the twenty-four-hour endurance test at Le Mans three times running, he was an accomplished skier and rider, he won a bet – he seems to have been a shrewd judge when backing his own abilities – that he would reduce his golf handicap from seven to scratch within a year, and he kept wicket for Surrey. He was also a discerning financier, who took control of Bentley Motors. It is true that this venture cost him money, but as a means of maintaining such a beautiful object as the Bentley racing car in being, the money was, in his judgment, well spent.

Woolf Barnato differed from his father, his uncle and his

cousins in that he rose, not from poverty, but from an assured position, so much so indeed that a Lord Mayor of London was present at a party held to celebrate his circumcision.

Of the many fortunes made by Englishmen in the nineteenth and early twentieth centuries not a few were disposed of on the Riviera. Some of the methods of disposal were spectacular, some were speedy, and some were both. Colonel Smith, a former officer in the service of the East India Company, built himself a smaller-scale version of the Taj Mahal, which was known on the Riviera as 'the Englishman's folly', and in which he consumed enormous quantities of whisky and soda. The band leader Bert Ambrose, whom society hostesses pursued relentlessly in the 1920s in the hope of persuading him to perform at their dances, estimated that he lost more than half-a-million pounds in casinos to the so-called Greek syndicate. The experience led him into reversing the roles and becoming manager of a *chemin-de-fer* club in London. Sir William Hopwood, who was known as the Napoleon of the Lancashire cotton industry, on being refused admission to the Monte Carlo casino because he was not wearing a dinner jacket, suggested, as a way of by-passing the rules, that he should buy the whole casino. He at least was spared the expense.

Spectacular spending by the newly rich attracted plenty of opprobrium. The fastidious Augustus Hare, returning to the Riviera in the 1890s, wrote of Cannes:

> The hills are covered with hideous villas, chiefly built by rich Englishmen, whose main object seems to be the effacement of all the natural beauties of the place – to sow grass which will never live, to import from the north shrubs which cannot grow, and to cut down and root up all the original woods and flowers.

He found Nice 'a great, ugly, modern town' and Menton 'vulgarized and ruined'.

An anonymous versifier whose work appeared in the *Menton and Monte Carlo News* was even more scathing. The principal character he created was known as Profiteera, who appeared in 1920 in the lines:

Once again to Montikarlo comes the awful Profiteera
With the lurid Maridorta from his Palace in Baisworta.

Profiteera may or may not have been based on a living original.
He is unlikely to have been a Yorkshireman. 'Not many
Yorkshiremen come to the casino in the season,' the *Menton and
Monte Carlo News* wrote, 'as they are too busy making money.' But
whether he existed in reality or not, he was sufficiently
recognizable to be featured regularly in the weekly paper:

In the deadly heat of summer, on the sun-scorched courts of
    Tennis,
See once more the Profiteera in an Oldarrovian Blaza.

War profiteers were an understandable target for abuse in 1920,
but there was a certain inconsistency in the *Menton and Monte Carlo
News*'s condemnation of them. The richest man on the Riviera at
the time derived his fortune entirely from the profits of war. In
February 1920 he was described in the *Menton and Monte Carlo News*
as 'Sir Basil Zaharoff, the great philanthropist'.

III

When asked what his nationality was Basil Zaharoff, according to
his biographer Donald McCormick, replied: 'I have almost
forgotten. I suppose I am all nationalities rolled into one. I was
born in Anatolia. My father was of Polish origin. My mother was
French with a Levantine strain.'
    In 1913 he acquired French citizenship, and the next year he
was made Commander of the Legion of Honour. He believed
France was the only country in which it was possible to lead a
civilized life but was accused of living there *comme un anglais*. In
1872 he married the daughter of a Bristol builder, whom he had
wooed in the guise of a Russian prince, and the next year he was
to be found trafficking in arms in Cyprus under the name of Z.Z.
Williamson. After making an enormous fortune by selling, to
use his own words, 'more arms than anyone else in the world',
he received an English knighthood. With strict impartiality in the
distribution of largesse he founded a chair of French literature at

Oxford and a chair of English literature at the Sorbonne, Oxford conferring on him an honorary degree for 'munificence to learning'.

In the early 1920s, largely because of the part he played in stimulating the Greco-Turkish war, Zaharoff was fiercely attacked in the House of Commons and in the British press, particularly the *Daily Express* and the *Daily Mail*, and he may well have served as the original of the protean international financier who was such a familiar villain in the English popular fiction of the period. It was during those years that Zaharoff controlled the Monte Carlo casino.

In 1918 Camille Blanc suggested to Prince Albert of Monaco that the annual payments for the casino concession should be reduced. The Prince disagreed and called in Zaharoff. This was not Zaharoff's first commercial venture on the Riviera, for earlier in his career he had established a number of brothels there which he used for entertaining and compromising politicians and generals. When Zaharoff assumed control of the Société des Bains de Mer one of the staff was another cosmopolitan figure named Nadel, who was almost certainly working for the French Sureté and who seems to have been making enquiries on its behalf into Zaharoff's birth certificate. Nadel was found dead in his room in Monte Carlo, having allegedly shot himself because of his gambling losses. He left about a million francs.

With the return of peace the Monte Carlo casino flourished again, Zaharoff doubling the amount of the minimum permitted stake. In 1925 he sold his casino interests to a consortium of French bankers, but he retained the ownership of the Hôtel de Paris, where he continued to live.

Zaharoff was not himself interested in playing the tables. In a letter to a newspaper he stated that during the forty winters he had spent in Monte Carlo he had never once entered the casino in order to gamble. Gambling for him was just another source of power, a power which derived from the fascination the tables exercised over people who might otherwise seem to have next to nothing in common, people of different backgrounds, different cultures and different nationalities. Arnold Bennett succeeded better than most in conveying the power of this fascination, for he had himself discovered that while he was in the casino winning forty-five francs 'the art of literature seemed a very small thing'. In an essay entitled *Monte* he wrote:

> Over the white-and-silver of the tea-table, in the falling twilight, with the incomparable mountain landscape in front of us, and the most *chic* and decadent Parisianism around us, we talked *roulette*. It is most extraordinary how the propinquity of a Grand Duke, experienced for the first time, affects even the proverbial phlegm of a British novelist.

There were probably larger individual gamblers among Russians, Americans and Greeks on the Riviera than there were among the British, but numerically British visitors to the casino for many years greatly exceeded those of any other nationality. Of the 5,346 people admitted to the International Sporting Club during the 1935–36 season 2,423, or about 45 per cent, were British. The French numbered 879, or about 16 per cent, the next largest contingents being Italians, Hungarians, Americans and Germans, in that order.

Before the First World War gold coins were still regularly used as stakes. 'A roulette table glittering with piles of golden louis was a wonderful sight', General Polovtsoff, President of the International Sporting Club, wrote: 'You felt that there was real money to be won.' There were also in the early years of the twentieth century a number of successes credited to Englishmen of the kind known as breaking the bank. One of the most celebrated of these was a combined performance by two addicts named Lord Rosslyn and Sam Lewis.

After Rosslyn and Lewis had won seven times consecutively a bell was rung and with some ceremony an employee of the casino was sent off to bring in more money. Rosslyn and Lewis continued to win, the bell was rung again, and still more money was fetched. After the ceremony had been performed a third time excitement in the casino was intense, but the observant Hiram Maxim remained sceptical.

> It had not been necessary for the bank to send for money at all [he wrote later]. This had been done for effect. It was telegraphed all over the world that Lord Rosslyn and Mr

Sam Lewis had broken the bank three consecutive times in a single evening. True, the bank had lost money, but they turned it into a valuable advertisement.

In the inter-war years the most successful baccarat players were the members of the Greek syndicate, whose guiding spirit, Nico Zographos, was the son of a professor of political economy in Athens. But even they decided that it would be desirable to have an Englishman playing the cards, and their choice fell on the acting manager of Lloyd's Bank in Monte Carlo, Reggie Simmons. Lloyd's had decided to amalgamate their Monte Carlo and Menton branches and Simmons was in danger of being transferred to Paris. He therefore accepted Zographos's offer, underwent a course of intensive training – Zographos once told Charles Graves that there was as great a difference between a good and a bad baccarat player as there was between a scratch and an 18-handicap golfer – and after service with the syndicate became banker of the municipal casino at Nice.

Lurid accounts abounded of the fate of people who had ruined themselves at the tables. A German naval officer named Captain Weihe, who spent three winter seasons in Monte Carlo, even wrote a book in which he declared that at the end of the season the bodies of suicides were packed into weighted cases and sunk far out at sea between the French mainland and Corsica. The earlier practice, he stated, had been to thrust the corpses into cracks in the limestone on which the casino and other buildings stood, but the smell had become so disagreeable that large numbers of Italian workmen were employed to transfer the corpses to the sea.

In reality the only provision which the casino authorities made for losers was the so-called *viatique*, the name given to the one-way ticket which was presented to people who were unable to pay for their journey home. The system continued to be operated up to 1939, although the Société des Bains de Mer was understandably reluctant to publicize it.

People who had been issued with *viatiques* were among the large number, estimated at one time to exceed 100,000, whom the authorities would not allow into the casino. To ensure their exclusion an elaborate card-index system was supplemented by the employment of a number of expert physiognomists, one of

9 La Croisette, Cannes

10 Carlton Hotel, Cannes, whose cupolas recalled the shape of la Belle Otéro

11 Dog's bar at the Carlton Hotel, Cannes

12 The battle of the flowers, Cannes, 1889

13 Lloyd George demonstrating golf to Aristide Briand, Prime Minister of France, at Cannes in January 1922

14 The Duke and Duchess of Windsor at the 'Bal des Petits Lits Blancs',
Cannes, August 1939

15 Cannes film festival—Gina Lollobrigida

16 Boulevard des Anglais, Nice

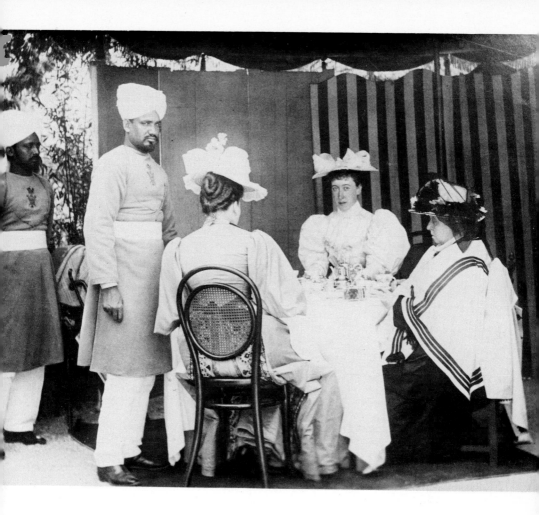

17 Russian church, Nice

18 Queen Victoria, with Beatrice, Princess Henry of Battenberg (*back view*), Princess Helena Victoria of Schleswig-Holstein (*facing*), and Indian attendants Sheikh Ghulam Mustafa and Sheikh Chidda, Nice, April 1895

19 *below* Prince Leopold (*left*) and Prince Maurice of Battenberg, Nice, April 1895

20 *opposite above* Monte Carlo, 1898

21 *below* Roulette at Monte Carlo

22 Nijinsky and Karsavina dancing *Le Spectre de la Rose*. The first
performance of the ballet was by Diaghilev's company at Monte Carlo in
April 1911, with Nijinsky and Karsavina in the leading roles

23 Monte Carlo, battle of the flowers, 1928

24 Baron de Kehrling at Monte Carlo

25 Tennis at Monte Carlo, 1928

26 *Le tir aux pigeons*

27 Monte Carlo rally, 1928

whom, named Le Broq, was reputed to be able to recognize 50,000 faces.

Among those who tried to defraud or otherwise outsmart the casino not a few were English. An engineer named Jaggers did profit for a time from discovering an imperfection in the roulette wheels. In 1936 a London broker issued cheques to the value of 600,000 francs without being able to meet them. This was a surprisingly large sum, for in 1907, in one of those extraordinary inversions of justice which periodically characterize the findings of English courts, it was ruled in the case of *Monks* v. *Owen* that an English cheque cashed for gambling in France could not be sued on in England. After that cheques became rather less easy to cash.

There were also plenty of hangers-on who offered to put their alleged skill at gambling at the disposal of visitors. One man even announced through the Paris edition of the *New York Herald*: 'I merely offer to double any small sum entrusted to me during my fortnight's stay at Monte Carlo.' He signed the letter 'Honour'. Of all these confidence tricksters the one who, indirectly at least, acquired the greatest fame was Charles Deville Wells.

Wells, who posed as a civil engineer, operated under thirty different aliases and was plausible enough to obtain £18,000 from the sister of an English judge to exploit some of the inventions he claimed to have patented. One of these was a means of reducing the consumption of fuel in steamships, and to test it required, as he pointed out, the use of a steam yacht. On a visit to Monte Carlo, Wells had an exceptional run of luck, turning £400 into £40,000 in three days, but not long afterwards enquiries pursued by various people whom he had defrauded led to his appearance at the Old Bailey, where on 14 March 1893 he was sentenced to eight years' penal servitude.

Before his past caught up with him Wells's fame had been such that he was the subject of a song which Carles Coburn sang for the first time at the Oxford music-hall in London on 23 April 1892. This was *The Man Who Broke the Bank at Monte Carlo*, a song which enjoyed undiminished success throughout the following two decades, when both the English music-hall and the Monte Carlo casino were at the pinnacle of their popular fame and plush glory.

IV

During her honeymoon in Monte Carlo after her marriage to the
ninth Duke of Marlborough in 1895 the Duchess, the former
Consuelo Vanderbilt, called her husband's attention to the
elegance and beauty of the women to be seen and was surprised
by the evasiveness of his comments. Without offering any explanation he forbade her to look at the women, and she was even
more puzzled when he insisted that in no circumstances must she
recognize the men who accompanied them. Yet some of the
men, she noted, had been her own suitors a few months earlier.
Only gradually did she realize that the elegant and beautiful
women were the leading courtesans of the Riviera.

From the years of the Second Empire to the outbreak of war in
1914 courtesans had a clearly recognized status in the relatively
stable social structure of the Riviera. It was a status which was
sometimes envied. An Austrian named Viktor Silberer, who
compiled a study of gambling practices in Monte Carlo in the latter part of the nineteenth century, wrote that when a dispute
arose in the casino about whose stake was on the winning number and the disputants were 'a demi-mondaine and a lady of
good character', it was 'usually decided in favour of the demi-
mondaine.' In *Monte Carlo and How to Do It* Goldberg and Piesse,
describing the procedure for admission to the casino, wrote:
'You will find yourself treated, in the main, with courtesy and
despatch; though you will be surprised to find that there is considerably less bother about giving the *entrée* to a notorious *cocotte*
than to a plain, decent Englishwoman or Gentleman.'

In a society designed largely to gratify the wishes of the rich the
process described by Arnold Bennett as 'the great daily con-
spiracy to persuade me, and those like me, that we are really the
Sultan', naturally ensured the availability of women at all price
levels, including the very highest.

Even to those British subjects whose social standing and wealth
were such that they were under little obligation to explain their
actions this provision, in the mid-Victorian era, was convenient.
Gioia no doubt fitted appreciably better into the Duke of
Hamilton's way of life in Nice than she would have done in Scotland. To the middle classes the convenience was even more evi-

dent. On the Riviera, it was discovered, a number of conventions which were *de rigueur* in British middle-class life could be waived with impunity. Goldberg and Piesse, for instance, assured their readers that they could confidently travel to the Riviera without 'that damnable contrivance, the British stove-pipe', a straw or 'squash-felt' hat being deemed suitable for all occasions. Such relaxations of standards were complemented, for the unattached male at least, by comparable ones in the application of the sexual code.

From the days when the principality of Monaco had begun to derive its main revenue from the casino there had always been a plentiful supply of women ready to relieve successful gamblers of their winnings. But of the many women who lived by their wits and by their bodies the few whose names have survived all played for much higher stakes than any gambler's winnings.

Among the most famous were Liane de Pougy and the part-gipsy Caroline, known as La Belle Otéro. The rivalry between these two was formidable. It was recorded that after La Belle Otéro had appeared in the casino one evening wearing an astounding collection of jewels, Liane de Pougy entered the following evening in a plain white dress followed by her maid, who was covered in even more jewels than La Belle Otéro had worn. Another version of the story is that Liane de Pougy's jewels were worn not by her maid but by her fox-terrier.

Others who acquired fame were La Juniory, who had a bed made in the shape of an enormous conch-shell, and Gina Palerme of the Folies Bergère, for whom a villa named L'Oiseau Bleu was built in Menton and who designed her own blue marble bathrooms. During the Second Empire the most notorious of all the courtesans in France was, by common consent, a young woman who was born in Plymouth, the sixteenth child of an impoverished music teacher, who died shortly after her birth. Her name was Emma Crunch, but at the age of thirteen she changed it to Cora Pearl.

At the same age she visited Paris for the first time in the company of an Englishman named William Bluckel, who had procured a joint passport in which she appeared as his wife. Through the efforts of her grandmother, who had been friendly with a retired French dancer, Cora Pearl had had some schooling in Boulogne and had learnt to speak French. It did not take her long to appreciate the attractions of Paris, and she surprised Bluckel by refusing to return to England with him. Instead she launched herself on a career in the course of which she amassed vast quantities of jewels as well as houses, carriages and horses provided by, among others, Prince Jérome, commonly known as Plon-Plon, who was the Emperor Napoleon III's cousin, Prince Murat and the Duc de Morny, who through two illicit unions was Napoleon III's half-brother and Talleyrand's grandson.

Cora Pearl was the barely disguised original of Laura Pearl in Ouida's novel *Puck*, in which she is depicted sitting in her box at the Paris opera 'blazing in the splendour of her beauty, and the living light of her sapphires, surrounded with princes'. Laura Pearl, Ouida wrote,

> was only capable of such joys as the drowsy jewelled snake may know in his Mexican swamps .... She was the courtesan of the nineteenth century, who, to all the licence of the wantons that turned their thumbs downward for their brawny paramours to die in Rome, has added all the vulgarities of modern ribaldry and all the chicaneries of modern civilization.

The original Cora Pearl suffered a setback when the son of a rich industrialist named Duval put a bullet through his chest after spending a fortune on her. The scandal which ensued was such that she was ordered to leave France. In fact she went to Monte Carlo.

Cora Pearl did not find the Riviera such a profitable hunting ground as Paris and Baden-Baden had been. She stayed for some time with another courtesan named La Léno and made the acquaintance of an Englishman known as the Nabob, but the police were put on her tracks, possibly through denunciation by La Léno, and she left for Nice. There too she stayed for a while, seldom going out except at night, but the police continued to pursue her, and she left for Milan. Cora Pearl's principal claim to distinction was her breathtaking extravagance, she was unable to save money, and her end was a sad and impoverished one.

Another Englishwoman to become the mistress of the great and to pass into relative obscurity on the Riviera had at one time entertained hopes of becoming Empress. This was Elizabeth

Howard, daughter of a shoemaker in Brighton, who met the future Napoleon III when he was in London in the 1840s. Elizabeth Howard had had an affair with an English officer of a rich family, had borne him a son and had received an extremely generous settlement.

During the early years of her association with Louis Napoleon it was she rather than he who was the paymaster, and she was reputed to have contributed £60,000 towards his campaign funds when he was preparing for his return to France. After his accession to power Louis Napoleon continued to live with her with little effort at concealment, and although she did not interfere in political matters and barely troubled to learn French, she felt she had fairly strong claims on his loyalty. This opinion, though reasonable enough from her point of view, was not shared by Louis Napoleon's ministers, nor did he himself seriously contemplate marrying her. Shortly after he was formally proclaimed Emperor he was married to Eugénie de Montijo. Elizabeth Howard received the title of Comtesse de Beauregard, and she retired from the public scene with a home on the Ile Ste-Marguerite in the bay of Cannes.

Of the many women who served as prizes for the rich and the pleasure-loving on the Riviera, the fame of one has been perpetuated, in part at least, in stone. When the Carlton Hotel was built in Cannes twin cupolas with nipple-like spikes were placed on the roof. These, it was generally acknowledged, represented the shape of La Belle Otéro. Like *The Man Who Broke the Bank at Monte Carlo* they remain as abiding monuments to an age that has passed.

7 The Literary Scene

I

In the autumn of 1882 Robert Louis Stevenson set off with his cousin Bob Stevenson to look for a new home in western Provence. A wet July in Scotland, when he had found Peeblesshire 'low, damp and mauchy', had aggravated his illness. The winters he had spent in Davos had been of limited benefit, and now he sought the southern sun.

This was not Robert Louis Stevenson's first visit to the south of France. He had stayed at Menton with his mother as a child, and he was sent there again in October 1873 at the age of twenty-two after the well-known physician Sir Andrew Clark had diagnosed phthisis. On this visit Stevenson was not altogether attuned to a southern landscape and southern habits. 'Being sent to the South', he wrote in a letter in November 1873, 'is not much good unless you take your soul with you, and my soul is seldom with me here.' He had, he declared, found more beauty in two wet, windy February afternoons in Scotland than in a week of olive gardens and grey hills. This he attributed to his 'low and lost estate, as the Shorter Catechism puts it'.

He saw Dr James Henry Bennet for a consultation and reported: 'He agrees with Clark that there is no disease.' He was enchanted by a Russian girl aged two-and-a-half who spoke six languages. But he still lacked the appreciation of French art and French customs which he was to acquire during the next ten years, largely through the influence of his cousin Bob, who had studied art in Paris and was regarded in Edinburgh and family circles as an advanced bohemian.

The visit to France in 1882 began badly. Robert Louis Stevenson had a severe haemorrhage in Montpellier, but he recovered sufficiently to make his way first to Marseilles and then to Nice. His wife Fanny, who followed him to Nice, was told that he had died on the wayside and had no reason to doubt the accuracy of the information until she found him sitting up in bed in the Grand Hotel reading.

In March 1883 Stevenson with his wife and stepson moved into a villa above the old town of Hyères some distance from the sea and beneath a ruined castle. It was known as La Solitude. After a month Stevenson described La Solitude as 'Eden and Beulah and the Delectable Mountains and Eldorado and the Hesperidean Isles'. Its attractions included roses, aloes, fig-marigolds, olives and 'a view of certain mountains as graceful as Apollo, as severe as Zeus'.

His first months in La Solitude were a period which in retrospect Stevenson often referred to as the happiest of his life. He wrote *The Black Arrow* and much of *A Child's Garden of Verses* there. He was in La Solitude when Cassell's published *Treasure Island* in book form and its acclaim by such influential arbiters of literary taste as Gladstone and Andrew Lang virtually assured its success. His health improved – for this reason he wrote rather less prose than usual, for he tended to be most prolific when confined to bed – and he even composed a mock epitaph in which, after describing himself as 'an active, austere, and not inelegant writer', he 'owned it to have been his crowning favour

TO INHABIT
LA SOLITUDE.'

He was then aged thirty-three.

Stevenson had his difficulties in Hyères as he had wherever he travelled. In November 1883 he described himself as continuing his 'uphill fight with the twin spirits of bankruptcy and indigestion'. The arrival the following January of his old friends W.E. Henley, who was in part at least the original of Long John Silver, and Charles Baxter led to a convivial excursion to Nice, in the course of which Stevenson contracted pneumonia. He was deemed by a French doctor to be dying, a diagnosis contradicted by a Scottish doctor, who held the opinion that Stevenson could live till he was seventy if he stopped 'the running about'. By July Stevenson was writing to Henley: 'My life dwindles ... I cannot read .... To play patience, or to see my wife play it, is become the be-all and end-all of my dim career.' Not long afterwards he was forced to leave the Riviera for good because of an outbreak of cholera in Hyères. But the memory of Hyères, or at least of the first months he spent there, remained unclouded. More than once on his first journey to Samoa Stevenson was heard to declare: 'Would to God I had died in Hyères!'

During part of the time that Stevenson was in Hyères another master of English prose, who was also to have a huge readership among the young, had also come to the Riviera in the vain search of a cure. This was John Richard Green, whose *Short History of the English People* with its cool, liberal interpretation of events, had an incalculable influence on the teaching of history in English schools.

Green was an Anglican clergyman, who carried out his parochial duties conscientiously, yet found time not only to create a standard work of history but to rewrite it twice, in addition to producing numerous essays and other historical pieces. Among the more attractive of his essays were those in which he examined various aspects of life on the Riviera, which he had visited as a holiday-maker several years before he was driven there by his final illness.

Cannes was the Riviera town which appealed to him most. Of the 'hundred little Britains' to be found on southern shores 'none', he wrote, 'is more lovely than Cannes.' Monaco he described as

> the one town of the Riviera which, instead of lying screened in the hollow of some bay, as though eager to escape from pirate or Saracen, juts boldly out into the sea as if on the look-out for prey.

To Menton he granted 'magnificence' of background, but in Cannes, he wrote, 'everywhere there is what Menton lacks – variety, largeness, picturesqueness of contrast and surprise.'

The activities of his fellow-countrymen on the Riviera

provided him with plenty of material for observation and reflexion. At carnival time he noticed 'the stout British merchant astride of a donkey, and exchanging good-humoured badinage with the labourers in the olive-terraces' and 'the impassive spinster whose voice never rises at home above the most polite whisper' screaming with delight when hit by a sugar-plum.

Green was among the first observers to deprecate the effects of the commercial power which the British had begun to exercise on the Riviera. After a visit to the Ile St Honorat he stated that a debt was owed to the Bishop of Fréjus for preventing the island from being turned into a tea-garden and picnic resort by 'English speculators'. The slow pacing of the monks under a carob-tree and the sound of boys' voices as they repeated their lesson to a lay brother must, he thought, be found preferable to 'the giggle of happy lovers and the pop of British champagne'.

These essays of Green's were published in book form in 1876. Six years later he returned to Menton. He was by then seriously ill, but he continued to work strenuously, and he was still struggling to finish another volume of *The Conquest of England* a few days before his death in March 1883. He was then forty-five. On his tombstone in Menton cemetery are inscribed the words: 'He died learning.'

Smollett and Stevenson, both sufferers from tuberculosis, came to the Riviera when they still had several creative years ahead of them. Other writers, like Green, had less to look forward to, and for some a sanatorium or nursing-home on or near the Riviera seemed to offer a last or nearly last hope.

Katherine Mansfield was among those who came to the French Riviera when little of her life remained, but the months she spent there were exceptionally productive ones. It was to seek relief from rheumatism that she first went to the south of France. Pulmonary tuberculosis was diagnosed towards the end of 1917, and she decided to make the journey south again in spite of war-time conditions. It was a discouraging experience. In a railway compartment she heard a large Frenchwoman tell a friend what a fatal place the Côte d'Azur was for anyone with lung trouble, the theory being illustrated by a description of how an American woman, 'belle et forte avec un simple bronchite', came to the Riviera to be cured and within three weeks had a haemorrhage and died.

After visits to Bandol early in 1918 and to San Remo the following year Katherine Mansfield, accompanied by her undemanding comforter, Ida Baker, came to a combined hotel and nursing-home in Menton called L'Hermitage in January 1920. Here her moods alternated between relishing the luxury and hating the noise and hospital atmosphere. It was in this period of her life too that she received the letter from D.H. Lawrence in which he wrote: 'You revolt me stewing in your consumption.'

In September 1920, after escaping the Riviera summer by returning to Hampstead, Katherine Mansfield moved into a villa in Menton named Isola Bella. It was, she wrote in a letter to her husband John Middleton Murry, 'up a side road *off* a side road standing high' with 'the smell of the full summer sea and the bay tree in the gardens and the smell of lemons.' She added: 'I could be content to stay here for years. In fact I love it as I've never loved any place but my home .... There's no division between one's work and one's external existence.'

Points of similarity between the Riviera and her New Zealand background struck her repeatedly – 'there's something about the rocks and stones that reminds me of New Zealand – volcanic' – and finding the setting more conducive to writing than almost any she had known, she produced some of her finest work, including *The Daughters of the Late Colonel*, *The Stranger*, *The Lady's Maid* and *The Life of Ma Parker*. Towards the end of her life Katherine Mansfield recorded in her journal: 'The only occasion I ever felt at leisure was when I was writing *The Daughters of the Late Colonel*.' Two months after moving into the villa she had written: 'You will find ISOLA BELLA in poker work on my heart.'

It was in Menton and its surroundings rather than in the Riviera as a whole that Katherine Mansfield found her deep contentment. Nice she dismissed as the *paradis des bourgeois*, and Monte Carlo was '*real Hell*, the cleanest, most polished place I've ever seen', with 'a continual procession of *whores*, pimps, governesses in thread gloves – Jews – old, old hags, ancient men, stiff and greyish, panting as they climb, rich fat capitalists, little girls tricked out to look like babies.'

With the sudden and extreme changes of mood characteristic of her temperament and her affliction Katherine Mansfield was unable to find lasting happiness even in the Villa Isola Bella. By

February 1921 she was writing to Lady Ottoline Morrell: 'I mean to leave the Riviera as soon as possible. I've *turned* frightfully against it and the French. Life seems to me ignoble here. It all turns on money.' She was forced to spend the next six weeks in bed, and this finally convinced her that she would not find a cure in the south of France. She believed the climate to be too relaxing.

Katherine Mansfield continued to search for a cure, in Switzerland and finally in the establishment which Serge Ivanovitch Gurdjieff, founder of the Institution for the Harmonious Development of the Mind, had set up at Fontainebleau. But with the existing knowledge of medicine nothing, it seemed, could be done to save her, and in January 1923 she died at the age of thirty-four.

Some seven years after Katherine Mansfield's death D.H. Lawrence himself came to the south of France in search of a cure. He too went first to Bandol, where he took a house in December 1929, but a month later he moved to Vence. From here he wrote to Aldous Huxley's wife Maria: 'I have submitted and come here to a sanatorium – sort of sanatorium – and Frieda is in the hotel.' A few days later he qualified this statement. 'It isn't a sanatorium really', he wrote, ' – an hotel where a nurse takes your temperature and two doctors look at you once a week.'

By then there was little the doctors or the nurse could do. Lawrence enjoyed the view from the balcony, and the mimosa, 'all out, in clouds', put him in mind of Australia. But when he noted this he was already near the end, and on 2 March 1930 he died aged forty-four, the age at which Stevenson also died.

Lawrence was buried in Vence cemetery, a peasant with whom he was briefly friendly carving a phoenix out of local stone to serve as a headstone. Few people attended the funeral. One of those who did, the poet Robert Nichols, wrote:

A huge wreath of dark crimson carnations arrived from two or three American painters who did not know Lawrence personally but much admired his work .... Every man took his hat off on the way – though one (Englishman of course) only did it at the last minute after I had stared him out of countenance and even then he kept his pipe in his mouth .... Frieda Lawrence was worse than useless.

Of the truly great writers of English, Americans excepted, who at some stage in their careers chose to live on the Riviera a high proportion, probably a majority, suffered from tuberculosis. Of the other British writers of distinction who took up residence there, some came to escape from the restrictions which the social conventions of their own country imposed, others to enjoy to the full the wealth which literary success had brought. One who was impelled by both these motives, who came first to enjoy the fleshpots and returned later because England was no longer a welcoming or convenient country to him, was Frank Harris.

II

The period when Frank Harris was at the height of his social success on the Riviera was from the mid-1880s to the late 1890s, when he was in his thirties and early forties. Not only could he be seen in the company of the Prince of Wales and Lord Randolph Churchill, but he was a close friend of the Princess of Monaco, and he was on terms of some intimacy with leading French literary figures.

In describing the French writers whom he met on the Riviera he tended, as he did with Shakespeare, to create them in his own image. The quality in Maupassant which particularly fascinated him was Maupassant's claim to be able to have an erection whenever he chose, and Pierre Loti startled him by insisting, at the age of forty, on doing a backward somersault. But of the devotion to Harris felt by Princess Alice of Monaco her letters leave little doubt. 'You are such a TRUE friend', she wrote on one occasion. 'How I love and admire your qualities. I am immensely grateful to Providence to have met you.'

Harris's Riviera successes were no more than a reflexion of those he had gained in London, where, arriving with no backing except his own, he had become editor of the *Evening News* at the age of twenty-seven. But the Riviera was also the scene of the first of the major financial reverses from which he never effectively recovered.

George Bernard Shaw, who wrote of Harris with both more

perception and more charity than most of their contemporaries, stated that when Frank Harris edited a paper he did it very well and that disasters occurred only when he left the editing to the office-boy because he was 'preoccupied by more fascinating activities'. It was at the height of Harris's success as editor of the *Fortnightly* that certain fascinating activities in the form of financial ventures on the Riviera began to preoccupy him seriously. The outcome of these depended to some extent on Princess Alice of Monaco.

The Princess, the former Alice Heine of New Orleans, whose first husband had been the Duc de Richelieu, was reputed to possess ten million dollars when she married Prince Albert. She was also something of an idealist and was horrified by her first sight of gambling in the casino. She even asked the Prince to close the gaming rooms, but her attitude gradually changed, and she and Harris evolved a plan for establishing, with financial backing from her father, an elite international sporting club. The plan was even brought to the point at which Harris confidently proposed himself to the Prince as permanent secretary at 'a decent salary'. Shortly afterwards Camille Blanc's concession was renewed, and Harris learnt that he himself had been used, without payment, as a means of frightening Blanc into offering more generous terms.

To promote another enterprise on the Riviera Harris, unfortunately for him, used his own money. After his successes in editing the *Evening News* and the *Fortnightly* he became both editor and proprietor of the *Saturday Review*. He sold this in 1898 to Lord Hardwicke and, with the encouragement of Princess Alice, left for the Riviera to work on the book on Shakespeare which he believed would be his masterpiece. He also used his money to buy a hotel and later to build a restaurant.

The hotel in Monte Carlo, whose windows looked out on to back streets, was not a good investment, but the restaurant built on an empty plot of land near Eze at a point where motorists, using the new road between Nice and Monte Carlo, could be expected to stop for lunch was a more imaginative venture. Unfortunately no provision was made for heating the restaurant. Unfortunately too Harris engaged for the setting up and running of both hotel and restaurant a maître d'hôtel named Cesari, a man of good taste and good faith but with little business capacity.

With the outbreak of the South African war Harris, switching interests once again, felt that the war required his presence. Cesari moved from extravagance to extravagance and a further blow was struck when Harris who had counted on Princess Alice's patronage of the restaurant at Eze, learnt that her husband had refused to allow her to visit it.

Creditors became clamant; Lord Alfred Douglas, whom Harris had talked into investing £2,000, lost it all; an accountant named Thomas Bell whom Harris had engaged found that neither the hotel nor the restaurant business had been properly registered; Cesari was put in prison in Nice; and Harris was launched on his thirty-year-long campaign of trying to maintain both credit and credibility, a struggle which ended only with his death.

It was while he was at work on his book on Shakespeare at La Napoule that Harris invited Oscar Wilde, now released from prison, to stay and treated him with no little kindness. Wilde during the comparatively brief period he spent on the Riviera was for much of the time in a wretched state. To reach Harris on one occasion he had to pledge his ring to raise the ten-franc fare, and English visitors would ostentatiously rise and leave restaurants when it was learnt that Oscar Wilde was present. But at least there was a flash of the incomparable and rarely unkind wit when he descibed Harris in La Napoule 'thinking about Shakespeare at the top of his voice'. There was an acknowledgment of the generosity too when Wilde dedicated *An Ideal Husband* with the words 'to Frank Harris a slight tribute to his power and distinction as an artist, his chivalry and nobility as a friend.'

In the first decade of the twentieth century, as financial pressures in London increased and the quality of the magazines with which he was associated declined, Harris's standard of living on his visits to the Riviera was gradually lowered. In 1910 he and Nellie O'Hara, the pretty, red-haired and probably rather extravagant and silly girl with whom he was living, took a villa in Nice with no bath and an outside lavatory. Augustus John, who stayed with them, noted that Harris had been reduced to cadging lifts from chauffeurs, not so much to avoid walking as to impress the local tradesmen. John also noted that they listened to the nightingales, adding 'as far as my host's conversational flow would permit'.

Imprisonment in England for contempt of court, escape to the United States to avoid bankruptcy and the overtly pro-German attitude which he adopted in the 1914–18 war combined to keep Harris permanently out of England after the war ended. In July 1914, when bankruptcy proceedings were pending, he had described himself as resident in Nice, born in Galway and an American citizen. The claim to citizenship was premature, but in 1921, when he and Nellie O'Hara returned to Nice, they had indeed both become citizens of the United States.

The work which Harris now hoped would bring him his fortune was his autobiography. This appeared in several volumes under the title *My Life and Loves*, but he was unfortunate in his timing. The descriptions of sexual encounters, which to readers in the 1970s may well seem both coy and fanciful, though imbued with a distinct period charm and clearly influenced by the translation from the *Arabian Nights* made by his friend Sir Richard Burton, were deemed to be obscene. The books were censored and impounded at frontiers, and though pirated editions appeared and customs officials supplemented their incomes by disposing of copies to advantage, Harris himself earned relatively little. But he did receive a large number of letters. Some of these, it seems, really were obscene, particularly those which came from virgins. There were also unexpected female callers at his flat in Nice. When these arrived Nellie O'Hara usually went out to do the household shopping, leaving Harris, who by then was impotent, to cope as best he could.

The furnishings of this flat reflected some of the complexities of Harris's character. There was a long entrance hall in which could be seen etchings by Whistler, photographs of Shaw and Maeterlinck and letters signed by Carlyle and Wilde. There was a crucifix in the library, for Jesus Christ was a character with whom Harris felt he had much in common. In the bedroom there were several paintings of nude women, all of which could be seen from the bed.

When Harris was seventy-one his second wife died, and he married Nellie O'Hara in the American church in Nice. They were still in Nice when Harris died four years later in 1931. Seven people attended his funeral.

III

In his novel *Dimanche* Georges Simenon described through the eyes of one of his characters a number of English visitors to the Riviera, who were intoxicated by a certain easy-going philosophy. They became more southern than the southerners and returned home only when they were obliged to. Others never returned, among them one 'who was said to be the son of a lord, who painted, went barefoot and walked hand-in-hand with other young men.'

A number of homosexual practitioners of the arts did come to the south of France, particularly after the trial of Oscar Wilde had made so many people in Britain overtly aware for the first time that homosexual acts existed and were therefore to be condemned. But the Riviera, where the British social code, modified only slightly by sun and distance, was so firmly established was not the ideal haven for practising homosexuals. In the inter-war years in particular they found themselves both freer and more welcome in Capri and in Florence, which Aldous Huxley in the 1920s described as 'a third-rate provincial town, colonized by English sodomites and middle-aged Lesbians'.

The greatest of the English writers to make a home for himself on the Riviera largely because of a homosexual relationship was, almost indisputably, W. Somerset Maugham. At the time of Wilde's trial Maugham had been twenty-one and therefore old enough and young enough to be duly impressed by its effects. He married and had a daughter, he chose not to alienate his readers by making any public confession of his homosexual inclinations, and he could no doubt have lived in England, had he chosen to do so, without harassment. His companion for many years, the American Gerald Haxton, was not so fortunate. He had been arrested in London in 1915 on a charge of gross indecency and though acquitted had been declared an undesirable alien and required to leave Britain. This was certainly among the reasons why Maugham in the 1920s decided to buy a house abroad. Haxton's predilection for gambling, which served to dispose of large sums earned by Maugham's writings, probably influenced the choice of site.

The house Maugham bought in 1928, the Villa Mauresque,

was situated near the tip of Cap Ferrat on land once owned by King Leopold II of the Belgians. Maugham himself described it as a square white house on the side of a hill which he had bought cheaply because it was ugly. He had some twelve acres of land, on which he planted avocado trees, whose seeds he had smuggled into France in a golf-bag. After a few years the trees, which Maugham claimed to have been the first ever cultivated in Europe, were yielding an annual crop of 300–400 pears.

In his autobiographical work *The Summing Up* Maugham wrote: 'The main thing I've always asked from my life is freedom, both in my way of living and my way of writing.' He added that although he was attached to England he had never felt at home there. 'To me England has been a country where I had obligations that I did not want to fulfil.' The way of living within which Maugham chose to find his freedom on the Riviera included a good deal of party-going, much entertaining and a high level of expenditure. E. Phillips Oppenheim wrote: 'Everyone on the Riviera accepts an invitation from Maugham at any time they are lucky enough to receive it, for they are always sure of being entertained.' Sir Gerald Kelly stated that at the Villa Mauresque one did as Maugham expected, for otherwise the invitation might not be repeated. The Duchess of Windsor dined at the Villa Mauresque on the Christmas immediately following her husband's abdication. Much bridge was also played, a game at which Maugham occasionally felt inhibited by his stammer. When he held a slam hand, he once told Elsa Maxwell, 'the s's won't come out'.

The Villa Mauresque gave Maugham a setting for a varied and, it seems, rewarding social life, and it was the most permanent home he ever knew. But the Riviera background did not appear prominently in his creative work, and it certainly did not inspire him to the degree that Spain and a variety of British colonial settings did. Yet it is from Maugham that we have perhaps the most vivid description to appear in print of the final hours of British colonial influence on the Riviera. It is to be found in *Strictly Personal*, which was published in 1942.

In the summer of 1940, after spending some months in England working for the Ministry of Information, Maugham returned to the Villa Mauresque via Paris. He expected to remain there for some time and ordered 20,000 bulbs to be delivered to him in September. A few days later the Germans invaded the Netherlands and Belgium.

After the defeat of the French armies Maugham made his way to the British Consulate in Nice, where he found a crowd of anxious people seeking information. The consul, 'a large, loose-limbed, amiable man, without a great deal of energy', had just received an order from the British Embassy in Paris to evacuate all British subjects willing to leave. They were to assemble in Cannes at eight o'clock the following morning, each bringing one piece of handluggage, a blanket and three days' provisions.

Two colliers, which had discharged their cargo in Marseilles, had been requisitioned to evacuate the British, who included invalids brought to Cannes on stretchers, governesses, chauffeurs, butlers and elderly retired people, many of whom had spent years in India and had come to the Riviera because the climate suited them and living was cheap.

On board the collier one woman asked where the games deck was, and another said she had never drunk tap water in her life. Four people went out of their minds during the voyage, but the great majority soon adapted themselves to the conditions.

> We had been in the ship for twenty days [Maugham wrote], without ever taking our clothes off. From beginning to end, with few exceptions, this crowd of refugees behaved with coolness and courage. Social distinctions went by the board. Our common dirt did that.

In fact social distinctions did not go entirely by the board. Among the passengers was the butler of a former neighbour of Maugham's at Cap Ferrat. He regularly brought Maugham a cup of tea at dawn, brushed his clothes and polished his shoes. 'They're a funny lot of people, sir,' he observed, 'not the sort of people we're accustomed to.'

When the war was over Maugham was one of the few British writers whose overseas earnings were large enough to enable him to return to his Riviera home and resume much of his former style of living. In some respects his style became rather more splendid, for it was after 1945 that he bought the bulk of his celebrated collection of French impressionist paintings.

The Villa Mauresque remained Maugham's home until his

death in 1968. He was then ninety-one, yet the first visit which he made to the Riviera, when he had stayed at Hyères and discovered Maupassant, had taken place more than seventy years earlier because, while still at school, he had been found to have an infected lung.

Many visitors came to the Villa Mauresque over the years, and between them they have created the various and contradictory pictures and legends of Maugham as host and writer, which have ranged from the daemonically evil to the generous and humane.

It is difficult to believe that any of the members of the Maugham family can have been quite as unpleasant as they have been stated to be in family memoirs and traditions. Willie Somerset Maugham's brother Frederic, the former Lord Chancellor, stayed at the Villa Mauresque in 1949. Fourteen years later the memory of the visit was still so powerful that Willie Maugham said to the former Lord Chancellor's son Robin: 'I have met many detestable men in my life, but your father was easily the mer-most detestable.' Frederic Maugham for his part published a lengthy autobiography in which he made, in all, three cool and brief references to his brother. Robin Maugham even recorded that his uncle once said of himself: 'I've been a horrible and evil man. Every single one of the few people who have ever got to know me well has ended up by hating me.'

That is one of the popularly accepted pictures. There have also been some shrill and uncharitable comments from former witnesses of the homosexual scene, but against them may be set the evidence of kindnesses and courtesy shown to a variety of visitors to the Villa Mauresque.

Frederic Raphael gave an attractive account of a call he paid on Maugham as a young and unknown, indeed unpublished, novelist. Maugham, after giving him much useful advice, revealed that he read on average some five manuscripts a week, on which he was asked to comment, as well as some four hundred letters. All his importunate correspondents seem to have been treated with consideration.

Maugham then a very old man, complained that doctors in the south of France had a tendency, which he deplored at his age, to let nature take its course. 'His philosophy was mundane,' Raphael wrote, 'but it was at least of this world. He deplored suffering and he despised bigotry. He was pitiful, but he had pity.'

The contradictory pictures will no doubt continue to be presented as the biographies and literary studies pile up. Maugham himself would have enjoyed watching this happening. The detached and enigmatic observer, who knows and tells much about others but reveals only small and carefully selected facets of his own personality, was the role he habitually chose for himself in literature, largely because it was a role which also suited him in life.

IV

Among those with whom Maugham played golf fairly regularly in the inter-war years was another writer who had tasted literary success early and had decided to enjoy the fruits of it on the Riviera. This was Michael Arlen, known as Dikran Kouyoum-djian until the publisher William Heinemann advised him to adopt a name more acceptable to the English.

Michael Arlen was engagingly sceptical of his own powers as a creative artist. 'It is more difficult for a second-rate writer not to be vulgar,' he wrote in *The Green Hat*, 'than for a camel to pass through a needle's eye', and all the praise heaped on him after *The Green Hat* appeared did not cause him to vary his judgment. But he enjoyed spending the money he earned. In London he drove the yellow Rolls-Royce, which he had bought from Lord Lansdowne, round Mayfair, and on the Riviera he operated a speedboat. All this was in conformity with his pronouncement that his literary career could be summed up in the phrase 'per ardua ad astrakhan'.

Michael Arlen and his future wife eloped to Cannes to be married. One reason for their choice of Cannes was that the bride's grandmother had a house there. The grandmother, who came from Cleveland, Ohio, had married Prince Karageorgevitch at the age of fifty-five, and after the Prince had been killed in a seaplane crash she derived evident satisfaction from being able to announce that it was one of the first seaplanes.

The marriage ceremony of Michael Arlen and his bride was performed in a Roman Catholic chapel, but a bearded Armenian priest of the Orthodox faith, who had been despatched from England by the bridegroom's mother, added variety to the proceedings by conducting his own form of service from a position a few feet to the bridegroom's rear. The bride was briefly disinherited by telegram by her father, Count Mercati, who had expressed the opinion that Michael Arlen was no better than an adventurer. This judgment Arlen, who had been known to describe himself as every other inch a gentleman and suffering from pernicious Armenia, would probably not have disputed.

Michael Arlen's son, Michael J. Arlen, recalling his childhood, described a white house on the side of a hill outside Cannes with wistaria, magnolia, lemon trees, 'the smell of kippers and all that sunlight'. In the afternoons, when his father was out on the golf course, an elderly secretary would come to a white room to type his manuscripts.

This was in the early 1930s, when Michael Arlen, in his son's words, was 'running out of success, and nerve, and stamina'. But in the 1920s Arlen had created in Iris Storm in *The Green Hat*, who had 'kicked through every restraint of caste and chastity' and who described herself as the slave of freedom, a figure who to many people seemed to symbolize a decade. As such it was fitting that she should gravitate towards Cannes, just as Nancy Cunard, from whom she was largely derived, had done in real life.

On arriving in Cannes the narrator in *The Green Hat* and Iris Storm 'were foul with dust, numbed with cold, aching with tiredness, and this because we had "done" the six hundred odd miles from Cannes in two days and a few hours.' Of the women surrounding Iris Storm, who had 'white oval faces, small breasts, blue eyes, thin arms, no expression', Arlen wrote that they danced to

> a beat like the throbbing of an agonised heart lost in an artery of the Underground ... at the Ambassadeurs at Cannes, with the masts of the yachts drawn ebony-black between the tall windows and the pale blue night over the sea.

The lives or, more exactly perhaps, the pastimes of the British and other rich foreigners on the Riviera provided themes for several novels by a writer who also enjoyed good living on the Riviera in the inter-war years, but who, unlike Arlen, was inhibited neither by success nor by self-doubt from continuing to produce a stream of best-sellers. This was E. Phillips Oppenheim.

In Oppenheim's *The Colossus of Arcadia* the characters, most of whom enjoy a fairly consistent diet of cocktails and caviare, include Lord Henry Maitland Lancaster, 'the third son of a genuine duke'. 'It is our duty to enjoy ourselves', he says, 'in order that we may pass on the spirit of enjoyment.' Others to be met on the Monte Carlo scene include Sir Julian Townleyes Bart, who seems to alternate in a confusing fashion between a seat in the Cabinet and employment in the Foreign Office, Phyllis Williams, 'the wellknown tennis player', and Colonel Brinlington, 'the secretary of the tennis club who had hurried up to play his respects to Lord Henry'.

The heroine, an American girl named Joan Haskell, has come into a legacy, 'one of those awkward-sized ones, too small to invest with the idea of adding to one's income, and too large to ignore.' So she comes to Monte Carlo and finds

> everything she had fancied it – the fantastic façade of that
> nightmare of architecture, the Casino, the wide-flung door
> of the Hôtel de Paris with its huge pots of scarlet geraniums,
> even the black Senegalese in his marvellous livery.

She has no reason to regret her choice. 'I have had plenty of tennis', she says, 'and I have been over to Cannes twice for golf. I think this is the most wonderful place in the world.'

Although there is a wealth of international intrigue, nearly enough indeed to precipitate a new world war, the indigenous inhabitants of the Riviera play little part in the events. But we do learn that there is an anarchist club in Nice, which is 'one of the most poisonous spots in Europe'. Similarly in *Murder in Monte Carlo* the gang of former American bootleggers who descend on the Riviera, and who are thwarted by a young American author educated at Oxford, include among their lesser minions a French gigolo. 'His cravat was florid, his shirt and collar were of French design but passable. The man himself was well groomed and perfumed.'

In his memoirs Oppenheim wrote: 'The Riviera is only a picnic ground for holiday-makers. Gaiety is its business.' He had discovered the Riviera in his twenties when he was still working in his family's leather business. A woman who had an affair with him at that time later told his biographer, Robert Standish, that Oppenheim was already confident that he would one day be rich. She had noticed how he envied the hard-faced men who surrounded the future King Edward VII and who won and lost large sums of money with an indifference which could not be counterfeited.

Recalling one late September day on the Riviera, Oppenheim wrote: 'I leaned back against the trunk of a pine tree, drew in one long breath of that sweet fragrance and swore that I had found my El Dorado, and that where I was I would live and die.'

Much of this resolve he kept. The home in which he spent many of his remaining years was a villa overlooking the eighteenth fairway of the golf course at Cagnes-sur-mer. He wrote some thirty novels there and gave innumerable cocktail parties. For variety he would sleep aboard his yacht, which became known as the floating double-bed, among the duties of the women who shared it being to remain awake at night and keep the mosquitoes at bay. At other times Oppenheim occupied a suite in the Hôtel de Paris in Monte Carlo, where the services of a valet, a masseur, a waiter, a secretary and a chauffeur – the chauffeur fetched the newspapers – were required before he would get up in the morning.

In 1935, when Oppenheim was nearly seventy, he and his American wife Elsie decided to take up residence in another popular haven for English expatriates, Guernsey. The experiment was not a success. They returned to the Riviera twice, the second time in 1939 after the outbreak of war. Oppenheim's professed reason for coming back the second time was to collect some manuscripts, but he lingered on, and when the two colliers came to Cannes to embark British citizens the Oppenheims decided that conditions aboard were too squalid for them to take passage. After a time they found the difficulties of housekeeping excessive and moved into an hotel. 'Here', Oppenheim wrote, 'we lived the quietest of lives. Neither my wife nor I ever cared for the films, the Country Club for golf was closed.'

With the virtual suppression of the British way of life on the Riviera it was not surprising that Oppenheim could find little entertainment or distraction. During all the years he had spent in France he had touched French life only peripherally. Robert

Standish noted that the names of only eight French people were mentioned in his memoirs. Mistinguett was one. Suzanne Lenglen was another.

Oppenheim was one of six people chosen by the *Menton and Monte Carlo News* for inclusion in a series of illustrated biographical sketches of Riviera celebrities which appeared early in 1925. Of the other five one was a politician, Sir William Joynson-Hicks; one was a naval officer, Vice-Admiral Sir John Parry; and one was a Frenchwoman. This foreseeably was Suzanne Lenglen. The remaining two, W.J. Locke and Baroness Orczy, were, like Oppenheim, successful novelists.

Locke was a popular figure among his fellow-novelists. Before settling on the Riviera he held the post of Secretary of the Royal Institute of British Architects, and in 1916 he was appointed Chairman of the War Emergency Fund Committee of the Society of Authors. In 1921 he decided to leave England, largely because of the state of his health. The villa in Cannes in which he and his wife settled was described by Oppenheim as the centre of literary hospitality on the Riviera.

In Aristide Pujol, who 'started life on his own account as a *chasseur* in a Nice café – one of those luckless children encased in bottle-green cloth by means of brass buttons', Locke created a character who promises for some time to become one of the memorable rogue-adventurers in English fiction. Unfortunately for his literary development a foundling child appears on the scene. The love they both feel for this child brings Pujol into contact with an English girl of irreproachable purity, and a manifestly unsuitable marriage is the outcome.

Among the writers who moved in the same Riviera milieu as Locke and Oppenheim was Katherine Mansfield's cousin Mary Beauchamp, who became in turn Countess von Arnim and Countess Russell, and whose best known work was *Elizabeth and her German Garden*. Others were the married couple who ostensibly collaborated as novelists under the names of C.N. and A.M. Williamson, although it was the wife who did nearly all the work.

In *Berry Goes to Monte Carlo*, which was first published in 1921, the Williamsons chose as their hero a slightly impoverished nobleman named Sir Berrian Borrodaile or Berry, whose efforts to adapt himself to post-war conditions on the Riviera provide the subject of the book. Berry has met a girl named Rosaleen while in hospital in Boulogne. ('She was a V.A.D. Love at first sight. Both broke to the wide.') To overcome his difficulties he evolves the evidently original idea of filling a house he has inherited in Monte Carlo with paying guests. These include a solicitor from Streatham, who speaks of 'the wife' and is presented as a figure of fun when he first encounters the glamour of the casino. A girl, who had been 'a flapper of sixteen' when war broke out, describes herself as leading a hand-to-mouth existence on the Riviera because she earns her living there. What she does in fact is to care for a countess's dogs. 'I've done nothing downright bad,' she says, 'and I don't think I ever will.' The bad woman of the plot, which revolves largely round the use of different systems at roulette, is crushed by Berry with the comment: 'You're so beastly rich, you don't need to worry whether you win or lose.'

The Baroness Orczy stated that it was the Williamsons' beautiful home in Roquebrune which finally induced her husband, Montagu Barstow, and herself to make a home of their own on the Riviera. Another reason, as the Baroness, with her remarkable command of a language she had first spoken at the age of fifteen, put it, was that English winters and springs were 'playing old Harry' with her husband's throat.

That the Baroness Orczy, who had made her reputation by writing of the triumphs of English aristocrats, should have settled on the Riviera was in many ways appropriate, not least because the French characters in her novels, apart from the Scarlet Pimpernel's wife, who has the good sense and good fortune to marry an Englishman, are markedly inferior to the British. But once she had come to live on the Riviera her literary output declined to the point at which she was producing only one historical romance a year. Her husband by contrast found that with American patronage it was easier to sell his paintings on the Riviera than it had been in England.

Both husband and wife led active social lives. They worked hard, in conjunction with the Duke of Connaught, to raise money for an English church. The large tea-and-cocktail party which they gave on New Year's Day was recognized as a social event of note, and the Baroness's standing was such that the *Menton and Monte Carlo News* was induced to write: 'What a wonderful person the Baroness Orczy is. She has made herself a charming home right in the middle of Monte.'

The Baroness Orczy remained on the Riviera throughout the Second World War. She and her husband were temporarily moved to Cannes, but they returned later to Monte Carlo, where they lived unmolested though advised not to speak English in the streets. Allied aircraft bombed Monaco in 1944, and on the morning following a bombardment a German officer rang the Baroness's front-door bell to ask whether she had been scared. It was a touching tribute, and one which she treasured, to personal dignity, literary distinction and a title.

V

Many British writers came for short periods to the Riviera or made passing reference to it in their works. Rudyard Kipling and Edward Lear were occasional visitors. Tennyson wrote of the 'Roman strength Turbia showed in ruin by the mountain road'. Matthew Arnold described the dying Rachel being carried up 'the steep pine-plumed paths of the Esterelle'.

There were also a number of writers who, though they never settled on the Riviera or even became habitual visitors, were strongly influenced by it in some of their work. One such was Arnold Bennett. At different times he was to be found staying with Eden Philpotts in order to collaborate on a play and installing himself in the Grand Hôtel Californie in Cannes. He met André Gide and made him envious by announcing that he could charge a shilling a word for what he wrote. He was also sufficiently overcome by what he saw to lapse into a rather undistinguished exercise in verse entitled *A Night on the Riviera*.

H.G. Wells was much involved in the social life of the Riviera during the winter of 1931–32. He was then nearing the end of his affair with Odette Keun, whom he had first encountered in bed in an hotel in Geneva before either of them had set eyes on the other. Odette Keun, who had been for three years in a nunnery, had sent Wells a book she had written entitled *Sous Lenin* and Wells had commented on it favourably. She came to Geneva from Grasse solely in order to meet him.

Wells and Odette Keun built a house near Grasse which they

called Lou Pidou, a contraction of Odette Keun's description of Wells as *le petit dieu*. Inscribed over the fireplace were the words 'Two lovers built this house.' Visitors could tell whether or not they had been quarrelling by the presence or absence of a screen covering the inscription.

One product of Wells's visits to the Riviera was his novel *Meanwhile. The Picture of a Lady*. In this a group of characters staying in a Riviera villa are drawn together by talk and inaction. They philosophize, but they also discuss Helen Wills's ankles and whether Suzanne Lenglen is likely to marry. An American named Plantagenet-Buchanan states: 'I perceive that I have been meanwhiling all my life.' The aristocratic English girls tend to throw themselves at the men. One of them known as Puppy Clarges, who departs hurriedly after a brief and unsatisfactory affair, leaves a note behind which reads: 'I've fled to the Superba at Dear Old Monty. Where my friends can find me, bless 'em.' All this is fairly convincing, but the second half of the book consists of one of those forays on to political sidetracks by which Wells in the 1920s squandered so much of his exceptional talent as a novelist.

In two novels by writers of distinction the lives of expatriates on the Riviera in the inter-war years and the way in which a young visitor from England reacts to their mode of living provided the theme. One was Cyril Connolly's *The Rock Pool*, the other Peter de Polnay's *A Door Ajar*.

In *The Rock Pool*, which was first published in Paris in 1936, the young visitor, whose name is Naylor, enjoys a private income of nearly £1,000 a year. He does a little work for a firm of stockbrokers and has barely formed literary ambitions. He goes first to Juan-les-Pins because he has heard that all the pretty women go there and that in September the rest of the coast is deserted. Then he is drawn to a resort which the author calls Trou-sur-mer. This consists largely of an ex-patriate colony of pederasts, lesbians, an unfrocked clergyman, artists, Corsicans and a Highlander who wears a kilt. Naylor also meets an American girl who has a studio and drinks Pernod for breakfast.

'Naylor began to grasp the rhythm of existence in Trou. About six they began to become alive. By dinner-time they were more or less their real selves, like small boats floating off the mud with the evening tide.' A Bessarabian painter advises Naylor on how to live on credit. ('It's no good trying to get tick from the natives. They're pretty shy by now.') By the end of the book Naylor has become an alcoholic and is living with the Pernod-drinking American, whom he periodically bashes.

The expatriates in *A Door Ajar* are of a strikingly different kind. Some of them are small-hotel dwellers: a Mrs Browne and her elderly daughter, who 'dressed alike, both looked like virgins, both carried canes'; a doctor who is the hotel's intellectual, has had two stories published in *Blackwood's Magazine*, and wears a beret; and a retired colonial governor, who 'liked to repeat daily a joke King George V when Duke of York made to him'. Rather higher on the monetary scale are a girl whose manners are said to be those of a Michael Arlen heroine and one who is called at half-past seven in the morning, reads in bed until nine, and starts to play tennis at half-past ten. 'After tennis her social life began.'

The characters in *A Door Ajar* are both more vivid and more convincing than those in *The Rock Pool*, no doubt because de Polnay is an accomplished novelist whereas Connolly, for all his merits as a critic, was not. Yet Connolly's characters, who were based on observation, existed. That they were to be found on the Riviera in the 1930s was partly a result of changes in fashion, changes in favour of summer pastimes and a summer season, which had the effect of noticeably reducing the average age of both expatriates and holiday-makers.

Peter de Polnay's book, which was published in 1959, recalls a past of which he wrote:

> I fell in love with the Riviera, a love that died only when I went to the Riviera after the Second World War. It wasn't the years: I maintain the Riviera of the nineteen-thirties was different altogether from the Riviera of today.

Once the important season had been the winter; now it was the summer. The Riviera he had formerly known he likened to a beautiful lady, the new one to a travel agent surrounded by a caravan site.

VI

In Anthony Powell's *Books Do Furnish a Room* Mark Members, the

poet who is addicted to congresses, says some two years after the
end of the Second World War that the only prospect he and
people of his kind seem to have of going abroad again is as
'emissaries of culture'. 'Unless something is done', he complains,
'we'll none of us ever see the Mediterranean again.'

So long as the post-war currency restrictions were in force
Mark Members's fears were partly justified, but in time a number of British writers did settle on the Riviera. They were either
gifted enough to earn substantial incomes from writing alone, or
they had other financial resources. Patrick Campbell contributed
a regular series of exquisitely constructed essays to the *Sunday
Times* from the Riviera and largely about the Riviera. In one of
these, after describing how readily friends gather round anyone
who has converted a ruined farmhouse in the south of France
into a villa, he wrote: 'There is, in fact, nothing that one friend
will not do for another, provided the party of the second part is
the owner of a villa in these marvellous mountains.'

David Niven, who had a villa on Cap Ferrat, added to success
as an actor success as an autobiographer, the sales of his first
book, *The Moon's a Balloon*, exceeding two-and-a-half-million
copies in Britain alone. He began work on this by dictating to a
severe lady from Nice, who, as he expressed it, 'disapproved of
all my four-letter words, so I ended up by writing in longhand.'

These were the hopeful voices. In English works of fiction set
on the Riviera after the Second World War, by contrast, new
notes were struck which had not been heard earlier. They
sounded perhaps most clearly in the work of Graham Greene,
who himself had a villa in Antibes. In the short story *Chagrin in
Three Parts* the action takes place in an Antibes restaurant, where
two Frenchwomen, one a widow, the other recently deserted by
her husband, are about to start a love affair with each other. The
narrator is an elderly English author. Of one of the women he
states: 'She took me in from balding top to shabby toe.' Of the
other: 'I didn't exist in her eyes now that she knew I was English.
I was less than human – I was only a reject from the Common
Market.'

Perhaps it was fortunate that Baroness Orczy did not live to
read these words.

8 The Last Colonial Years

I

The Riviera, whose charms Smollett and Dr Bennet had proclaimed and to which invalids had come in the hope of cures, writers and artists of genius among them; which Queen Victoria and her family patronized; where Brougham and Woolfield built, statesmen recuperated, millionaires gambled and courtesans flourished; where Anglican divines proclaimed their faith and British sportsmen imposed their habits, underwent a new transformation in the years between the two world wars. This was brought about by the presence of thousands of British subjects who had come to the Riviera with the intention of living there permanently.

Many of these people were of modest means, but only a fraction of them had any gainful employment. They lived on pensions and dividends, and they were attracted to the Riviera by the rate of exchange as much as by the climate. These settlers combined with the visitors, who after 1919 came from Britain in increasing numbers, to ensure that a British way of life was imposed on the Riviera even more widely and deeply than it had been before 1914.

There was also one numerically large group of British subjects on the Riviera who did have to earn their living. These were the chauffeurs and butlers, nannies, ladies' maids and governesses, most of whom were employed by other British subjects. The *ren-*

tiers and the domestic servants between them were to form the bulk of the passengers on board the two colliers which left Cannes in the summer of 1940 in the last and decisive British evacuation.

During the First World War the British on the Riviera led on the whole restrained social lives. The energies of many were directed towards the care of the wounded and the convalescent. One Englishman even bought a large hotel in Menton and handed it over for use as a hospital, staffing it largely with nurses brought from Britain to work for wages appreciably above the accepted norm. Variety was provided by the presence of British soldiers on their way to and from the Italian front. The gravest shortage generally experienced was that of meat, which officially could be bought on only two days a week. British families also found that the shortage of sugar prevented them from having the puddings to which they were accustomed.

Some of those who returned shortly after the end of the war found the Riviera shabby and empty in comparison with what they had known. Princess Daisy of Pless described 1920 as 'a dreadful year'. But it did not take the British long to regain their hold. The *Menton and Monte Carlo News* resumed publishing week after week the names of visitors who had just arrived and were staying in the principal hotels. By January 1920 three to four pages were needed to list those who had come to Menton alone. By the winter of 1921 the paper was able to announce: 'Already, before Christmas, English seems to be the all pervading language on the Promenade des Anglais.'

The manner in which many of the newcomers took their pleasures was both louder and faster than had been customary before 1914. A coloured dance-band known as The Versatile Four enjoyed a new kind of success. In February 1921 the *Menton and Monte Carlo News* published a letter signed 'Visitors', which complained of disorderly scenes in the streets of Menton on Sundays and on weekday nights between 10 p.m. and 3 a.m., when 'parties of men and women' could be heard 'shouting and singing at the tops of their voices'. There was no suggestion that this might be discourteous to the indigenous inhabitants, but the writers did make the point that it was 'injurious to invalids'.

In conflicts of interest between British pleasure-seekers and British invalids on the Riviera it was the pleasure-seekers who increasingly tended to win. Menton and Hyères continued, in part at least, to be outposts of the invalids, but elsewhere the British pursued their pleasures with the vigour and self-assurance which characterized so much of British conduct abroad in the 1920s and 1930s. In particular they indulged their taste for outdoor games with such evident relish that a growing number of the indigenous inhabitants began to adopt their habits.

II

Tennis was the game which conferred the greatest prestige and drew the largest British crowds on the Riviera. Hercule Poirot, searching for clues to the identity of the murderer in *The Mystery of the Blue Train*, observed: 'At the tennis one meets everyone.'

The Riviera tournaments constituted the beginning of the international tennis season in the 1920s, and their standing was generally acknowledged to be higher than that of any tournaments in the world except Wimbledon, Forest Hills and the French championships in Paris.

Among the women players Suzanne Lenglen continued to have no serious rival for years, such resistance as she met coming mainly from Elizabeth Ryan of California and the leading British players, Mrs Lambert Chambers, Mrs Satterthwaite and Mrs Beamish. In 1920 F. Gordon Lowe of Britain was acclaimed as the champion of the Riviera, but British supremacy in men's tennis did not last long. In one of his finals in 1921 Lowe was confronted by a Frenchman named Alain Gerbault, and the tournaments soon began to be won by representatives of the new school of French players, Jacques Brugnon and Henri Cochet, or by the two tennis-playing barons, di Morpurgo of Italy and Kehrling of Hungary. But the administration remained under the control of the British, A.E. Madge, who officiated as referee and manager at the first Monte Carlo tournament in 1903, still being in charge more than twenty years later.

The administration of golf also remained almost wholly a British preserve. The Secretary of the Mougins Country Club was a lieutenant-colonel named Bunbury. The Secretary of the Mandelieu Club was a major named Harvey. The Mougins committee did include the Duc de Nemours and the Grand Duke Cyril,

28 Shopping aboard the Mistral train

29 Mistral restaurant

30 Bay of Garavan, Menton

31 Anglican church, Menton

32 Queen Victoria at Grasse, April 1891, with (*left to right*) Long, Francis Clarke and Alexander Rankin

33 Lady Patricia Ramsay unveiling the statue of Queen Victoria at Menton

34 Menton lemon festival

35 Isola 2000 skiing resort. The brainchild of an Englishman, Peter
Boumphrey

but its other eleven members in 1924 were all British, several having double-barrelled names and several using naval or military ranks. When Nice played Cannes in a twelve-a-side golf match in 1921 the only non-British name in either team was Vagliano.

Football was a game which the British were readier to share with the native inhabitants, no doubt because it was played mainly by touring teams coming from England. At the end of March 1923 the *Menton and Monte Carlo News* announced with evident excitement that Cannes was to be 'treated to a real Franco-British Football game with a visit by the Oxford University team'. The main football event the following year was a match between Old Carthusians and Cannes Olympique, which the British team won only narrowly by 3 goals to 2. By 1928, when a team from HMS *Valiant* was held to a 1–1 draw by Menton, the sailors were reported to be 'literally astonished at the footballing knowledge of the Mentonnais'. The following year the *Menton and Monte Carlo News* felt justified in stating: 'The local teams are keen and play a wonderfully good game.' A similar pat of encouragement had been given earlier to local boxers when it was reported that 'the French youth has taken to this manly sport and is rapidly learning the fine art of the game.'

In contests of almost any kind with the indigenous inhabitants the British on the Riviera expected to win, and they usually did. At the Monte Carlo dog show in 1924 all the main prizes were won by British owners, though a French countess did get a second prize with a pekinese. Sporting contests staged in Britain were assumed to be inherently superior to those staged on the Riviera or indeed anywhere else. When the International Sporting Club in Monte Carlo decided to hold a series of so-called 'monster sweepstakes' in 1928 the race chosen for the first of these was the Aintree Grand National. The British continued to introduce sports which they had invented, the Riviera's first squash rackets courts being opened in the Carlton Hotel in Cannes in 1929. In the administration of sports which they were largely prevented from practising at home because of the nature of their climate the British also assumed positions of authority. In the late 1920s the popularity of skiing suddenly began to increase on the Riviera. In 1932 the man chosen to be President of the Menton Ski Club was George Hay of Barclay's Bank.

Perhaps only in motor racing did the British, as they had done in the early days of the sport, expect both to compete as equals and to have no monopoly of administration. The first great motor race through the streets of Monaco, known as the Monaco Grand Prix, was staged in 1929 largely through the initiative and tenacity of a Monégasque, Antony Noghès, and aroused excitement of a kind never experienced in the principality before. People watched from rooftops, and yachts in the harbour served as grandstands. For much of the race the lead changed between Williams of Britain and Carraciolla of Germany, and when Williams finally won it was reported that British spectators 'went crazy with delight'. Their only regret was that Williams was driving an Italian car.

In the other great motoring event popularly associated with the name of Monte Carlo, the rally, the British increasingly imposed their presence. In the first Monte Carlo rally held in 1911 the winner was a Frenchman, Henri Rougier, and all the competitors set out from the continent of Europe. By 1934, of the total of 161 competitors no fewer than sixty came from Britain.

III

'The sporting parson', the *Menton and Monte Carlo News* stated in January 1920, 'is not an uncommon figure in English social life.' The paper was reporting the appointment of the Rev. W. Armstrong Buck as chaplain at Monte Carlo. After listing his skills at football, rowing, cricket and tennis the writer continued: 'These qualifications, added to those of a strictly Clerical nature, must make him particularly well fitted for his duties.'

This was probably a sound judgment. The opportunities for church-going offered to the British on the Riviera in the 1920s were plentiful. In Menton alone there were two Anglican churches and one Scottish one. But the old evangelical zeal had been largely dissipated. Anglican clergymen in the 1920s were to attribute the excellent relations they enjoyed with the French authorities partly to the fact that the Anglican Church on the Riviera had not been a proselytizing body, and certainly for half a century their claim was justified. Indeed the spirit of religious tolerance became so general that a committee was formed in

Nice in 1928 to 'further the interests of English-speaking Catholics on the Riviera'.

With the loss of fervour belief in the essential iniquity of Monte Carlo also faded. In 1921 a book was published entitled *The Riviera of the Corniche Road*. The author, Sir Frederick Treves, had become famous nineteen years earlier, when King Edward VII had been taken suddenly ill two days before the date chosen for his coronation and Treves had been called upon to perform an emergency operation. Treves received a baronetcy and was appointed Sergeant-Surgeon to the King. In his later years he took to authorship, producing, among other works, a book entitled *Highways and By-Ways of Dorset*. In *The Riviera of the Corniche Road*, after stating that the moral climate of Monte Carlo was 'not so vitiated as in London or Paris', he wrote that 'the young lady, when necessity demands, can walk from the Opera House to her hotel without fear of being incommoded, a venture that she would not essay in either London or Paris.' He added that young men were also less likely to be 'molested' in the boulevards of Monte Carlo than in Regent Street in London, and he even made the remarkable claim that 'those who want to live the plain, unemotional life of a French country town will find that Monte Carlo fulfils their needs.'

As doctrinal fervour diminished the charitable activities of the British on the Riviera intensified. Year after year on 11 November British women could be seen selling Remembrance Day poppies on the streets of the Riviera, those who were permitted to do so having been approved by British consuls or vice-consuls. In 1922 companies of Girl Guides and Brownies came into being in Menton. In 1928 a Masonic lodge was formed in Nice.

There was also an abundance of British local charities. In 1922 it was discovered that the consular fund for helping distressed British subjects passing through Menton had been allowed to fall into abeyance and subscriptions were invited. Charitable contributions helped to support a convalescent home for British clergy and other professional men, who were provided with board, lodging and wine for fifty shillings a week. In 1924 a holiday home was instituted for the dogs of those British residents who had occasion to leave the Riviera temporarily. To raise funds for this water colours were sold and the services of a palmist were engaged. Both the water colours and the palmist were English.

The British subjects on the Riviera for whom charitable provision was principally made were the domestic workers. Many of these had better service conditions and led more comfortable lives than they could have expected to enjoy in Britain. The more menial household tasks were normally performed by local labour, the British filling the responsible and supervisory roles. British nannies enjoyed a special status even in French households. One who had the care of a French child during and after the First World War found that, in contrast with the responsibilities conferred on her, French wet-nurses were prized mainly for their milk and were chosen and fed accordingly, and that French day-nurses belonged to the servant category.

There were of course those who thought domestic employees were too leniently treated and that the quality of their work had declined in consequence. A regular feature of the *Menton and Monte Carlo News* was entitled 'The Rooms by One who Knows Them'. In March 1921 the writer of this addressed himself to what he called 'The Chauffeur Peril'.

> In the good old days, [he wrote] the men had first of all the horses to attend to, a good hour's work. After that they would take their dinners quietly with a good bottle of wine. Now-a-days the auto is shoved into a garage and after that there is nothing whatever to do, so the men go and soak, soak, soak in some little buvette.

In spite of these strictures, or perhaps because of them, it was widely recognized that some kind of provision should be made for the innocent entertainment of domestic staff when off duty. It was also accepted that funds were needed to relieve distress among those who suffered from sickness, old age or loss of employment. When plans were prepared in 1928 for building a clubhouse in Cannes for visiting yachtsmen it was agreed that something must also be provided for the chauffeurs who were expected to accompany the British and American yacht-owners. In the same year a whist drive was held in St Paul's church-room in Menton in aid of the Maid's Club. There was too a Hotel Servants Mutual Aid Society. To support this a ball was held annually.

In their charitable activities, as in their social life, the bulk of the British more often than not ignored the local inhabitants. The Mayor of Menton was known to preside over meetings of the Société Protectrice des Animaux, but such an arrangement was probably regarded as one of those concessions to the spirit of the *entente cordiale* which from time to time were deemed appropriate.

Of all the charitable activities of the British on the Riviera in the inter-war years none perhaps was a more unequivocal example of beneficent colonialism than the achievement of the Society of the Friends of Cannes, who in 1928 raised enough money to buy a Citroën car. This they presented to the French police in order to provide them with rapid transport when they were engaged on urgent duties. The car seems to have been handed over without a suggestion of criticism and to have been accepted in an equally obliging spirit.

IV

In 1925 Messrs Batchelor and Woolrych, solicitors, received permission to open offices in Monaco. They were the first English solicitors to enjoy this privilege. In 1923 a Miss Christine Mead opened a boarding-school for British and American girls in Menton. This, she claimed, would enable many more English-speaking families to take up permanent residence on the Riviera. In the same year a Miss McHardie established a home for British nurses in Hyères. Her professed aim was to ensure that a qualified British nurse would always be available for urgent cases.

Food and cooking of kinds the British were accustomed to at home were also readily available to them on the Riviera. This convenience seems to have been particularly appreciated by the Scots and, to a lesser extent, by the northern English. In *Monte Carlo and How to Do It* published in 1891 Goldberg and Piesse had suggested that one of the most welcome gifts a British visitor to the Riviera could bring was 'Finnan haddies'. These, they told their readers, would almost certainly be found preferable to the local *bouillabaisse*. In the 1920s a number of Scotch Tea Houses were established. The one in Monte Carlo was generally considered the smartest, but a new teahouse opened in Nice in 1921 was said to have 'delicacies made by an expert in Glasgow'. Six years later a Yorkshirewoman opened the Richmond Restaurant and Tea Rooms in Menton. Roast beef and Yorkshire pudding were frequently on the menu, and the proprietress claimed that she specialized in catering for British people who spent the winter in Menton in small flats 'with perhaps one servant'.

Many of the British on the other hand conceded that *cuisine* was one of the fields of human activity in which the French could reasonably claim superiority, and it became increasingly fashionable to hold this opinion. In 1926 the *Menton and Monte Carlo News* instituted a new feature headed 'Quaint Restaurants of the Riviera' with the sub-title 'Places for Provençal Dishes'. It was sufficiently popular to be repeated for a number of years.

In the inter-war years the way of life of many of the British on the Riviera was affected appreciably by the complexities of fluctuating exchange rates and tax laws. The exchange rate at all times enabled the British who were on fixed incomes to enjoy a higher standard of living than they could have had at home. In 1926 the franc dropped briefly to a level of 244 to the pound and so became worth less than the penny. One consequence of this was that British people could be seen on the Riviera streets with sterling notes in their hands waiting for the banks to open. It was a sight which can hardly have endeared them to French and Monégasque citizens.

When Britain abandoned the gold standard in 1931 there was some adjustment in the rate of exchange, but through most of the inter-war period it was not difficult for British expatriates to live a comfortable but unspectacular life in a Riviera villa with perhaps two servants on £300 a year. There were *pensions* which provided adequate board, lodging and service for about half that amount.

A number of the British, on receiving their monthly cheques, would promptly visit a casino, and the outcome of this would decide how well they ate for the rest of the month. The inveterate and impoverished haunters of casinos, particularly the old women among them, were generally considered the most melancholy spectacle of any to be encountered in the lives of the British expatriates. Such people were to be found in all the larger Riviera towns in the 1930s after Monte Carlo's monopoly had been broken by the French Government's decision to legalize roulette in casinos on French territory.

The reliefs from income tax which British Governments allowed helped appreciably those expatriates who lived on fixed incomes or dividends, and of all the Englishmen who practised their trades or professions on the Riviera in the inter-war years few seem to have been more generally welcome than an income tax consultant named Wilfred T. Fry.

Announcing a return visit which Fry was to make to the Riviera early in 1923, the *Menton and Monte Carlo News* called attention to the fact that British subjects resident on the Riviera were entitled to a refund of all or part of the British income tax which was deducted at source from their dividends and interests. The writer went on: 'It behoves all those who are in any way affected to make an early application to Mr Fry for a free consultation.'

There are few benefits more likely to induce visitors and ex patriates to adopt a patronizing attitude towards the native inhabitants of a country than a rate of exchange which is highly favourable to themselves. The British on the Riviera were already heirs to a considerable tradition of national self-assurance. That the disparity between the pound and the franc should have served to enhance this is hardly surprising.

The British did not indulge much in expressions of patriotic fervour, largely no doubt because these were not thought to be necessary. In the first battle of flowers of the 1921 season a driver of one of the cars did wear a John Bull outfit, a Union Jack serving as his shirtfront, but as the entry represented an hotel named Iles Britanniques this may have come about through an excess of zeal on the part of a French manager.

It was in a tacit assumption of superiority that the British on the Riviera normally expressed their attitude to people of other nationalities. Sometimes the assumption was carried to excess. In November 1927 a retired British officer, who was stopped by the French police and asked to show his identity papers, refused to co-operate, giving as his reason that he was above the law. He was expelled from France. But his attitude was not altogether different from that of the British motorists who complained bitterly that the police were seeing fit to enforce traffic regulations in Nice. A similar attitude was revealed in a report in the *Menton and Monte Carlo News* of a street accident which occurred on the

Promenade des Anglais at 3 a.m. on an April morning in 1924. In this it was stated that the driver, who had three of his Cambridge friends in his car, 'was unfortunate enough to kill a shoemaker aged 51.'

The British seem to have been largely responsible for preventing the spread of bullfighting on the Riviera in the early 1920s, but in general in the inter-war years they were more reluctant to interfere with local practices than the generation of their fathers and grandfathers had been. They were also less censorious. One reason for this may have been that the standards they applied within their own social circles became less rigid. Charles Graves, who had wide first-hand knowledge of the Riviera social life of the period, stated that apart from the local correspondent of the *Herald Tribune*, Francis Brantingham, who was exceptionally discreet and forbearing, there were 'no newspapermen to draw attention to the intrigues, naughtinesses and excesses of the distinguished visitors'. He went on to cite the absence of *demi-mondaines* in Cannes as evidence of the general promiscuity to be found there.

In public pronouncements the predominant British attitude towards the French on the Riviera was expressed from time to time in the phrase 'our Gallic friends'. This effectively combined a desire to appear courteous with an unmistakable suggestion of condescension. 'Our Gallic friends', the *Menton and Monte Carlo News* wrote, when reporting the determination with which French newspaper readers devoured details of the Landru murders, 'are wonderfully stoic and have more grit than you can believe.' It was a characteristic comment from a newspaper which in 1930 celebrated thirty-three years of existence by departing from its normal practice and expressing Christmas and New Year greetings in French.

Entente cordiale was another phrase with which public pronouncements were peppered. The range of its application was wide, one of its more curious uses being in two letters left by a man named Benjamin Hackett, who originally came from Leicester. In 1926 Hackett committed suicide at the age of eighty-four by throwing himself from a third floor building in Nice. One of the letters he left was addressed to the British consul, the other to the Commissioner of Police. Both ended *vive l'entente cordiale*. No other explanation of his suicide was offered.

That there was resentment among the French on the Riviera of the general British assumption of superiority was to be expected. What may seem surprising in retrospect is that it was not more forcefully expressed. Good manners may account for part of the restraint. The importance of the British presence to the economy of a region which had little industry and was poor in a number of natural resources could never be overlooked. But whatever the reasons, there is little doubt that the peculiar social standing of the British and the pre-eminence they enjoyed in a number of spheres were readily accepted. It is difficult to account in any other way for the existence in the 1920s in Nice, which was one of France's principal cities, of a body which engaged in various social activities, such as *soirées dansantes*, and which chose to call itself *l'association des dames françaises*.

V

In the early 1920s the great majority of the British who came to the Riviera continued to regard it as a region to be avoided in the summer. The term *hivernants* was used to denote those who remained on the Riviera for what was considered the whole of the habitable year, as distinct from those who came for only a month or two in winter or spring.

The advent of summer was marked by the sight of mattresses put out to air from windows of hotels and *pensions*. The summer too was the season when major works of reconstruction or renovation were normally carried out in the big hotels. In the early 1920s these consisted largely of the installation of private bathrooms, which were described in a contemporary account of work in progress as 'very necessary luxuries'.

The medical theories which gave rise to the manufacture in Britain of huge quantities of sola topees still prevailed, and carefully brought up British children on the Riviera were obliged to wear hats whenever they went out of doors, even in winter. The development of the Riviera towns as summer bathing resorts was also hampered by the practice of dumping huge quantities of rubbish at sea a mile or two from the shore and by the widespread belief that bathers were liable to be at the mercy of octopuses.

In the development of the Riviera's summer season in the inter-war years American influence was of major importance, and the ways in which it was exercised will be considered later in this work. But a major part was also played by the British as organizers, *entrepreneurs*, publicists and, of course, as patrons.

In 1922 a decision was taken to keep the courts of the Nice tennis club open throughout the summer, and a number of the members took advantage of this extension of the season. Whether the new policy was due to the initiative of the French secretary, Charles Lenglen, or to that of the British committee members is not clear. The attractions of yachting noticeably increased the number of summer holiday-makers in the 1920s, and in spite of the hazards, real or imaginary, more and more people took to bathing.

In 1923 a committee which had been formed in Cannes to make plans for a summer season recommended, among other attractions, the provision of better bathing facilities from the Croisette, firework displays and a cinema show every evening. Four of the leading hotels, including the Hôtel des Anglais, signified their willingness to remain open in the summer.

Soon afterwards the *Menton and Monte Carlo News* turned its attention to the problem of popularizing Menton as a summer resort. After dismissing what he called 'the prevalent idea that it is much too hot on this coast' as 'a very erroneous one', the writer of an article which appeared in April 1924 listed the main improvements needed to attract summer visitors. These included allowing the orchestra to continue to perform after the end of May, improving bathing facilities, opening a summer casino, getting rid of mosquitoes and reducing dust. The writer also made the point that there was still only one hotel which remained open in Menton in the summer, the Hôtel des Anglais. Seven years later the newspaper reported that a British resident had prepared a scheme for presentation to the authorities which would provide Menton with a sandy beach, a swimming-pool and facilities for what was described as 'that now popular pastime – which comes in for so much criticism in England – Sunbathing.'

The increasing readiness of both men and women to undress greatly enhanced the popularity of Mediterranean bathing resorts in the inter-war years and also added to the comfort of those who did the undressing. In an article which appeared in the publication *Paris − Côte d'Azur* in June 1974 Fernand Dartigues argued that too little credit had been given to the Riviera for instituting a revolution in social habits. It was, he claimed, 'this privileged region' which first gave men and women the opportunity to appear in public with scarcely any clothes. By the early 1930s it was already a commonplace to describe Cannes as 'a pyjama playground'.

A number of scientific and technological advances which later helped to make summer in hot climates more agreeable were still in an early stage of development in the 1920s. These included air-conditioning and insecticides. When the new International Sporting Club building was erected in Monte Carlo in 1932 the coolness of the air in the night-club, restaurant, ball-room and bar was widely commented on. The air-conditioning which produced this was nearly all the work of British firms.

Progress in the control of mosquitoes, on the other hand, was slight until the general introduction of DDT. The first year in which the *Menton and Monte Carlo News* appeared throughout the summer was 1934, and it was significant that the first summer issue contained detailed advice on how to eliminate 'the mosquito pest'. Removing stagnant water and cleaning ponds and banks were among the methods recommended. Refrigeration too was still widely regarded as a luxury. Something of a stir was caused in Nice in 1926 when a Frenchman displayed a forerunner of the modern mobile caravan fitted with a refrigerator.

To attract enough visitors to make the summer season profitable in the 1930s widespread publicity was needed. The general economic recession in the early years of the decade had already severely affected the whole of the tourist industry on the Riviera, and to solve new problems new methods of tourist promotion were introduced. In the planning and execution of these the French authorities recognized that they had much to learn from American and British expertise and example. One early manifestation of the new methods was the parading of girls.

The introduction of the girls known as *les cornuchettes* from Maxim's in Paris to Cannes in the 1920s had been a fairly discreet venture, for the girls were not flying their own colours but posing as heiresses. In 1934 by contrast Miss Europe and fourteen other beauty queens made a triumphant progress through the main Rivièra towns, large crowds assembling outside the Hôtel Negresco in Nice in the hope of catching sight of them. Two years later a competition for the title of Miss Riviera was staged for the first time under the auspices of the Nice casino.

In 1932 the President of the Menton Syndicat d'Initiative, whose name was Rouat, sent a circular letter to business people in the district proposing the formation of a joint publicity committee 'to overcome the difficulties of the moment'. The *Menton and Monte Carlo News* promptly proclaimed its wish 'to be associated with M. Rouat's wise action'. In doing so it described itself as 'the recognised organ of the Winter Colony in Menton' and stated that it had been engaged in active propaganda for Menton since its inception.

Both these claims could be substantiated. British visitors who wrote of the Riviera in a derogatory manner were liable to be fiercely attacked in editorial comment. In February 1928 the newspaper reported that the novelist Ethel Mannin had notified the local press of her arrival in Cannes, supplied a photograph of herself and announced that she was looking for local colour for future novels. She had then written two articles for the *Daily Express* commenting unfavourably on the Riviera's climate and on the age of its visitors. The report was headed 'Visitors We Don't Want'. Two years later there was a protest against 'the odious campaign of calumny waged against the Riviera by the Beaverbrook Press'.

There were also successes to be recorded. In January 1932 one of the headlines in the *Menton and Monte Carlo News* was 'Return of Confidence on the Riviera'. The article which followed stated: 'We have been optimists and have tried to turn some of the Riviera business people into the same happy state.' Justification for this policy was found in an item of news received just as the paper was about to go to press. This was that a villa had been taken in Monte Carlo for three years at an annual rental of £2,950.

Of all the events planned in the 1930s to bring visitors to the Riviera in the summer holiday months none was to be more effective in the long run than the Cannes film festival. It was a measure of the confidence felt in the political and economic conditions of the time that the first of the film festivals was due to be staged from 3 to 17 September 1939.

VI

The 1939 summer season on the Riviera was described as the gayest on record. During the preceding winter men who were at the centre of the great political events of the world maintained the tradition of coming to the Riviera to combine a holiday with unofficial discussions. One of these was Colonel Jósef Beck, the Polish Foreign Minister. Another was Sir Robert Vansittart, the former permanent head of the British Foreign Office, whose warnings of German intentions Neville Chamberlain persistently ignored. Crown Prince Umberto of Italy was also present.

In December 1938 Dr E. Wightman Ginner began a series of lectures on air raid precautions which he gave in the Hôtel Beaulieu in Cannes. They were based on measures then being introduced in Britain. In April 1939, when the traditional military parade was held in Nice, Hermann Goering, who was ostensibly holidaying in San Remo, was seen to be present in a large car discreetly placed. During the summer there were several reports, or rumours, of spies being put ashore clandestinely at Cap Ferrat and Cap Martin.

In spite of, or perhaps because of, such rumbling warnings spending was lavish, and new kinds of sports enjoyed new vogues. Among them were water-skiing, which was yet another British importation to the Riviera, and underwater fishing. When news was received of the Soviet-German non-aggression pact in August international university games were being held in a splendid new stadium recently opened by Prince Louis of Monaco.

The French mobilization which followed suddenly removed large numbers of Frenchmen from their normal employment on the Riviera. It was also the signal for the first major exodus of British subjects. Many remained behind, some to leave later on board one of the colliers which sailed from Cannes, some to be interned.

When war began the British on the Riviera no doubt entertained hopes and fears similar to those experienced by the British at home, ranging from extravagant confidence to the belief that London and other great cities would be totally destroyed. Few can have foreseen that one of the consequences of a war in which the British were to be victorious, and in which France was to be liberated by the combined efforts of British and American forces and French resistance, would be the final elimination of the unique standing, the privileges and the prestige which the British on the Riviera had enjoyed for so long and which many of them had come to regard as a part of the natural order.

9 The American Impact

I

The subject of this book is the life of the British on the Riviera. But for a full understanding of how they could live as they did and how they acquired their peculiar position it may be helpful to consider the experiences of people of other nationalities who also came to the Riviera in large numbers and who also formed more or less cohesive groups. Of these other peoples the two who made the most powerful impact were the Americans and the Russians.

Some of the first Americans to make their presence felt on the Riviera were also some of the richest. Among them was James Gordon Bennett the younger, proprietor of the *New York Herald*, which his father had founded in 1835.

The younger Bennett was involved in one of the last recorded duels in the United States. In 1876 he became engaged to a Maryland beauty named Caroline May, and on the following New Year's Day he called at her family home in Manhattan. There he seems to have urinated into the fireplace, the alternative story that he used the grand piano for the purpose being rather less convincing. The next day he was horsewhipped by the girl's brother, but the duel which followed was a rather innocuous affair. Soon afterwards Bennett left the United States, to which he was to return only for short visits. He made one home in Paris and another in Beaulieu.

Bennett's extravagances were enormous in scale and varied in kind. One of them was the Paris edition of the *New York Herald*, which conferred social distinction on its proprietor but incurred persistent losses. Another was his yacht *Lysistrata*, which he kept in the Mediterranean. This was designed by G.L. Watson of Glasgow in 1900 and cost 625,000 dollars. On board were to be found a suite of rooms on each of three decks, a full-scale Turkish bath, a crew of 100 and an Alderney cow. On one occasion Bennett arranged for a party of his guests on board the yacht to be taken to sea without warning any of them that this was happening. The guests included two American women who had acquired English titles by marriage as well as the whole of a musical comedy company from Amsterdam. Bennett made his peace with the two titled women by giving them diamond tiaras and with a third guest, who had no title, by giving her a pearl necklace.

Bennett had an unfortunate weakness which made him liable to become fighting drunk after a couple of glasses of champagne. He was known to throw rolls of banknotes into fires, and he made a habit of passing between a row of tables in a restaurant and pulling all the tablecloths from under the plates and glasses.

In Monte Carlo Bennett frequently patronized a small restaurant which passed with distinction a test he habitually applied, the ability to cook mutton chops to his liking. On one occasion when he arrived there he found all the best tables on the terrace occupied. He immediately bought the restaurant for a sum reputed to have been 40,000 dollars, and when a waiter arrived with his mutton chops, the story goes, he made him a gift of the restaurant by way of a tip. The waiter, whose name was Ciro, was thereby launched on a career of some distinction.

In newspaper history James Gordon Bennett the younger is known principally as the man who despatched Stanley to find Livingstone. On the Riviera he was thought of primarily as the owner of the Villa Namouna in Beaulieu, where he died in 1918. In its garden he demonstrated his fondness for animals by covering the lawn with a huge assortment of animal figures perpetrated in pottery, iron and other materials. The street in Beaulieu which today bears his name leads into another which bears the name of Franklin D. Roosevelt.

The man whose name symbolized American wealth more clearly in the first decades of the twentieth century than that of anyone else, the elder J. Pierpont Morgan, has been harshly criticized by at least one French historian of the Riviera for buying a number of Fragonard paintings and removing them from Grasse, where Fragonard was born. The wealth of paintings executed by French artists on the Riviera being what it is, the judgment may seem unnecessarily carping, particularly in the light of Morgan's discrimination as a collector and the munificence of his gifts to New York's Metropolitan Museum.

Morgan, whose father died in Monte Carlo as a result of injuries received in a train accident, did not become a true devotee of the Riviera. Rome, Paris and Aix-les-Bains all served him as satisfactory alternatives. But he and the effervescent Bennett had at least one taste in common. Whenever they were near the sea both indicated a preference for being addressed as 'Commodore'.

Shortly after the union of the interests of Morgan and Andrew Carnegie, which led to the formation of the United States Steel Corporation, the man who was appointed president of the corporation, Charles M. Schwab, found himself in trouble with both these financial giants because of his activities in Monte Carlo. In January 1902 Schwab motored from Paris to Monte Carlo, visited the casino with two business acquaintances, played a little at the tables, and had a night-cap at the bar. The next day the *New York Sun* carried a front-page report of how Schwab had broken the bank and been loudly cheered for doing so. Carnegie was much distressed and wrote to Morgan that he felt as if a son had disgraced the family. Schwab, he declared, had shown 'a sad lack of solid qualities' and his influence on thousands of young men would be 'pernicious in the extreme'. When Schwab gave Morgan his own account of the incident, explaining that he had indeed gambled but had not done so behind closed doors, Morgan pointed out to him that that was what doors were for.

As a prolific spender Schwab, who had a refrigerator designed to hold twenty tons of meat, retained Caruso to sing for his dinner guests for a 10,000 dollar fee and died with liabilities greatly exceeding his assets, was naturally drawn to the Riviera. Mrs Whitelaw Reid, widow of the man who succeeded Horace Greeley as proprietor of the *New York Tribune*, found on the Riviera evidence of a distinction of which she was proud. When she travelled in the United States or Europe, she liked to point out, it was never necessary for her to stay under a roof which was not her own. She died in 1931 under the roof of the villa in Cap Ferrat belonging to her daughter, Lady John Ward.

Spencer Penrose, a mining millionaire, whose reaction to the advent of prohibition was to instal enough liquor at his home in Colorado Springs to keep himself supplied for fifty years, followed a pretty widow, whom he met at a dance, across the Atlantic to Nice. There he showed her a letter from his father expressing approval of the idea that they should be married. They remained married for thirty-one years.

Evelyn McLean and her husband, purchasers of the Hope diamond, raced the Blue Train from Monte Carlo to Paris in order to put in their bid. Before her marriage to Ned McLean Evelyn Walsh, as she was then named, and her father, a prospector, who had come from Clonmel, Co. Tipperary, and had found gold, often visited the Riviera. In the Hôtel de Paris in Monte Carlo Evelyn Walsh met the daughter of a barber in California named Mrs John W. Mackay, who had also come into a fortune from the extraction of minerals from the ground. Mrs Mackay, who wore a large red wig, stayed in bed every day until she was ready to play at the casino. She then lost persistently. When her losses were mentioned to her she would reply: 'I am buying wares you do not see.'

Of all those who came to the Riviera from the United States to enjoy fortunes which had been made or inherited from railroads or steel, banking or newspapers, none left a more lasting imprint on the physical appearance of the Riviera than Frank Jay Gould.

Frank Jay Gould was one of the six children of the railroad king, Jay Gould, commonly known as 'the robber baron', who has some claim to be considered the most evil of all those who made huge and quick fortunes in the United States. His children too were not generally loved. Lucius Beebe in *The Big Spenders* wrote that socially the Goulds were 'unacceptable over a longer period of probation than most *arrivistes*.' Jay Gould himself was too much of a valetudinarian to derive much pleasure from spending his money, apart from indulging his tastes for yachts and orchids. But two of his children, who were strongly drawn to France, disposed of considerable sums there. One of them, Anna, married a French count and then a French marquis, and found both undertakings expensive. Her brother, Frank Jay, created much of the modern Juan-les-Pins.

Frank Jay Gould, a man with a large nose and a mournful air, gave his second wife five motor-cars, all at the same time, as an engagement present. He also put up the purse for the world heavyweight title fight between Primo Carnera and Max Schmeling. His extensive commercial interests on the Riviera included casinos in Nice and Cannes. He also built and owned hotels, and in these he introduced a number of innovations. One was to equip every bedroom in a new hotel with a private bathroom. Another was to provide every hotel guest on arrival with a new piece of soap.

It was for his development of Juan-les-Pins that Gould mainly earned the distinction conferred on him by the French Government when he was made Commander of the Legion of Honour in 1928. Juan-les-Pins was designed for summer visitors. That it was already a popular resort in the late 1920s was one of the clearest indications that before long the principal holiday season on the Riviera would be the summer and not the winter.

II

The Americans who first set the fashion for spending summers on the Riviera were not the millionaires but a small group of writers, painters, composers and discriminating art patrons, most of whom had come to France largely because they could live there more cheaply than they could in the United States. At the centre of this group for a number of years were Gerald and Sara Murphy.

Gerald and Sara Murphy were the originals of Dick and Nicole Diver as they appear in the first part of *Tender is the Night* before they are transformed into characters representing Fitzgerald himself and his wife Zelda. On a June morning in 1925 in a setting which is clearly Antibes Rosemary Hoyt, the eighteen-year-old film star in *Tender is the Night*, asks whether the Divers 'like it here'. She is told: 'They have to like it. They invented it.' 'The theory is', Dick Diver explains, 'that all the northern places, like Deauville, were picked out by Russians and English who don't mind the cold, while half of us Americans come from tropical climates – that's why we're beginning to come here.'

Murphy himself came from Boston. In 1921 he set off for Europe, knowing that there would be enough money to keep himself and his family there in comfort. In Paris an early acquaintance with the work of Braque and of Picasso decided him to devote his energies to painting. Though he remained essentially an amateur he exhibited at the Salon des Indépendents, and he and his wife worked as unpaid apprentices when they learnt that some of the scenery for Diaghilev's ballet company had been destroyed by fire.

The Murphys were introduced to the Riviera by Cole Porter, with whom Gerald Murphy had become friendly at Yale, largely through the enthusiasm they shared for Gilbert and Sullivan. Cole Porter was reputed to have a flair for finding little known places, and in 1922 he spent part of the summer at Antibes. His ambitious wife, who wanted him to write what she considered serious music, tried while they were there to persuade Stravinsky to teach him harmony and composition. Stravinsky declined the invitation.

The Murphys came to Antibes the following year and stayed at a small hotel called the Hôtel du Cap. Its owner, Antoine Sella, and his family had managed it for the past thirty-five years and had always closed it down for the summer on 1 May. Murphy persuaded Sella to keep the hotel open during the summer of 1923 with the services of a cook, a waiter and a chambermaid. The hotel is the original of Gausse's Hotel in *Tender is the Night*. 'Deferential palms cool its flushed façade, and before it stretches a short dazzling beach.... It was almost deserted after its English clientele went north in April.'

Later in 1923 Gerald and Sara Murphy found a villa just below Antibes lighthouse, which they bought. They named it Villa America, and for a number of years it was their principal home. Here they entertained Picasso and Stravinsky and, among their American friends, John Dos Passos, Archibald MacLeish, Gertrude Stein, Alice B. Toklas, Robert Benchley and Dorothy Parker. MacLeish seems to have expressed the general opinion when he described the Murphys as masters in the art of living.

The Murphys' other guests in the Villa America included Scott and Zelda Fitzgerald and Ernest Hemingway and his first wife, Hadley. The Fitzgeralds sailed for Europe in April 1924 in the hope both of being able to live more cheaply and of re-establishing some order in their lives. They reached the Riviera at the end of May and stayed first in St Raphael, which Fitzgerald described as 'a red little town built close to the sea, with gay red-roofed houses and an air of repressed carnival about it'.

Their visit began well. Fitzgerald worked every day, and in a letter to Edmund Wilson, Zelda expressed the hope that some-one could spread around New York an account of the idyllic existence they were leading. All her life Zelda had delighted in swimming, and, coming as she did from Montgomery, Alabama, she found the Riviera summer the ideal contrast with the bleak winter she had spent in St Paul's, Minnesota, after the birth of her daughter. 'Zelda and Scott', a French airman named Edouard Jozan told Zelda's biographer, Nancy Milford, 'were brimming over with life. Rich and free, they brought into our little provincial circle brilliance, imagination and familiarity with a Parisian and international world to which we had no access.'

Disturbances did occur during their first Riviera summer, Zelda on one occasion nearly committing suicide by taking an overdose of sleeping pills. The next year, when they left Paris for Antibes in August, Fitzgerald's attitude was summed up in his statement: 'One could get away with more on the summer Riviera, and whatever happened seemed to have something to do with art.' But it was on their subsequent visits that the most spectacular and most distressing incidents occurred.

At a restaurant in St Paul-de-Vence Zelda threw herself down the well of a stairway after Isadora Duncan had openly admired her husband. Early one morning a French farmer found both Scott and Zelda asleep in a car at a point on the railway track where they would shortly have been run down by a train. At a dinner party given by the Murphys Fitzgerald threw a fig soaked in sherbet at a countess, socked Archibald MacLeish on the jaw, and hurled three Venetian glasses over the garden wall. It was a measure of the Murphy–Fitzgerald relationship that his punishment for all this was to be banished from the Villa America for only three weeks. When they learnt that the Fitzgeralds were to return to the Riviera in 1928 both Gerald and Sara Murphy seem to have been genuinely pleased.

Scott and Zelda Fitzgerald paid their last visit to the Riviera in the summer of 1929, when they stayed in Cannes. Zelda had by then added to her accomplishments as writer and painter an ability to dance sufficiently well to give her first professional performances in Cannes and Nice. It was in that year too that while being driven on the Grande Corniche she tried to seize the steering-wheel of a car, in which her husband was also sitting, and to force it over the precipice. The next year she was diagnosed as a schizophrenic and was admitted to a home for prolonged psychiatric treatment.

Hemingway was attracted to Europe in the early 1920s for a variety of reasons: cheapness, gratifying memories of a war in which he had behaved with conspicuous gallantry during his brief period of action, and opportunities of learning the author's craft, of which he sensibly took advantage when he taught Ezra Pound how to box in exchange for receiving instruction in how to write. It was therefore almost inevitable that he should gravitate towards the Murphys, first in their flat in Paris on the left bank, and then in their villa in Antibes.

Hemingway was somewhat overawed by both Gerald and Sara Murphy and once described himself as feeling like 'a trusting and stupid bird dog in their presence'. He also took a véhement dislike to Zelda Fitzgerald, which was reciprocated, Zelda extending her distaste to Hemingway's prose, which she described as 'pretty damned Biblical'.

Hemingway and his first wife were guests of the Murphys at Antibes in 1926. Later that year he took two rooms in an hotel in Juan-les-Pins, of which one was occupied by Pauline Pfeiffer, who was to become his second wife. But even in this tangled situation Hemingway escaped for three weeks to Spain, the country which already exercised over him as man and writer, a fascination which he could never feel for the French Riviera.

The Murphys spent a year and a half in Switzerland because one of their children had contracted tuberculosis. They returned to Antibes in the early 1930s but found, in the words of their biographer, Calvin Tomkins, that 'the Riviera had lost its innocence'. The Hôtel du Cap had become the Grand Hôtel du Cap, and its Eden-Roc swimming pool was a favourite resort of the American film colony. Gerald Murphy too had changed, for he no longer even attempted to paint. He closed the Villa America in 1933, sailed for New York and never returned.

The Murphys had experienced something which could not be

recaptured. They had known Antibes when the telephone service in the summer closed down for two hours at noon and did not operate after 7 p.m., and when the town's only cinema had a film show on one evening a week. That they did not find it easy to adapt to the startling changes which occurred in a decade is not altogether surprising, even though their own example and way of living had done much to set these changes in motion. They lived well on the Riviera for much of a decade. Calvin Tomkins acknowledged this when he gave to his study of their lives the title *Living Well is the Best Revenge*.

III

There were great creative artists among Americans living on the Riviera in the inter-war years who did not belong to the coterie of the Murphys. They included a novelist of the calibre of Edith Wharton and a dancer of the stature of Isadora Duncan.

Henry James called Edith Wharton 'the Pendulum Woman' because of the frequency with which she crossed and re-crossed the Atlantic. She herself wrote of her family background in New York that it was peopled by 'heirs of an old tradition of European culture which the country has now totally rejected'. It was mainly a consciousness of this rejection which throughout her adult life gave her a stronger urge to cross the Atlantic eastwards than westwards.

In 1879 at the age of seventeen Edith (or Pussy) Jones, as she was then named, came to Cannes with her parents. At that time, she recalled later, 'the wooded background of Cannes descended almost to the shore.' The social circle in which she was allowed to move was a restricted one. 'The Americans who forced their way into good society in Europe', she wrote when recalling that period in her life, 'were said to be those who were shut out from it at home; and the self-respecting American on his travels frequented only the little "colonies" of his compatriots already settled in the European capitals.' Nevertheless her mother was delighted during this visit to greet two old friends from Boston, both of whom occupied near-by villas. One had become Comtesse de Sartiges. The other was also a countess with the name of Banuelos.

After her marriage Edith Wharton continued to travel, spending winter after winter before the First World War with her husband in what she described as 'rather aimless drifting on the French and Italian Rivieras'. Hyères, where they were lent 'a peach-coloured villa above the peach-orchards of Costebelle', by the French man of letters, Paul Bourget, was the only Riviera town which pleased her. It was to Hyères that she was to return after her divorce and after the Second World War, when she bought a large house set in a large park called Sainte-Claire le Château. Lord Clark described it as a 'dotty, comfortable, converted convent'.

In 1925 Edith Wharton wrote to Scott Fitzgerald: 'To your generation, which has taken such a flying leap into the future, I must represent the literary equivalent of tufted furniture and gas chandeliers.' With the passage of time the literary generation-gap may seem to have been narrowed. But nothing could bridge the gulf between the life-styles of these two great American novelists, both of whom spent so much time on the French Riviera, the one with a literary and personal life which were barely distinguishable from each other while both were made painfully public, the other separating her work as a writer from the rest of her disciplined and discreet existence as completely as is possible for any literary artist.

As a child Pussy Jones was discouraged from writing. Being excessively shy, she became a writer in secret, and as all her life she had plenty of space in the houses she occupied she was able to maintain the physical as well as the social barriers which suited her temperament. None of her friends, it seems, ever saw her in the act of writing, and she chose not to discuss her work except with those directly concerned.

At Sainte-Claire le Château she lived comfortably and hospitably. She described herself as 'a rather housekeeperish person', and she cultivated her garden with care. She contributed generously to local charities, and near her main property she bought a small house which, in memory of Stevenson, she named La Solitude and which she let from time to time to young writers.

To many of those whom she met she was a forbidding figure. The former Consuelo Vanderbilt wrote that 'in appearance she had the precise primness of an old maid', and that her husband 'seemed more of an equerry than an equal, walking behind her and carrying whatever paraphernalia she happened to discard'. These frequently included an ostrich boa which she had a habit of dropping. Lord Clark described her as living in 'a social fortress of which the doors were occasionally opened for a second to admit a newcomer'. The few who were admitted, and who included Lord Clark as a young man, usually commented on her kindness.

Like that of Scott Fitzgerald, the mode of living which Isadora Duncan adopted on the Riviera during her last years could have made little appeal to Edith Wharton, who was nevertheless a dedicated admirer of Isadora Duncan's art. 'I beheld the dance I had always dreamed of', she wrote after watching Isadora Duncan dance in Paris, 'a flowing of movement with movement, an endless interweaving of motion and music.' This was an extension of Isadora Duncan's own comment that it was a mistake to call her a dancer. She considered herself rather 'the magnetic centre to convey the emotional expression of the orchestra'.

Isadora Duncan knew the Riviera both during her times of triumph and in her final years when success seemed to have passed her by and fame had become fused with notoriety. She parted from Gordon Craig, the brilliant stage designer and producer, who was the father of her daughter Deirdre, in Nice. She gave birth to her son Patrick, whose father was Eugene Singer, the grandson of the inventor of the sewing machine, in Beaulieu. At the end of the First World War she and the pianist Walter Rummel set up a joint studio at Cap Ferrat.

She came to Nice again in 1925, when she was nearly destitute and was being helped by her brother Raymond, who had by then built up a flourishing business. This was based on the weaving by his vegetarian pupils of togas, sandals and other garments deemed suitable for the emancipated. To sell these he established one shop in Paris and another in Nice.

Sandwiched between these experiences were the years of Isadora Duncan's public acclaim and personal tragedies, when Diaghilev acknowledged that she had given an irreparable jolt to the Russian classical ballet and Lenin was moved to lean forward in his box and cry 'Bravo, bravo, Miss Duncan'; when Isadora was married to the Russian poet with whom she could communicate in no spoken language; when her two children were drowned in the Seine; and when a section of American opinion found its mouthpiece in the voice from the pulpit which proclaimed: 'That Bolshevik hussy doesn't wear enough clothes to pad a crutch.' This last comment was made during Isadora Duncan's visit to the United States in 1923, when she resolved never again to return to the country of her birth.

The final period of Isadora Duncan's life was largely spent in the Hôtel Negresco in Nice, which she was unable to leave because of the size of the bill she had accumulated. 'That nice hotel where we had credit' was how she described it. Her bedroom on the third floor had all the appearance of an actress's dressing-room littered with newspapers. Here, as the bills piled up, she worked on her memoirs in the hope of being able to escape from debt.

She had a continual fear of being alone and at least once attempted to commit suicide. She put on weight, admitting that her weaknesses included potatoes and young men. Sometimes she consoled herself by pointing out that she had good arms which, she declared, were 'the last of a woman's glories to fade'.

She clung to her dream of re-establishing the school to propagate and perpetuate her method through the instruction of young girls, to which so much of her money and her energy had been devoted. Spasmodically she planned a come-back, and she did give a Good Friday performance in Nice not long before she died, for which a hundred tickets were sold. She remained faithful to her concept of the dance as an art form when she declined an invitation to see the Russian ballet in Monte Carlo with the comment: 'I don't care much for acrobats.' But she seemed unable to escape from the poverty with which she was ill equipped to deal and of which she was continually made aware.

On a September day in 1927 Isadora Duncan set off on a journey by car wearing a scarf wrapped round her neck. The heavy fringe of the scarf was caught in the front wheel of the car, and she was killed by strangulation. She was aged forty-nine.

Neither Edith Wharton nor Isadora Duncan produced her best creative work on the Riviera. The sculptor, Henry Clews, by contrast, found on the Riviera the ideal setting for his work. This was the castle of La Napoule, which the Saracens had occupied in the tenth century. Being a rich man Clews was able to buy the castle in 1918, and he and his wife Marie, an architect, began a work of restoration which was to last them nearly twenty years. The only labour employed, apart from their own, was that of a local master-mason and his son.

Formal gardens were created where doves and peacocks roamed. In the castle itself Henry and Marie Clews dined in the huge hall dressed in carefully designed medieval styles, waited on by servants in Provençal costume and entertained by musicians performing in the minstrels' gallery.

For five years Henry Clews never left his property, dedicating himself to his work as a sculptor, creating in marble, alabaster, bronze and wood, monkeys, satirical figures with such titles as Autocracy, Plutocracy and Democracy, and busts of Edgar Allan Poe and Frederick Delius among a mass of other work.

Clews died shortly before the outbreak of the Second World War. His widow, after hiding much of his work and refusing to leave the castle even when German occupying troops moved in, opened the castle after the war as a museum in which a superb collection of Clews's sculpture can be seen today. Critics have described him as the greatest sculptor the United States has produced. This is clearly debatable, but he must surely have a strong claim to be considered the wittiest.

IV

The United States Government and American concerns generally were slow in providing their nationals on the Riviera with services which the British, among others, had long been accustomed to receive.

American Express opened an office in Nice for the first time in 1920. Chile, Roumania and Sweden were all ahead of the United States in establishing consulates in Cannes, and such consular representatives as the United States did have on the Riviera in the 1920s were not expected to be overburdened with duties or responsibilities. Dr Otis A. Glazebrook, who held the post of Consul in the Maritime Alps for eight years from 1921, was a doctor of divinity whom President Wilson had appointed to be United States Consul in Jerusalem at the age of sixty-five. When he retired in 1929 he was eighty-three. In spite of the influx of summer visitors in the 1920s the American church in Nice remained closed during the summer months for a number of years after the First World War.

In the administration of sport Americans on the Riviera seem to have sought none of the authority which the British habitually assumed. But when their sporting champions did appear on the Riviera they usually won. A match which aroused exceptional interest and speculation was that between Suzanne Lenglen and Helen Wills at the Carlton Club in Cannes in November 1926. So great was the crush to see the game that would-be spectators were shaken off the branches of a eucalyptus tree by the police. Suzanne Lenglen won 6–2 8–6, but before long Helen Wills had succeeded her as the acknowledged champion of the world. William T. Tilden showed a comparable mastery when he appeared on the Riviera tennis scene in the late 1920s. Americans also helped to fill the few gaps in the sporting scene which the British left vacant. When a leading French basketball team came from Paris to Nice in 1938 opposition was provided by a team from USS *Raleigh*.

In the provision of social services there was a tendency for Americans to join with the British rather than establish institutions of their own. The principal lending library in Nice was known as the English-American Library, and an Anglo-American clinic sprang up in the 1920s in Juan-les-Pins.

A number of individual Americans made a memorable impact on the Riviera scene in the inter-war years by sheer force of personality. A certain social eminence was accorded for instance to Ralph Curtis of Boston. On being asked by Lord Harris whether he knew the Vanderbilts Curtis replied that when he left the United States they were 'still vanderbuilding'. Elsa Maxwell enjoyed a standing as a hostess which was in some respects unique. Believing the human race to be consumed, almost without exception, by burning social ambitions – 'as a person climbs,' she once wrote, 'whether it's in international society or the local garden club, progress is measured by the length and thickness of assembled press clippings' – she became a central figure in what she described as 'a menage of celebrities – semi-, would-be, and truly immortal – who made Europe during the twenties and thirties the glittering mecca it became.' Noël Coward's song, 'I went to a marvellous party', was, she claimed, based on one she herself gave in Cap Ferrat in the late 1930s. This may well have been so.

In her book of reminiscences, *The Celebrity Circus*, she described how in the inter-war years she filled the role of what today would be called a public relations consultant for the development of Monte Carlo as a summer resort. The extent to which her advice was taken has not been clearly established.

Other Americans left abiding physical reminders of their presence. Perhaps the most sought after architect specializing in Riviera villas was Barry Dierks of Pittsburg. He designed the Villa l'Horizon for Maxine Elliott and made extensive alterations to Maugham's Villa Mauresque. The fashions he set soon affected market values. Villas which their owners wished to let had once been judged largely by the beauty of their gardens. In the 1930s they were being assessed by the size of their swimming pools.

One of the more spectacular works of restoration carried out in the mountains immediately behind the Riviera coast was at Gourdon, the old Roman fortress overlooking the gorges of the river Loup, which had withstood repeated Saracen attacks. Here the castle and the hanging gardens were largely recreated at the expense of an American benefactress named Miss Norris.

Mary Garden, the singer, who was born in Aberdeen and who was nearly the cause of a duel between Maeterlinck and Debussy – Maeterlinck did in fact shoot his cat while practising for the duel – was a benefactress of the village of Peille near Monte Carlo, where a war memorial and a new road leading to it were built almost entirely at her expense. But the costliest and perhaps the most impressive constructional work for which the Riviera is indebted to an individual American took place at La Turbie.

Here the great monument known as the Trophée des Alpes, which had been completed in the year 5 BC to commemorate the Roman conquest of the Alps and the submission of forty-four hostile tribes, was found by Edward Tuck, who was already a considerable benefactor of the city of Paris, to be in ruins. In 1929 he offered to finance the restoration of the monument, to be carried out under the direction of the Services des Monuments Historiques. Nearly three thousand pieces belonging to the original monument were uncovered, and to enable the work to be completed twenty-two private houses and an hotel had to be demolished.

In spite of such benefactions it is yet arguable that there were only two fields of social activity on the Riviera in which the

influence of Americans in the inter-war years was more pro-
nounced and more effective than that of other foreign nationals.
One was the development of the summer season. The other was
the establishment of the Riviera as one of the world's principal
social centres for those engaged in the film industry. In the creation of the Palm Beach Casino in Cannes the two trends clearly
converged.

V

A proposal to build a summer casino at the end of the Croisette
in Cannes was examined seriously by the so-called Cannes Bains
de Mer committee set up in 1923. There was plenty of well
organized and vocal opposition, most of it from owners of shops
who did not welcome the prospect of having to operate one
establishment near the end of the Croisette in the summer and
another in the main part of the town in the winter. The hotelier
Henri Ruhl, who was the main proponent of the scheme, gradually wore the opposition down, and on 5 April 1929 the new
casino was formally opened.

Ruhl had counted largely on American patronage, as the
choice of the name 'Palm Beach' indicated. This had been suggested to him by the Princess Elisabeth de Caraman-Chimay, an
American who had been a friend of Marcel Proust and who
claimed to be a direct descendant of Peter Stuyvesant. The gala
opening dinner was attended by the Aga Khan, by André
Citroën and, in the words of *Nice-Matin*, by 'de très nombreuses
jeunes et jolies Américaines'. Among the principal events in the
casino's first season were the Independence Day gala, a personal
appearance by Maurice Chevalier on his return from the United
States and a *concours d'élégance*, in which the first prize was won by
an American girl in a Studebaker. When thirty-three directors
drawn from the leading American travel agencies came ashore at
Cannes from the French naval vessel *Le Brestois*, the prospects for
the casino seemed encouraging. Then, at the end of its first
season, came the crash on Wall Street.

The number of American visitors to the Riviera dropped
sharply after October 1929, but among those who continued to
come and to spend as freely as they had ever done were some of

the leading film stars. The American film industry had discovered the Riviera as a desirable location some years earlier, and in 1923 the *Menton and Monte Carlo News* was already suggesting that Nice might become the Los Angeles of France. As a holiday resort for the stars the Riviera made a natural appeal, and neither Wall Street crash nor subsequent slump could prevent Charles Chaplin or Gloria Swanson, Ronald Colman or William Powell from holidaying there in a manner to which they were accustomed.

With the restoration of confidence and the consequent return of American visitors in large numbers the demand for American and American-style entertainment grew. In 1938 the athletic American dancer Veronica, wearing a swimsuit, performed ten thousand consecutive high kicks on the beach at Cannes. In the same season the Palm Beach Casino's principal attraction was Marlene Dietrich, who was reported during this visit to Cannes to have indulged in sunbathing for the first time in her life.

By then the Riviera was also being patronized by leading American political figures. They too came in summer, among those engaged in what was called swimsuit diplomacy being Henry Morgenthau, Secretary of the United States Treasury, and Joseph Kennedy, United States Ambassador to Britain, who brought with him the future American President and others of his numerous children.

Until the attack on Pearl Harbor converted what had been predominantly a European war into a world war the United States had a non-belligerent status and even after the defeat of the French armies was able to maintain diplomatic relations with the Vichy Government. But after September 1939 Americans ceased as abruptly as the British to be attracted to the Riviera as a playground. Not until they returned again in a new role nearly five years after the outbreak of war in Europe did American faces and American voices become familiar once more to the inhabitants of the Riviera.

VI

Americans came to the Riviera later than the British and in smaller numbers. Before the first big exodus in 1939 there were between thirty and forty thousand British residents on the Riviera. The number of American residents was about a tenth of that figure. But American influence was to persist after British influence had declined almost to the point of being negligible.

The land forces which invaded southern France in August 1944 were under the command of Lieutenant-General Alexander M. Patch of the United States Seventh Army and were predominantly American in their composition. After the fighting was over Cannes was made a leave centre for American officers, and for some years after the war, before President de Gaulle decided to remove France from the operational area of the North Atlantic Treaty Organisation, a powerful American fleet was based at Villefranche.

After the war Americans suffered from none of the currency restrictions which afflicted the British, and American service personnel, at first, and American tourists later, played a major part in reviving the Riviera's economy. An indication of what the future held was given in July 1948 when Conrad Hilton, who was staying in the Carlton Hotel in Cannes, held a press conference in which he startled those present by describing hotels which would have 3,000 bedrooms all equipped with their own radio and television sets.

The Cannes film festival, which had had to be abandoned so suddenly in 1939, was held for the first time in 1947. The first festival was a modest affair, but American participation soon helped to make it one of the principal events in the film industry's calendar. In 1955 an American star of exceptional beauty appeared in Cannes at the time of the festival to promote a film in which she was appearing. This was Grace Kelly, whose meeting with Prince Rainier III of Monaco and subsequent marriage to him provided a modern fairy-tale as well as a union which, both personally and in the interests of the principality, seems to have been as successful as any in the history of the house of Grimaldi.

In the winter of 1953–54, of the 51,000 tourists who came to Cannes 39,000 were French, 4,500 were Americans and 3,400 British. The next largest foreign contingents were the Swiss and the Belgians. As economic recovery continued the proportion of visitors who came from the mainland of Europe to the Riviera, from Germany in particular, grew consistently. Americans for their part found that air travel gave them a new ease of access to holiday resorts in different continents which, in climate and scenery at least, compared not unfavourably with the Riviera.

Some twenty years after the end of the Second World War Americans meant less to the Riviera and the Riviera meant less to Americans than in the first decade-and-a-half after Cole Porter's and the Murphys' discovery of Antibes as a summer resort, the period when the Eden-Roc swimming-pool glittered with Hollywood stars and Les Girls made their presence felt all along the Riviera. Yet though their influence declined, the Americans never suffered that sudden eclipse of power and prestige experienced, not only by the British, but, even more decidedly, by the Russians.

10 Russians, other Foreigners and the French

I

When the Emperor Alexander II of Russia and his Empress came by train to Nice a week after the railway line had been opened they set a fashion which was to shape the social life of the French Riviera in new ways. It was then that the annual large-scale winter migration of Russian land-owning families began. With them they brought new levels of extravagance and new forms of eccentricity which neither the local inhabitants nor most of the other foreign visitors to the Riviera had ever experienced.

A number of Russians had made an impact on the region before the coming of the railway. A colony of Russian grain merchants and seamen was established in Nice in the 1770s. The Russian navy acquired certain rights in Villefranche from the Sardinian Government. In the 1850s the Russian Admiral Popov conducted negotiations, which he evidently believed might succeed, and whose purpose was the outright purchase of Monaco. In the 1850s too the Grand Duchess Helena, whom Maargaret Brewster descriibed as suffering from 'rheumatic gout' and who made a practice of bathing naked in the sea in winter, was a leading hostess in Nice. On one occasion she entertained some 5,000 people in the garden of her villa. But it was not until after the railway came that the annual disposal of large incomes derived from property in Russia, supplemented from time to time by the disposal of valuable items of jewellery, became of major importance to the Riviera economy.

Prince Cherkassky, who had a villa on the heights of Californie above Cannes, liked to see a different display in his flower-beds every morning and employed forty-eight gardeners to change the plants during the night. Count Apraxin, who arrived every year at his villa in Cannes on 15 November and left on 15 March, kept a number of distinguished cellists on permanent duty throughout the period of his stay. They were required to play at any time of day or night that he chose, and as the music tended to make him feel suicidal a servant had to stand behind his chair to prevent him from shooting himself. Once the crisis had been overcome he would drink seven or eight glasses of a mixture consisting of cognac and a distillation of violets poured over sugar and then fall asleep. He refused to receive any visitors, even the Grand Duke Michael, apart from the Mayor of Cannes, M. Capron, who was permitted to call from time to time.

Such forms of conduct were not confined to the dwellers in private villas. Antoine Sella, proprietor of the Hôtel du Cap d'Antibes, recalled one Russian guest who ordered a kilo of strawberries daily. After sniffing the scent of these he would hand them over to his valet to dispose of as he thought fit.

The number of Russian grand dukes and grand duchesses who spent much of their time on the Riviera was considerable, and to protect them and the emperors and empresses themselves from assassination provided the local police with one of their more exacting duties. It was a duty carried out with consistent success. In 1884 one grand duke did kill a police inspector, who was guarding him, in the belief that he was a nihilist assassin, but the affair was hushed up. Otherwise there were no serious incidents. On her visits to the Riviera the Empress Maria Feodorovna made a point of presenting members of the police force with a watch and a glass of champagne shortly before her departure. The rewards were well justified by results.

A number of Russians expected to enjoy to the full while on the Riviera the social privileges to which they were entitled at home. The widow of the Grand Duke Constantine, for instance, on being told that a steamer from Marseilles would be calling at Nice and could take her to Genoa which she planned to visit, refused to travel with the common people and persuaded the Emperor Napoleon III to send a frigate for her. When she reached Genoa, deciding she could not entrust her grand piano to a pinnace which had been sent out, she remained on board the frigate for two weeks until a jetty had been constructed. In death too the distinctions accorded to members of the Russian royal family tended be unique. When the heir to the imperial throne died of tuberculosis in the Villa Bermond in Nice in 1864 it was thought fit to demolish the villa in its entirety and erect a memorial chapel in its place.

Some of the members of the Russian royal family, the Grand Duke Michael most noticeably, were conscious of social obligations, but in general they did not greatly endear themselves to those whom they met. Describing a dinner party held in Cannes in April 1905, Princess Daisy of Pless wrote: 'The dinner was awful. The Grand Duke George shouted and yelled and behaved too dreadfully. Michael himself, poor dear, is not anything particular, *mais mis contre son frère*, there is no comparison.' In the same diary entry she wrote: 'I can understand still better now why and how the Japs are beating the Russians at every turn.'

The dinner party Princess Daisy described was held in the villa of the Grand Duchess Anastasia. Her husband, the Grand Duke of Mecklenburg-Schwerin, committed suicide by jumping over the parapet of his villa in Cannes. After his death she bought a villa in Eze, from which she regularly sallied out in search of handsome young men. Among those who trod it the pathway to her house became known after a time as the *route nationale*. The Baroness Orczy wrote of the Grand Duchess: 'I have seldom seen a more unpleasant looking old woman with the face of a lizard, and claw-like hands.' In her later years the Grand Duchess was regularly to be seen in the middle of the day in the Café de Paris in Monte Carlo surrounded by young girls, 'amongst whom', the Baroness Orczy wrote, 'I was really sorry to note a few English ones.'

There were of course people of real distinction among members of the Russian ruling classes who visited the Riviera or settled there. Count Leo Tolstoy came to Hyères in 1860 with his brother Nicholas who suffered from tuberculosis. The Armenian General Loris-Melikov, after conducting himself ably in the Russo-Turkish war of 1877–8 and as Governor of Astrakhan, where he remained at his post during an outbreak of plague, retired from the political scene with dignity on the succession of the Emperor Alexander III and settled permanently in Nice. But of those enduring products which did emanate from Russians on the Riviera during the period known to them as the *belle époque* one of the most satisfying was the work of a girl belonging to a family who were excluded from what was considered polite Russian society. This was the journal of the young Marie Bashkirtseff.

II

In 1870 Marie Bashkirtseff's mother set off on a tour abroad, leaving her husband, an easy-going small landowner with a taste for women, behind. The touring party numbered seven: the mother, Marie herself, Marie's grandfather, her aunt, her brother Paul, her cousin Dina and a rather long-suffering Polish doctor. After wandering for some two years, with stays in Vienna, Geneva and Baden-Baden, the party finally arrived in Nice. Here Marie, while still little more than a child and infatuated with the Duke of Hamilton, began the journal which Gladstone was to describe as 'a book without parallel' and work of 'a true genius'.

There were a number of reasons why the Bashkirtseff family were not accepted in certain social circles in Nice. The absence of a husband for Marie's mother was one. The way in which Marie was allowed to run along the Promenade des Anglais without a hat and to appear as a little girl in short dresses in the Monte Carlo casino was another. There were also some rather deplorable incidents, including the occasion when the Bashkirtseff monkey bit Anna Tolstoy's son. By way of revenge Madame Tolstoy showed some friends over the villa which the Bashkirtseff family had rented furnished, treating them as prospective tenants, whereupon Marie's uncle George, who had also joined the family group, rose in a drunken rage and began to beat Madame Tolstoy.

To escape the consequences Uncle George fled over the border to Monaco, where he was later found living, rather dismally in Marie Bashkirtseff's view, in a suite of three rooms with a mistress. In his absence he had been sentenced to a term of imprisonment and a fine, and the Russian consul insisted that for the honour of Russia he should return to Nice. After a time he did so, the sentence of imprisonment was quashed, and the damages he had to pay to Madame Tolstoy were reduced.

For all the affection she evidently felt for them Marie was not sparing in her descriptions of her family's shortcomings. Of a train journey from Paris to Nice she wrote: 'Mama with her thirty-six packages reduced me to despair. Her cries, her fears, her boxes are sickeningly bourgeois.' She was no less frank about her own conduct. There was for instance the occasion when she threw a plate of macaroni on the floor and burnt several chairs because she had not been invited to a ball. Another time she wrote:

> Yesterday evening I had such a fit of despair that I groaned aloud, and felt impelled to throw the dining-room clock into the sea. Dina ran after me, fearing that I had some sinister design, but it was only the clock, after all.

Perhaps the most revealing journal entry of any was that in which she recorded simply that the family 'spoke quietly for almost the first time in my life'.

There are elements in Marie Bashkirtseff's journal which cry out for the kind of parody Stephen Leacock offered in *The Sorrows of a Super Soul: or, The Memoirs of Marie Mushenough*. But as an exercise in self-revelation it became a best-seller soon after its first publication in France in 1887, that is to say three years after her death from tuberculosis. It remains compelling reading today.

As a record of how one Russian family lived in Nice in the 1870s the journal is unique. 'I love Nice,' Marie Bashkirtseff wrote in September 1874, when she was in Paris. 'Nice is my country; Nice made me grow; Nice gave me health and a beautiful complexion. It is so beautiful.'

Though some members of the royal family and some noblemen preferred Cannes, Nice remained throughout their *belle époque* the principal centre of Russians on the Riviera, and it was appropriate that the exotic church provided by the Emperor Nicholas II and his mother should have been erected in Nice. To the western European eye it may appear as a startling exercise of oriental fantasy, but as a complement to Marie Bashkirtseff's journal in providing a memorial to what Nice meant to Russians and how Russians lived in Nice it offers an absorbing study.

III

Most of all [Scott Fitzgerald wrote in *Tender is the Night*], there was the scent of the Russians along the coast – their closed bookshops and grocery stores. Ten years ago, when the season ended in April, the doors of the Orthodox Church were locked, and the sweet champagnes they favoured were put away until their return. 'We'll be back next season,' they said, but this was premature, for they were never coming back any more.

Some did come back and some stayed. Between them there were enough to make possible in the 1920s on the Riviera an extraordinary flowering of Russian creative talents. Its centre was Monte Carlo, and the form much of it took was shaped by the artistic sensibility and strength of personality of one man, Serge Diaghilev.

In Russia Diaghilev had controlled a magazine dedicated to improving tastes and standards in all the arts. When he came to western Europe he organized an exhibition of Russian painting in Paris and then arranged a series of Russian concerts. In 1911 he came to Monte Carlo, presented *Scheherazade* and so began to develop the process of allying to the dance the work of great composers, great painters and poets in forms which had not been attempted before.

At the end of the 1914–18 war Diaghilev was in serious financial difficulties. His company of dancers was kept in being largely through the generosity of a member of the American Singer family, the Princess Edmond de Polignac. Then in 1922 he made a satisfactory agreement for their employment. There was a small permanent troupe of dancers in Monte Carlo. Diaghilev offered to supplement this with most of his own dancers in the winter and to continue, as formerly, to have his own season in Paris beginning in April. In this way the Ballets Russes de Monte Carlo came into being.

The meetings which Diaghilev held in Monte Carlo, often in the Café de Paris, were likened by the Aga Khan to councils of war.

> I often used to be present [the Aga Khan wrote] at his conferences with all his leading associate 'heads of departments' as he called them: Stravinsky, Bakst, Nijinsky, Karsavina, his ballet-master, his choreographer in chief, a young poet perhaps, a venerable and venerated artist like Rodin.

Diaghilev would describe himself to newspaper reporters as the man who looked after the lighting and claim that his only measurable gains were board and lodging in the best hotels and the privilege of a seat at the Russian ballet. But, as Igor Stravinsky expressed it, 'Diaghilev was more strong-willed than all his artists and controlled every detail of every ballet he produced.'

As a homosexual Diaghilev enjoyed a freedom in France which he would not have been permitted in Russia. Until he left Russia his inclinations seem to have been known to virtually no one other than those with whom he was sexually involved. In Monte Carlo he was surrounded by what Stravinsky described as 'a kind of homosexual Swiss guard'. He would frequently argue with Stravinsky his proposition that the exclusive love of women was a morbid taste. 'I don't know', Stravinsky commented drily, 'how he could have known very much about that.'

Stravinsky himself had also visited the Riviera before 1914. It was in Beaulieu that he composed the music for the first scene of *Petrushka*, a work which caused members of the Russian colony in Monte Carlo to send a deputation headed by a general to the president of the local music society asking him to ban it. After the war, which he spent for the most part in Switzerland, Stravinsky came to Monte Carlo a number of times at Diaghilev's invitation, and in 1924 he established his home in Nice. Here for a few years he stayed during the summer months composing and resting after his tours as conductor or pianist in Europe and the United States.

The great Russian composers and painters, singers, dancers and choreographers, Stravinsky, Chagall, Chaliapin, Pavlova, Nijinsky and others who came to the Riviera were able to practise their art there. Most of them too were able to enjoy richly the pleasures which the Riviera afforded, though Anna Pavlova's enjoyment of the Monte Carlo casino may have been somewhat restricted, for her memory was so poor that she had to ask her friends to stay with her and inform her which numbers she had put a stake on.

Other members of the Russian colony were not so fortunate in the 1920s, though one who did succeed in a post of some importance not primarily concerned with the arts was the former military attaché in London, General Pierre Polovtsoff.

IV

General Polovtsoff had been familiar with the Riviera in his youth, for his father had owned a large villa on Monaco's eastern boundary with France. The father had disposed of a considerable fortune at roulette, being a determined believer in systems and employing a secretary to note the numbers which came up during his absences from the tables. The son found his best chances of winning lay in staking against his father.

After being commander-in-chief of the Petrograd military division General Polovtsoff escaped from Russia to Persia disguised as an American missionary and eventually arrived in Monte Carlo. Zaharoff had by then disposed of his interests in the casino, and René Blum, who was later to die in a German concentration camp, had become chief administrator responsible only to the board and to the Prince of Monaco. It was he who suggested the appointment of General Polovtsoff as President of the International Sporting Club, putting forward the argument that it was high time there was a gentleman in the administration. The appointment seems to have been a considerable success.

Relatively few of the Russians on the Riviera were able to adapt themselves as successfully as Polovtsoff to new circumstances. For many the ideal to which they aspired was the maintenance as nearly as possible of the old traditions. One such was the well-known dancer Kschessinska, who had had a varied association with the Russian royal family.

As a young girl she had attracted the attention of the future Emperor Nicholas II, who had provided her with a flat which her parents allowed her to share with her sister. After the Emperor's marriage the Grand Duke Serge did his best, as she put it, to 'comfort and entertain' her and also provided her with a *dacha*.

Then the Grand Duke André, who was seven years younger than she was, began to haunt the theatre, and in due course she bore him a son in Biarritz.

The Grand Duke André bought a villa in Cap d'Ail, where he and Kschessinska were living in 1913. In 1920 they made their way back there and found that their indoor servants and an old gardener had faithfully maintained their property. To pay their wages the Grand Duke had to mortgage the villa. Through the sale of jewellery and dancing lessons given by Kschessinska she and the Grand Duke gradually restored some of their old way of life, and they decided it might be appropriate for them to be married, provided they could obtain the consent of the Grand Duke Cyril, the head of the imperial family. Consent was given, the marriage took place, Kschessinska was made a princess and given the family name of Krassinsky, and her son was made a prince. When the Grand Duke Cyril decided to allow the morganatic wives and children of unions such as that of the Grand Duke André to use the name of Romanovsky the family titles became even more impressive.

Those who found it hardest to part from the old traditions were of course among the likeliest to become economic casualties. In December 1922 the *Menton and Monte Carlo News* reported that a private lottery was being organized for 'a former wealthy Russian family now in great distress'. Some two years later the same paper published a photograph of a princess, who preferred to remain anonymous selling English newspapers on the Promenade des Anglais. Why she chose to remain anonymous when she had agreed to pose for the press photographer was not explained.

Charity helped to relieve some of the distress. A number of cheap lodging-houses were supported in this way. An establishment in Cannes fed, clothed and educated some sixty Russian children, and there were similar homes in Nice and Menton. But to a number of the Russians on the Riviera hope no doubt lay largely in a restoration of the *status quo* in Russia, a hope which was revived in the mind of not a few by the German invasion of Russia in 1941.

V

Among the dancers whom Diaghilev launched in Monte Carlo was Serge Lifar. After the revolution Diaghilev asked Bronislava Nijinska, sister of the great dancer, who was herself to become one of Diaghilev's principal choreographers, to send him five of her best pupils from Kiev to Paris. One of the five failed to turn up when required to leave, and the seventeen-year-old Lifar took his place. He met Diaghilev in Paris, found him to be, as he later expressed it, 'art incarnate', and was despatched to Monte Carlo to join the troupe.

There he danced a number of leading roles and formed the habit of going night after night to the point of the rock of Monaco to rehearse by himself.

When the German–Russian treaty of non-aggression was announced in 1939 Lifar was in Cannes attending a ball under the patronage of the Duke and Duchess of Windsor. After his return to Paris he became *maître de ballet* of the Paris Opera and accepted it as his duty, as he put it, 'to preserve under the tidal wave of Occupation that part of the national patrimony represented by the Opera, its stage, its dancers, its treasures, its archives.'

It was a duty which he was able to combine with being received by Hitler, who expressed appreciation of the work he was doing, with plenty of champagne parties in Paris and with more than one visit to the Riviera. In February 1944 Lifar dined with the German Admiral von Spiegel and then went to the Monte Carlo casino, where he heard rumours that the local civilian population was to be evacuated. In his autobiography he later described how he asked von Spiegel to cancel the order, how von Spiegel promptly did so, and how he himself announced the news over the radio.

It was over a different radio that Lifar heard, as the Allied armies approached Paris, his own name picked out as one of those who was to be handed over to the Russian people. In fact he had to face a five-week trial by the Purge Committee of Lyric Theatres and was banned from further association with the Opera and the State theatres. The ban did not apply to the Monte Carlo Opera and before the end of 1945 Lifar had accepted an invitation to become director of the Nouveaux Ballets de Monte Carlo.

In his autobiography, which he dedicated 'To My Country Russia', Lifar wrote that some Russians in France were 'sincerely persuaded' that it was their patriotic duty to believe in a German victory. On the Riviera the number who acted accordingly was large enough to damage by association the reputation of most of the others, and after the liberation many found it prudent not to emphasize too strongly their Russian origins. Added to the natural process of assimilation, of which the decision to conduct services in the Russian church in Nice in the French language was symptomatic, it was to have the effect of steadily eliminating most of the traces of the former Russian presence.

The Russian churches remained open, but they attracted dwindling and aging congregations, which were supplemented here and there by French students of Russian who enjoyed taking part in the singing. In 1974 a link with the past was lost when a grandson of the Emperor Alexander III and a nephew of Nicholas II, Prince Nikita, who had been sent by King George V to the Crimea in an attempt to rescue the imperial family, died in Cannes. Then in November 1975 what might have been considered a symbolic act to mark the end of the era of Russian influence on the Riviera occurred when Sotheby's and the Société des Bains de Mer sold by auction in Monaco the great library assembled by Diaghilev, who was a dedicated bibliophile, a library containing, among other treasures, the first book printed in Moscow, the first Russian grammar printed in the western world and the manuscripts of Pushkin's *Eugene Onegin* and Stravinsky's *The Firebird*.

VI

Picasso had a house called La Californie in the district of that name, where a goat lived indoors in a packing-case, and to which a continual stream of visitors came; he revitalized the pottery industry of Vallauris and was largely responsible for the institution of a *corrida* there. He worked for a time in the Grimaldi castle in Antibes, where there is a permanent exhibition of his pictures. Another distinguished Spanish creative artist, Blasco Ibañez, lived in Menton.

Nico Zographos, who gave away large sums of money in his lifetime, died in 1953, leaving more than £5 million, all of which he had acquired by playing baccarat. One of the other members of the Greek baccarat syndicate, Athanase Vagliano, was unable to read. When he visited a restaurant he would insist on the whole of a chicken being cut up in his presence in order to make sure that he missed nothing. The Greek tradition of success was maintained when Aristotle Onassis acquired control of the Monte Carlo casino.

Dr Guglielminetti carried out what is believed to have been the world's first successful experiment in the tarring of roads in Monaco in 1902. Caruso sang with Patti in the Monte Carlo opera as a baritone. Paganini died in Nice.

Nietzsche witnessed an earthquake in Nice in 1887 and compared his own feelings of irony and cool curiosity favourably with the general excitement around him.

Maeterlinck had a villa in Nice named Les Abeilles. Simenon set a number of his stories on the Riviera. The road which leads from Menton to the Italian frontier is named Promenade Reine Astrid to commemorate the death there in a road accident of the wife of King Leopold III of the Belgians.

Henryk Sienkiewicz wrote a short novel entitled *In Monte Carlo*. Paderewski gave a number of piano recitals on the Riviera in the 1920s after his retirement from the post of Prime Minister of Poland.

Le Corbusier died by drowning off Roquebrune. Sir Mortimer Davies, President of the Imperial Tobacco Company of Canada, died of a heart attack while playing baccarat in the Monte Carlo casino. John MacCormack enlarged his range of experience by singing in opera in Monte Carlo, where Melba was often heard.

The list of eminent visitors to the Riviera from a variety of countries could clearly be prolonged. But none of these other peoples, Spaniards or Greeks, Germans, Belgians, Poles, Swiss, Canadians, Irish or Australians, could claim before 1940 an influence on the social life of the Riviera seriously comparable with that of the British, the Russians or, latterly, the Americans. Even the Italians who, because of their proximity, were usually the most numerous of the foreign visitors were seldom the most dominant.

It was perhaps an instinctive understanding of the degrees of importance enjoyed by the different nationalities on the Riviera which led to the choice of the reception party to meet Félix Faure, President of the French Republic, when he paid an official visit to the Riviera in 1896 accompanied by the President of the Council and the Minister of Marine and Commerce. Minor royalty was represented by the Grand Duke of Mecklenburg-Schwerin (husband of the Grand Duchess Anastasia) and the Prince and Princess of Nassau. The other members of the party were the Grand Duke Michael, Prince and Princess Galitzine, the Countess Torby, the second Viscount Brougham and W.E. Gladstone.

VII

Of that part of the Riviera which lies between the River Var and the present Italian frontier Talleyrand is reputed to have said in 1816 that if he had known how beautiful it was he would never have agreed to its coming under Sardinian rule. Such relative ignorance was not unusual in French ruling circles at the time. The attitude of mind fostered among courtiers in the reign of Louis XIV, which accepted that the countryside was a desert and that to be banished to it was a disgrace, died hard. The Riviera was many miles from Paris or Versailles or Fontainebleau; it was a poor district served by bad communications; and before the works of Rousseau became popular a liking for the proximity of both sea and mountains was an eccentric taste.

Famous Frenchmen had passed through the region or stayed there for a time before Talleyrand made his comment. The mysterious Man in the Iron Mask was held prisoner on the Île St Honorat from 1687 to 1698. The Chevalier de Lamarck, while serving as a lieutenant in the French garrison in Monaco in 1763, was so impressed by the vegetation of the rock, and particularly by the shapes of the Barbary fig trees, that he decided his vocation must be that of botanist. Napoleon Bonaparte made more than one landing on the Riviera, near St Raphael in 1799 on his triumphant return from Egypt, and at Golfe-Juan sixteen years later after his escape from Elba. But such visits were transitory or enforced.

For a long time the region was too remote to acquire a clear identity in the minds of French people generally other than as a territory which lay beyond Provence and did not properly belong to it. 'Le niçard n'est pas le provençal', Camille Mauclair wrote in his work, *La Provence*. 'Le ciel, et en partie les sites, sont les mêmes: l'âme est tout autre.' A true Provençal, he stated, would describe himself as leaving his country at some point near St Raphael or possibly at the River Var. The very name Côte d'Azur, which may be regarded as the French equivalent of the English term 'French Riviera', was not known until 1887, when it was first used by the Burgundian poet Stéphen Liégeard, author of the verses inscribed on the Brougham statue in Cannes.

Prosper Mérimée may be considered the first well-known French public figure to make a cult of a Riviera town. In May 1834 he was appointed Inspector-General of Historic Monuments, a post he was to fill with distinction for more than eighteen years. Two months after assuming office he made his first tour of southern France. He found himself increasingly drawn to Cannes, and in 1856, after renting part of a house there for eight weeks, decided he would return every year.

Once the railway was built he fell into a regular rhythm. In November or December he would take the train from Paris to Cannes, the two English sisters, Emma Lagden and Fanny Ewer, who looked after his household affairs and whom Brougham had described as 'scarcely appropriate Psyches for such a large Cupid', having been despatched in advance. He would remain in Cannes, where he was often to be seen wearing yellow Chinese pantaloons and an English panama hat, until late February or early March, when he would return with some reluctance to Paris. July and August he spent in England in spite of having once been nearly driven to suicide by the English Sunday.

'I have the feeling', Mérimée wrote from Cannes in 1865, 'that in this part of the world I am at *home*, which I scarcely am in Paris.' He returned to Cannes for the last time on 10 September 1870, when he was met at the railway station by his physician, Dr Maure. France, Mérimée said, was dying, and he wished to die with her.

Within a fortnight his wish was granted, but his spirit of contradiction and anti-clericalism still found expression after death. In order to be assured of a decent burial he had declared in his will that he belonged to the Augsburg confession. The French Protestant minister in Cannes therefore conducted the funeral service and took the opportunity to make a virulent attack on the Catholic church. Dr Maure was convinced that this was a plot hatched by the two English sisters, angrily interrupted the service, and brought the proceedings to a close.

VIII

Another French man of letters made an important contribution to the economy of the Riviera soon after the coming of the railway. This was Alphonse Karr, novelist, critic, editor of *Figaro* and celebrated wit, who was knifed by a girl named Louise Collet, with whom he was living. He afterwards kept the knife framed on a wall with the inscription 'donné par Mme Collet (dans le dos).' He was the originator of the phrase *plus ça change, plus c'est la même chose*.

The growing of flowers for commercial purposes, roses, carnations, jasmin, lavender, orange-blossom, geraniums and others, had long been one of the principal sources of revenue of the Riviera region, providing, as it did, the raw materials for the Grasse scent factories. Karr seems to have been the first to appreciate the opportunities the railways offered for selling the cut flowers in Paris and elsewhere. He opened a flower shop in the public gardens in Nice and established a mail order business linked with Paris, Lyons and Marseilles. For a time this was generally thought to be the harmless eccentricity of a well-known literary figure, but when Karr received the patronage of crowned heads or future kings of Bavaria, Sweden and Sardinia it began to be recognized than an important new business enterprise had been launched.

Victor Hugo visited Napoleon's landing-point at Golfe-Juan twenty-four years after the event and walked for two hours without seeing another human being. Jules Verne stayed in a villa in Antibes while writing *Vingt Mille Lieues sous les Mers*. Maupassant, who stated that he had never seen anything so surprising or beautiful as a sunset at Antibes, was one of the first distinguished patrons of St Tropez, which he discovered when its links with the outer world were a sailing boat from St Raphael and the *diligence* which brought the mail over the Maures mountains. In the years of his health and vigour he would sail his yacht *Le Bel-Ami* off the Riviera, but as physical disintegration set in he was largely confined to Nice and to Cannes, where in January 1892 he tried to kill himself. The attempt failed, and he was removed to Paris, where after suffering appalling pain he died some eighteen months later.

Colette bought a house near St Tropez in 1926. Two years later she published *La Naissance du Jour*, in which the action, such as it is, takes place in St Tropez in July. After a month all the male characters in the book have been beautified by sun, sea and nakedness, and almost the only inconvenience suffered by anyone is a shortage of materials for the French painters. This arises because 'hectares' of canvas have been devastated by Americans and other foreigners grouped under the generic term 'les Tchéco-Slovaques'.

The St Tropez Colette depicted was a place in which the characters were driven by *un caprice unanime*, a place for idling, for siestas, for making love, perhaps for growing fat, as Colette herself did, a fact she duly recognized when she made a practice of asking for beef-steaks as thick as her own thighs.

Eminent French composers also came to the Riviera, largely because of the enlightened policy consistently followed in Monte Carlo, where Camille Blanc commissioned new operas from both Massenet and Saint-Saëns. But it was not through composers or writers that the French artistic heritage was principally enriched as a consequence of the belated discovery by Frenchmen of their own Côte d'Azur. This came about with the arrival on a little known part of the Riviera of a number of French post-impressionist painters in the early 1890s.

IX

In 1892 Paul Signac, disciple of Seurat and principal theorist of the neo-impressionist school, landed from his yacht at St Tropez. Twelve years later Henri Matisse, who had just had his first one-man show, spent the summer at St Tropez with Signac. Other artists joined them in forming the *école méditerranée*, Paul Bonnard being one.

To go south in the summer to paint was still widely regarded in Paris around the turn of the century as an eccentric habit. One of the later adherents of Signac's group, André Dunoyer de Segonzac, who lived until 1974 and who appears under his own name as one of the characters in Colette's *La Naissance du Jour*, recalled being asked in 1908, after he announced that he was going south, whether it was his intention to spend the summer in the Sahara.

One of Signac's own better known paintings was *St Tropez – le port en fête*. St Tropez itself became recognized as a centre of post-impressionist painting, and Georges Grammont, a rich manufacturer of submarine cables, bought a deconsecrated chapel there which he converted into a museum. It came to house one of the best collections of early twentieth-century French paintings.

St-Paul-de-Vence, the small hill-town which stands above Vence, also attracted a number of artists. The far-seeing proprietor of one of its restaurants, La Colombe d'Or, acquired a number of paintings from young artists as payment for meals, and in time he built up a collection which included works by Bonnard, Matisse, Dufy and Léger as well as by Picasso, Utrillo, Vlaminck and Modigliani.

Other Riviera towns attracted other French painters. Auguste Renoir, crippled by arthritis, decide to settle in Bas-de-Cagnes, where he spent his last sixteen years. Towards the end of his life he worked from an invalid chair; his brushes were tied to his impotent fingers, and he had to paint by the movement of his arms.

Bonnard bought a small villa in Le Cannet in 1926. He came to live there three years later and did not visit Paris again until 1945. Matisse lived in Cimiez as well as in Vence, where the chapel on which he worked from 1944 until 1951 was one of the masterpieces of his later period. Fernand Léger chose the small foothill town of Biot, where the Musée Léger was opened in 1960, five years after his death. Raoul Dufy, who came to Hyères for the first time in 1913, probably presented more of the Riviera landscape on canvas than any other of his great contemporaries.

The French post-impressionist painters on the Riviera tended for the most part to live outside the main centres of the foreign population in places which were little known to the outside world before the cult of the summer season and the advent of the motor-coach. St Tropez in particular, which faces north, seemed to offer little to those foreign visitors who came to the Riviera for the winter. St-Paul-de-Vence was popularized largely by its inclusion in excursion tours.

In consequence two groups, both of which played parts of major importance in the history of the Riviera region, the British and other foreign residents and visitors on the one hand and the French painters on the other, seem to have had little contact socially or otherwise, coexisting within a comparatively small region in a kind of mutually acceptable *apartheid*.

X

The great French painters and, to a lesser extent, the French writers and composers who came to the Riviera before the Second World War left permanent memorials behind them. The region also had a long tradition of association with famous figures of the French theatre, from Rachel, who died in Le Cannet in 1858, through Sarah Bernhardt to Sacha Guitry, who bought a villa in Cap d'Ail in 1927, and Jean Cocteau.

By contrast, in the creation of the prosperity of the region, a prosperity which derived almost entirely from what is known today as the tourist industry, the part played by French people themselves was strangely secondary and muted. The two most celebrated of the Riviera's hoteliers, for instance, were both foreigners. Ruhl was a Swiss, Negresco a Roumanian. Facts such as these give substance to the opinion of an historian of Monaco, who stated: 'Les étrangers ont créé la Côte d'Azur.' As a generalization it was not inaccurate.

The French creative artists were able to pursue their professions while they were on the Riviera, but to other eminent French people the region was a place for retirement and old age. Philippe Pétain had a house in Villeneuve-Loubet, which was later converted into a children's home. The contents of the Menton municipal museum suggest that the most distinguished citizen whom Menton can claim as its own was André Tardieu, the faithful supporter of the policies of Clemenceau, who became Prime Minister in 1929 and again in 1932. But Tardieu himself came to Menton to retire and to cultivate vines and vegetables. He had been living there quietly for a number of years before his death in 1945.

As a birthplace for eminent people the region was peculiarly infertile. Some early painters, such as Louis Bréa of Nice, are known to art historians, but of world-famous figures, those whose names are well known outside their own countries, no more than four, it may reasonably be claimed, were born in the whole of the region which we know as the French Riviera: Garibaldi and Masséna in Nice, Fragonard in Grasse, and the famous chef, Auguste Escoffier, in Villeneuve-Loubet. Of these, all except Fragonard had to travel beyond the frontiers of France to achieve the distinctions with which their names are still associated, Garibaldi and Masséna to Italy and Escoffier to England. Even Fragonard spent most of his working life in Paris. For a region of such exceptional beauty, which has today acquired such exceptional riches, the tally is a meagre one.

XI

The foreign domination of the Riviera by wealth and by numbers first began to be seriously threatened in the 1930s with the requirement that employees in France should receive holidays with pay. As a consequence many French families of modest means came to the Riviera for the first time, nearly all of them in the summer.

Some thirty years after that the French could be said to have come at last into full possession of this favoured part of their country, but before they did so another war had to be fought, involving a series of new foreign occupations.

11 Epilogue: War and Aftermath

I

After the two colliers which the British Government had diverted to Cannes in 1940 departed, a number of British subjects remained behind. Many of them were frail and old. To its credit the British Government arranged for these people to be supplied with funds through the agency of the United States consul in Nice, who found it difficult to understand why they did not return home. In fact the only home most of them knew was the Riviera.

One of those who remained, Miss Amy Paget, who died in 1947 at the age of ninety, continued to live in the Château de Garibondy above Cannes, where she flew the Union Jack throughout the various occupations. The Anglican chaplain in Beaulieu, an elderly man, regularly left home at five o'clock in the morning, travelling one day to Nice, another to Vence, another to Monte Carlo and another to Cannes in order to minister to his flock. According to the Baroness Orczy, about eighty to ninety people, some of them Americans, formed his congregation in Monte Carlo and rather more in Nice and Cannes during the period when southern France was known as the unoccupied zone.

During this period the British who remained at large were treated by the authorities as rather undesirable aliens. Some of the restrictions imposed on them also applied to British women married to Frenchmen, one of whom did however open the

Lavender Tea Rooms in Nice, which she conducted with some success. Expressions of pro-British feeling by the French population were prohibited in print and discouraged in private conversation, not only because the Vichy Government was anti-British in sentiment but because it feared, rightly in the event, that too much provocation might cause the Germans to cancel the terms of the armistice and occupy southern France.

The armistice terms were in fact abrogated on 11 November 1942 as a direct consequence of the successful landing of Anglo-American forces in French territories in North Africa. Italian troops occupied the Riviera, where they remained until the Allied armistice agreement with Italy in September 1943, after which they were replaced by Germans. British subjects were nearly all interned at Uriage near Grenoble, where they had fairly good accommodation and were able to while away the time by playing bridge.

In Monaco a frail form of neutrality was maintained. Italian troops did enter the principality and were greeted by the waving of numerous Italian flags, but they left before long. From then until the Allied invasion in 1944 Monaco served largely as a recreation centre for those in the Axis camp who had profited in one way or another from the conduct of the war. To a number of British citizens the Monégasque Government acted with considerable magnanimity, advancing them money on the understanding that the debts would be repaid when the war ended. According to Charles Graves, a deplorably large number of these debts were not honoured.

The young and able-bodied among the British had disappeared from the Riviera on the outbreak of war or afterwards. But in 1942 some of them began to return clandestinely as agents despatched by the Special Operations Executive, generally known as SOE. Their number was never large but the influence they were to have in helping to develop the French resistance movement was profound.

II

In 1942 Captain Peter Churchill was conveyed by submarine to a point near the French coast from which he came ashore by canoe. The landing-point he had chosen, at the western tip of the bay of La Napoule was in the grounds of an hotel where he had spent two summers. He remembered it well enough to know that when he reached the iron steps, which the hotel had provided for bathers, he could not be overlooked from the coastal road. The first people to give him refuge were a couple who had acted as gardener and cook to some English friends with whom he had stayed in the summer of 1939.

Churchill had been instructed to contact Dr Lévy, who lived in the Boulevard Maréchal Foch in Antibes and who was later to die during a forced march from a German concentration camp. As he made his way through Cannes towards the bus which would take him to Antibes Churchill reflected on the differences between the summer scenes of the Riviera he had known just before the war and the rue d'Antibes now largely deserted on a late January afternoon. Through a shop-window he saw three big polished cars with 'GB' plates, a Rolls-Royce, a Bentley and an MG, which their owners had evidently left behind in sudden flight. But in the food-shops there was little to be seen. He wondered, as he wrote later in one of his books on his experiences in France, *Of Their Own Choice*, 'how the people survived in the absence of the holiday trade. The hotels must be empty. There was no money, little food and, apart from the flower business, there was precious little else to live on.'

Through Dr Lévy Churchill was put in touch with Baron d'Astier de la Vigerie, a poet and the head of a growing resistance group, who later came out by submarine to report to General de Gaulle. The baron in turn brought him into contact with other members of the underground organization based largely on Lyons, which included a courageous and resourceful American journalist named Virginia Hall. The most pressing needs of the organization were money to give them freedom to operate and a radio operator to keep them in contact with London. Churchill was able to supply them with money immediately, and with the help of some highly skilled guides he crossed over the Pyrenees and through Spain on his way to London to report the other requirements.

Churchill made four visits to southern France, arriving either by submarine or by parachute. Altogether he spent 255 days on

French soil before being betrayed and captured. During much of that time his radio operator and close associate was Alec Rabinowitch, a half-Russian, half-Egyptian entomologist, who had been a light-heavyweight boxer and had served in the French Foreign Legion and to whose posthumous memory Churchill dedicated one of his books. With him at the time of his arrest was a courier who had been sent to him from London, Odette Sansom, whom he later married. She was to have all her toenails pulled out and to be kept in total darkness for some two-and-a-half months in Ravensbrück concentration camp in vain attempts to persuade her to reveal what she knew about the French underground movement.

Sidney Jones, a former representative of Elizabeth Arden in France, was landed clandestinely on the Riviera when he was nearly forty and organized extensive sabotage. John Goldsmith held classes in the use of explosives in Nice and in Juan-les-Pins. John Roper, a future British ambassador, had occasion to spend a night in a cinema in Antibes. Arguably the most successful of all SOE agents in southern France, Francis Cammaerts, the son of an eminent Belgian man of letters and an English mother, spent more than a month in Cannes passing as a schoolmaster convalescing after jaundice.

One reason for the successes Cammaerts achieved was the rigorous self-discipline with which he applied the precepts of the SOE training schools. One of these was to change his place of residence continually. To members of the underground movement in Cannes and the other Riviera towns the need for such precautions was less evident. Unlike some central European countries, France was fortunate in having no tradition of underground warfare; in the comparatively lax atmosphere of the Riviera potential resistance workers were all too ready to express their real feelings towards the Vichy Government; and disregard of security precautions was encouraged by numerous examples of connivance by Vichy-controlled officials at acts of defiance.

Much of the transporting of secret agents to southern France was carried out by two Poles named Buchowski and Krajewski, who operated a 20-ton Spanish felucca, which made the journey from Gibralter to the Riviera and back in twelve to eighteen days according to the state of the weather. Both were awarded the

DSO for their services. The scenes accompanying the arrival of the felucca on one occasion were described by Lieutenant Alastair Mars, the commander of a submarine which was transporting Peter Churchill, as reminiscent of Henley regatta. Policemen enjoyed grandstand views of the proceedings, and members of a youth club, who dredged for stores brought by the felucca, made a practice of marking their whereabouts by a buoy.

It was largely because of such incidents that Cammaerts decided to move the centre of his operations from Cannes to the interior. The decision was a prudent one. When, some time later, thirty members of the French resistance, including the second-in-command of the circuit in Cannes, were arrested the security precautions and system of cut-outs, which Cammaerts had adopted, were largely responsible for preventing the arrests of key figures from spreading much further.

The Italian forces during this period of occupation showed no excessive zeal in suppressing incipient French resistance. To some French citizens their presence even provided a respite, for there was noticeably less persecution of Jews during the Italian occupation than there had been under Vichy rule. SOE agents for their part were instructed to do nothing to impede the Italian occupation. Their principal task had by then become that of helping to prepare the French resistance movement for the culmination of all its efforts, direct action in support of invading Allied armies.

M.R.D. Foot, the historian of SOE in France, estimated that in France as a whole no fewer than eight German divisions were kept from the main battlefields after the landings in the north and in the south by the efforts of the resistance movement. In the Riviera sector in particular the resistance groups with which Francis Cammaerts was associated and some neighbouring groups succeeded in holding open the whole of the *route Napoléon* from Cannes through Digne to Grenoble.

The British agents sent to France were for the most part young men with no political experience. To serve any useful purpose they had to play a commanding role. Not only did they provide the link which brought money and arms and explosives, but they were also highly trained specialists in sabotage, secret communications and guerilla warfare, and it was necessary for them to act as instructors in the skills they had acquired. In doing so they were confronted by proud and sensitive resistance leaders of a nation which had suffered a deep humiliation. For the SOE agents to succeed at all required generosity of spirit in their hosts and powers of leadership in themselves. It was also necessary that they should know and understand the part of France to which they had been sent and desirable that they should feel affection for it.

To Englishmen who had come to know the Riviera before 1939, as Peter Churchill had done, affection for it came easily. On returning to the Riviera by parachute in August 1942 Churchill was provoked by the sights around him to reflexions somewhat different from those he had had in January in the Rue d'Antibes in Cannes. 'So much beauty', he wrote later, 'was a prodigious compensation for the hard days that lay ahead.' He also recalled a decision he had made some time earlier that by preference he would live and die, no matter what his circumstances, in a land where weeds were called mimosa.

This decision he adhered to. After the war, while staying in a villa near Grasse belonging to one of his French comrades in the resistance, he wrote *The Spirit in the Cage*, an account of his experiences as a prisoner of the Germans. He had been living on the Riviera for some years, writing books and working as an estate agent, when he died in 1972 at the age of sixty-three.

III

There were other clandestine activities which linked the British and the French on the Riviera during the wartime years. One of these was the organization of the land and sea lines along which members of the British armed forces were secretly conveyed back to Britain.

In the first months after the end of the campaign in France in 1940 the German high command was not greatly concerned by the knowledge that remnants of the British armies, men who had neither been evacuated from Dunkirk nor taken prisoner, were trying to make their way slowly home through southern France and Spain. On the Riviera the British residents who had remained even formed a committee under the chairmanship of the Duke of Westminster to raise funds to help these men on their journey.

It was also relatively easy for a time for those who had been wounded to receive medical certificates which the Vichy Government accepted as valid grounds for despatching them across the Spanish frontier. One who did so, James Langley, a one-armed Guards officer, spent Christmas and New Year at the end of 1940 with a Swiss family in Cap d'Ail. On reaching England he reported for duty and became one of the leading figures in MI9, the organization concerned with bringing back fighting men from enemy-occupied territory.

By 1941 helping the British to evade capture had already become a hazardous undertaking, and the dangers increased as the war progressed. Even the production of medical certificates was sometimes attended by grave risks. One prisoner of war who was accepted for repatriation on medical grounds was Squadron-Leader Whitney Straight, an American who had joined the Royal Air Force and who had acquired a considerable reputation both as a pre-war racing driver and as a wartime pilot. The medical board which declared Whitney Straight unfit for service was induced to do so by a determined member of the escape organization, Dr Rodocanachi. Because of his supposed condition Straight was directed to the Pasteur Hospital in Nice. There a nurse, after advising him of the best escape route, provided him with a sedative for putting into the wine of the hospital guards.

Whitney Straight's escape was largely organized by a former officer in the Belgian army medical service, Albert-Marie Guérisse. ·This resourceful man, who had been second-in-command of a British naval vessel engaged in clandestine operations off the south coast of France, had acquired the rank and name of Lieut-Commander Patrick O'Leary and was to become in many ways the outstanding figure in the organization of escapes through the south of France.

Another of O'Leary's exploits was the planning and execution of an escape from Fort de la Revère at La Turbie, a few miles from Monaco, where the Vichy authorities held a number of British servicemen as prisoners. One of these was Squadron-Leader F.W. Higginson, who received instructions to escape together with five other airmen. O'Leary arranged for a hacksaw blade to be smuggled to him together with other useful implements.

One of the agents used by O'Leary to contact Higginson was a Polish priest named Father Myrda. Another was Viktor Bouryschkine, also known as Val Williams, who had been born in Moscow and brought up in the United States, where he became a well-known basketball player. Williams found himself a cover job as coach to the Monaco basketball team, and in this capacity he persuaded the Vichy authorities that the prisoners in Fort de la Revère were entitled by the Geneva convention to have periodical physical exercise and that he should act as their instructor.

With the help of the implements provided Higginson and the others escaped down a coal-shute, through a moat and along a sewer. Near Cap d'Ail railway station they were found by two other agents of O'Leary's, a Frenchman and an Australian, and brought to Monte Carlo. Here they were housed and fed by two Scotswomen, the Trenchard sisters, who kept a teashop, until they were passed along the line to Marseilles. After the escape by Higginson and his party all British officers were removed from Fort de la Revère to Italy. A mass escape of other ranks from the fortress followed later. Of the various prisoners of war who reached Monaco the more adventurous and the more dutiful made their way home through Spain, but a number continued to enjoy the benefits of Monaco's form of neutrality until August 1944.

Airey Neave, who after the war became a Member of Parliament and the chief organizer of Margaret Thatcher's accession to the leadership of the Conservative party, discovered, following his own escape from Colditz in 1941, that there was already a highly developed organization to bring him from Switzerland through southern France to Spain. On returning to England he joined Langley in MI 9, where for the rest of the war he operated under the code-name 'Saturday'. His organization's principal concern was not so much the fate of escaped prisoners of war as the recovery of the many airmen, British, Americans, Poles and others, who were shot down over enemy territory. In his book *Saturday at M.I.9* Neave stated that before the Normandy landings more than 3,000 of the Allied airmen who were shot down in north-west Europe avoided imprisonment. 90 per cent of them arrived in Spain.

That they returned was due to the efforts of thousands of volunteers of different nationalities who risked extreme penalties. O'Leary himself was captured in March 1943, tortured and sent to a number of concentration camps before being released from Dachau. About a hundred and fifty French people who helped form the escape routes were betrayed to the Germans by the actions of a single British traitor. This was Harold Cole, who, after absconding with the funds of his sergeants' mess, had remained in France, infiltrated himself into the escape organization and then sold his services to the Germans. Some fifty of the French people captured as a consequence of Cole's treachery were killed, among them being Whitney Straight's benefactor, Dr Rodocanachi.

IV

The date chosen for the invasion of southern France by Allied forces under American command was 15 August 1944. The invasion plans were among the less well kept secrets of the Second World War, not least because of the frequency with which officers who were to take part in the operations themselves, or in their planning, asked for guide-books to southern France in the bookshops of Rome.

The initial assault was made by the First Airborne Task Force under the command of Major-General Robert T. Frederick, then the youngest major-general in the United States Army. As this force had no previous operational experience of an enterprise on such a scale it was not surprising that there was a good deal of confusion in the early stages of the assault and that immediate losses occurred. According to the estimate made by the chroniclers of the campaign in southern France, Robert H. Adleman and Colonel George Walton, of the total losses of the First Airborne Task Force some 40 per cent occurred in the actual droppings and landings.

Almost the first action of General Frederick on landing on French soil was to seize a man round the throat and begin the process of breaking his neck, which he was well qualified to complete. He then discovered that the man, whose uniform he had mistaken for a German's, belonged to the British Second Independent Parachute Brigade, which was under his command. One airborne unit, which was dropped a long way from its target, moved into St Tropez and captured an hotel in which a German headquarters was housed. Then somebody remembered that the Allied bombardment of the town was due to start in half an hour, and the unit left hurriedly. But in spite of such variants of the original plan the task force attained its immediate objective, which was to seize the passes behind Fréjus, through which the main seaborne force could advance.

The seaborne force, which consisted of the United States Sixth Corps, followed by four French divisions under the command of General Jean de Lattre de Tasisigny, met little opposition, for the German high command had decided to concentrate on the defence of Marseilles and Toulon in order to deny to the Allies the use of these great ports for bringing large quantities of war materials to the main battlefields of western Europe. In this they failed. Marseilles and Toulon both fell within about a fortnight of the first American landings, and on 1 September, after some street fighting between German troops and French resistance forces, Nice was also liberated.

Apart from those places selected for the bombardment which preceded the landings, St Tropez in particular, the Riviera towns for the most part suffered little damage, and in sparing them from heavy shelling the American command showed commendable restraint. While surveying Cannes, which was still under enemy control, from above, Colonel William P. Yarborough, commander of the 509th Parachute Infantry Battalion, was asked by Herbert Mathews of the *New York Times* to refrain from causing any damage to the Carlton Hotel on the grounds that it was, in Mathews's opinion, the best hotel in the world. The request seems to have been acceded to.

The American liberating armies were immediately made welcome on the Riviera, and there were the customary scenes of rejoicing. But the welcome did not last long. People looking forward to liberation from alien rule are frequently disillusioned when they find themselves face to face with soldiers of the liberating armies. On the Riviera the arrival of the Americans brought a clash of cultures and of habits of life which was too fierce for there to be much chance of accommodation on either side.

Friendships were made. The readiness with which American soldiers shared their very ample rations in a period of food shortage was appreciated, and the generous concern with children, which characterized American forces wherever they went during the Second World War, was noted. But the Americans had barely arrived before French people were reminding themselves and each other that, humiliating though German rule had been, German uniformed troops had obeyed orders and had normally remained sober. Few of the French would have advanced both these claims for the generality of American troops.

In a letter to a United States civil affairs officer, which Adleman and Walton quote, the editor of a Nice newspaper stated that no troops had ever been so well received in the south of France as Americans and that everything had been open to them, 'the homes and the hearts'. When the paratroopers finally left Nice, he concluded, 'there was a great sigh of relief all over the town.'

Garry Page, an American Red Cross official, estimated that the period between the initial welcome and the asking of the question 'Why don't you go home?' usually lasted about three days. The Americans, he stated, expected the French to admire them and to be grateful to them for the fact of liberation. The French, he added, found this attitude difficult to endure.

Monaco saw less of the American troops than Nice or Cannes because before long it was declared 'off limits'. But the order not to go there was obeyed only sporadically. As one American soldier expressed it, 'some of the wheels that wouldn't turn for less than a thousand dollar bet in peacetime were now spinning for cans of our C-rations'.

The disparity between the rations which the Americans enjoyed and the food available to the civilian population was indeed one of the principal reasons for the deterioration in relations. The American authorities did something to put this right by shipping in some thousands of tons of wheat. Before it happened the management of the Hotel Negresco in Nice had called attention to the prevailing difficulties in a dignified but unequivocal fashion. The full hotel service would be provided, American officers were told, if the Americans would themselves supply the food.

In retrospect the American invasion of southern France can be seen as a highly successful operation. Its purpose was achieved swiftly and loss of life and damage to property were both comparatively light. Nor did the presence of American troops on the Riviera last long enough to be the direct cause of serious deterioration in Franco-American relations. But local scars did remain, scars which began to heal when, on the insistence of President de Gaulle, the United States Navy abandoned its base in Villefranche.

V

When peace came to Europe efforts were made in official and other circles to re-establish something of the traditional British presence on the Riviera. Sir Duff Cooper, the British ambassador, arrived aboard the aircraft carrier *Colossus* and laid a wreath on a war memorial. Accompanying him was a detachment of Argyll and Sutherland Highlanders, whose kilts caused widespread comment. The British Council staged an exhibition of English books in the Hotel Negresco in Nice. Billy Butlin arrived by private aircraft, and there were reports that he had been invited to become a director of Carlton Hotel in Cannes. A Franco-British club was formed in Cannes, and on 31 May 1947 the *Menton and Monte Carlo News* resumed publication.

If hopes were aroused by these or similar happenings of an effective revival of British influence they were soon to be disappointed for reasons which were made clear in the first post-war number of the *Menton and Monte Carlo News*. In this attention was called to an article by Charles Graves which had appeared in the *Sunday Express* under the heading 'The 75 pounders on the Riviera'. It was Graves's contention that some two thousand British subjects had cashed cheques on the Riviera to supplement the sum they were legally entitled to take abroad, which was no more than £75. Far from querying Graves's figures the *Menton and Monte Carlo News* made the point that his descriptions of whispering barmen and dark alcoves had been exaggerated and that transactions of the kind he had mentioned were discussed quite openly. 'We agree', the paper declared, 'that Britons abroad are not always the scrupulous and honest citizens they are in the British Isles.'

It did not take the British Treasury long to reach conclusions similar to those of Charles Graves, and a watch began to be kept on conspicuous spenders. Except for a small number of people who had overseas resources or business interests British citizens on the Riviera soon found it impossible, if they were law-abiding, and dangerous, if they were not, to enjoy a high standard of living. The easy assumption of superiority which a plentiful supply of money can promote became increasingly difficult to sustain, and when the amount of the permitted travel allowance was cut even further the phrase 'we poor British' began to creep into common parlance.

Protests by example against the drabness which had begun to be evident in the lives of British visitors to the Riviera were made by the colourful wife of a captain of industry, Nora, Lady Docker. But she was swimming against the current of the time. British newspapers, whose readers were conditioned to austerity, were less concerned with her belief, which was almost certainly justified, that a certain amount of quite legitimate panache made her in effect an excellent saleswoman for her husband's overseas interests than in her occasional *contretemps* in the Monte Carlo casino and the zebra-skin upholstery of her Daimler car. Mink, she was reputed to have said, was too hot to sit on. To the British Government in the early post-war years the condition of the British on the Riviera was understandably a subject of minor concern, as was shown in the new policy for the establishment of consulates. Before the outbreak of war in 1939 there had been British Vice-Consulates in Cannes, Menton and Monaco in addition to the Consulate in Nice. After the war there was only the Nice Consulate, and in 1960 even this was closed on grounds of economy. More than ten years before this happened the *Menton and Monte Carlo News* had published its last number.

VI

Prosperity returned to the Riviera after the Second World War through the summer season, of which the Cannes film festival was a central feature. There was a new cult of youth and nudity. Brigitte Bardot became a symbol of sex and of St Tropez. Françoise Sagan was one of the abler portrayers of the scene. The bikini, later to be followed by the fashion of the topless, became standard wear on beach and in café.

With the easing of the travel restrictions holiday-makers from Britain were again able to discover or rediscover the Riviera in appreciable numbers. In 1963, according to the official statistics, the figure for visitors from Britain and Ireland to the Côte d'Azur (excluding Monaco) was 64,380. 610,131 came from other parts of France, 77,149 from the United States and 30,320 from Germany.

The great majority of the British visitors came for short summer holidays, but their numbers were large enough for the British Consulate in Nice to be reopened in 1962 in new and modest premises, the first floor of an office block being shared with a car hire firm and a hairdresser. After the reopening an appreciable portion of the time of the British consular officials was devoted to the repatriation of British subjects who had had brushes with the police or run out of money, or both. The officials could however console themselves with the knowledge that a good deal less was demanded of them by this form of activity than of their opposite numbers in Spain.

Permanent British residents also came or returned, but they tended, significantly perhaps, to live among the foothills around Haut-de-Cagnes, Vence or Grasse rather than in the towns which their forerunners had done so much to create. One practitioner of the arts did however have the distinction of being made an honorary citizen of Menton in 1968. This was Graham Sutherland.

In the 1960s the Riviera enjoyed a boom period, which extended well into the 1970s, with an enormous investment in apartment blocks and motorways, marinas, motels and supermarkets. In this the British participated to some extent. They were prominent in providing services for yachtsmen, particularly in chartering and ship's chandlery. Some British property companies and banks did good business. Grand Metropolitan Hotels took over the Carlton Hotel in Cannes, and a major new enterprise was the brainchild of an Englishman, Peter Boumphrey. This was Isola 2000, a spectacular new skiing resort more than 6,000 feet above sea level and some fifty miles from Nice, whose first operational season was the winter of 1971–2. Its construction was financed by the Bernard Sunley

Investment Trust group of companies.

Nevertheless the total contribution of the British to the creation of all the new amenities and all the new properties remained relatively slight. As the general prosperity of the French began in the 1960s to outstrip that of the British, building took place on the Riviera on a scale and with an imagination which the British for the most part found stunning, and there was an acceptance of a standard of living of which few among the British had much awareness. This was particularly true of the great apartment blocks at the Baie des Anges designed by the Greek architect André Minangoy and of the developments of the mid-1970s in Monte Carlo which extended out over the sea.

Having been forced for a number of years by shortage of funds to play a minor role in the life of the Riviera, the British were unable in the years of expansion to acquire more than a small part of the power and prestige they had once enjoyed. As a result, a new relationship between the British and the French developed, in a number of respects a more cordial one. The less dominant and the less envied they were, the less arrogant and the less resented the British tended to become. Among the French, especially those who had memories of the wartime and pre-war years, an increased appreciation could be found of the contribution which the British had made to the Riviera's development. An acknowledgment of the value attached to one kind of British export was to be found, for example, in an event staged in Menton in February 1972.

Among the graves in Menton cemetery is that of the Rev. William Webb-Ellis, former rector of St. Clement Danes church in London, who had achieved lasting distinction as a schoolboy at Rugby by running with the ball in his hands and so establishing one of the principal features of the game which became known as rugby football. Webb-Ellis died in 1872, and after his grave had been discovered by Ross McWhirter in the course of researches he was making for a rugby football centenary history, an Old Rugbeian colonel, known as Tiger White, who lived among the Riviera foothills, suggested that the hundredth anniversary of Webb-Ellis's death should be marked by a match between a team of former pupils of Rugby school and the Menton rugby club. The match took place; a commemoration service was held in the English church;

trumpeters of the Menton municipal band sounded a fanfare in the cemetery; and wreaths were ceremonially laid on Webb-Ellis's grave. From then on the French rugby football federation undertook the responsibility of maintaining the grave. In evident contrast with the decayed condition of most of the British graves in Menton cemetery it is permanently adorned with fresh flowers. Beside it stands a plaque on which are reproduced the words of the commemorative plaque in the close at Rugby school.

Whereas in 1963 the number of visitors to the Riviera from Britain and Ireland was greater than that from any other European country, apart from France, in the years which followed the pattern changed. For 1968 the official figures, which again excluded Monaco, showed that visitors from Britain and Ireland numbered only 32,906 – that is to say roughly half the figure for 1963 – and that more visitors came from Belgium and Luxemburg than from Britain and Ireland. By 1974 the number of visitors from Germany exceeded the British-Irish total by more than 20 per cent.

In recognition of these trends, and again in the interests of economy, the British Government announced in November 1975 that its consulate in Nice was to be closed. The month chosen for the announcement was the same as that in which a chapter in the history of the Russians on the Riviera was closed with the sale by public auction of the Diaghilev library.

VII

If a British ghost from the time of King Edward VII or from the 1920s were to return to the Riviera today he would no doubt be startled by the scale of the new developments, but after a time he might well reflect that, grossly though man has overbuilt, he seems, mercifully, incapable of destroying the charm of the Riviera or its visual beauty.

The ghost would find much evidence around him of the impact his fellow-countrymen made in the past, in the names of the hotels, Bristol and Balmoral, Claridge's and Richmond, in the ubiquitous use of the English language in signs and notices calling attention to such institutions as the yacht club and the snack bar, in the names of streets and squares, familiar names such as James Henry Bennet and new ones such as Peter Churchill.

If he came in the summer he would be impressed by the number of the British who spent their holidays in a manner unknown to him by trailing their mobile homes behind them. If he came in the winter he might notice small groups of his fellow-countrymen near the Anglican churches and the lending libraries associated with them, elderly people for the most part, whose words he would readily understand, for all would be speaking in accents which at one time were *de rigueur* for BBC announcers.

As his vision became accustomed to the changes in fashion and in traffic he might have the feeling that another important change had taken place whose significance he could not immediately analyse. This might puzzle him. Then, as he wandered among the familiar sights, which had barely changed since his time, the *pétanque* players and the sunshine, the bougainvillea and the jasmin, the *pâtisseries* and the palm-trees, he might suddenly come to understand what this other change was. Apart from the small principality of Monaco the whole of the region from the present frontier with Italy in the east to Hyères in the west had finally come fully into the possession of the French. If he were a sensitive and generous ghost he might well come to the conclusion that the region was none the worse for that.

Bibliography

I have obtained much valuable information from newspapers, particularly from the back numbers of the *Menton and Monte Carlo News*, which can be studied in the Newspaper Library in Colindale, although unfortunately the collection is incomplete.

I have found all the following works useful in the preparation of this book:

Adleman, Robert H. and Walton, Colonel George, *The Champagne Campaign* (Leslie Frewin, 1973).

Aga Khan, The, *World Enough and Time* (Cassell, 1954).

Alpers, Antony, *Katherine Mansfield* (Jonathan Cape, 1954).

Anspach, Margravine of, *Memoirs* (Henry Colburn, 1826).

Antier, Jean-Jacques, *La Côte d'Azur. Ombres et Lumières* (Editions France-Empire, 1972).

Arlen, Michael, *The Green Hat. A Romance for a few People* with introduction by A.S. Frere (Cassell, 1968, first published by Collins, 1924).

Arlen, Michael J., *Exiles* (André Deutsch, 1971).

Armand, Louis and others, *Histoire des chemins de fer en France* (Presses Modernes, 1963).

Avon, Earl of, *The Eden Memoirs. Facing the Dictators* (Cassell, 1962).

Baker, Carlos, *Ernest Hemingway. A Life Story* (Collins, 1969).

Balsan, Consuelo Vanderbilt, *The Glitter and the Gold* (Heinemann, 1953).

Baring-Gould, S., *Book of the Riviera* (Methuen, 1905).

Bashkirtseff, Marie, *Journal*, translated with introduction by Mathilde Blind (Cassell, 1890).

Baussy, Alex, *Cannes hier et aujourd'hui* (Robaudy, 1966).

Beardsley, Aubrey, *Letters*, edited by Henry Maas, J.L. Duncan and W.G. Good (Cassell, 1971).

Bedford, Sybille, *Aldous Huxley. A Biography, vol. I: 1894–1939* (Chatto & Windus in association with Collins, 1973).

Beebe, Lucius, *The Big Spenders* (Doubleday, 1966).

Behrend, George, *Grand European Expresses* (Allen & Unwin, 1962).

Bénézit, Emmanuel, *Dictionnaire des peintres, sculpteurs, dessinateurs, et graveurs* (Gründ, 1954).

Bennet, James Henry, *Winter and Spring on the Shores of the Mediterranean* (J. & A. Churchill, 3rd edition, 1865).

Bennett, Arnold, *Paris Nights* (Hodder & Stoughton, 1913).

Bentley, W.O., *My Life and My Cars* (Hutchinson, 1967).

Bernardy, Françoise de, *Princes of Monaco. The Remarkable History of the Grimaldi Family*, translated by Len Ortzen (Arthur Barker, 1961).

Borel, Pierre, *Côte D'Azur* (Arthaud, 1957).

Bresson, Jean, *Palm Beach Story*, a series of seven articles in *Nice Matin*, 23–31 October 1973.

Brewster, Margaret Maria, *Letters from Cannes and Nice* (Constable and Hamilton, Adams, 1857).

Brion, Marcel, *Provence* (Arthaud, 1954).

Brougham, Henry, Lord, *Life and Times* (Blackwood, 1871).

Calder, Robert Lorin, *W. Somerset Maugham and the Quest for Freedom* (Heinemann, 1972).

Campbell, Patrick, *A Bunch of New Roses* (Anthony Blond, 1967).

Cecil, Lady Gwendolen, *Life of Robert, Marquis of Salisbury* (Hodder & Stoughton, 1932).

Célarie, Henriette, *Une lionne: Cora Pearl* (Fayard, 1947).

Christie, Agatha, *The Mystery of the Blue Train* (Collins, 1928).

Churchill, Peter, *Of Their Own Choice* (Hodder & Stoughton, 1952).

Churchill, Peter, *Duel of Wits* (Hodder & Stoughton, 1953).

Churchill, Peter, *The Spirit in the Cage* (Hodder & Stoughton, 1954).

Churchill, Winston S., *The Second World War*, volume VI: *Triumph and Tragedy* (Cassell, 1954).

Clark, Kenneth, *Another Part of the Wood* (John Murray, 1974).

Colette, *La Naissance du Jour* (Flammarion, 1928).

Connolly, Cyril, *The Rock Pool* (Hamish Hamilton, 1947).

Connolly, Cyril, *Ideas and Places* (Weidenfeld & Nicolson, 1953).

Cordell, Richard, *Somerset Maugham. A Biographical and Critical Study* (Heinemann, 1961).

Corley, T.A.B., *Democratic Despot. A Life of Napoleon III* (Barrie & Rockcliff, 1961).

Corvol, Robert, *La Côte d'Azur à la belle époque* (Fayard, 1958).

Coward, Noël, *Private Lives*, printed in *Play Parade* (Garden City, 1933).

Cowles, Virginia, *Edward VII and His Circle* (Hamish Hamilton, 1956).

Creston, Dormer, *The Life of Marie Bashkirtseff* (Eyre & Spottiswoode, 1943).

Crosland, Margaret, *Colette. The Difficulty of Loving* (Peter Owen, 1973).

Curtis, Anthony, *The Pattern of Maugham* (Hamish Hamilton, 1974).

Dartigues, Fernand, article in *Paris-Côte d'Azur*, 15 June 1974.

Donaldson, Frances, *Edward VIII* (Weidenfeld & Nicolson, 1974).

Driberg, Tom, *Beaverbrook* (Weidenfeld & Nicolson, 1956).

Duff, David, *Victoria Travels. Journeys of Queen Victoria Between 1830 and 1900 with Extracts from her Journal* (Frederick Muller, 1970).

Ellis, H.F., *Origin of Rugby Football*, Old Rugbeian Society letter, April 1972.

Epton, Nina, *Victoria and Her Daughters* (Weidenfeld & Nicolson, 1971).

Faber, Richard, *French and English* (Faber & Faber, 1975).

Fielding, Daphne, *Emerald and Nancy. Lady Cunard and her Daughter* (Eyre & Spottiswoode, 1968).

Fitzgerald, F. Scott, *Tender is the Night* (Scribner, 1934).

Foot, M.R.D., *SOE in France. An Account of the British Special Operations Executive in France 1940-1944* (HMSO, 1966).

Frischauer, Willi, *Onassis* (Bodley Head, 1968).

Garratt, G.T., *Lord Brougham* (Macmillan, 1935).

Goldberg, W.F. and Piesse, G. Chaplin, *Monte Carlo and How to Do It* (J.W. Arrowsmith, 1891).

Graves, Charles, *The Big Gamble. The Story of Monte Carlo* (Hutchinson, 1951).

Graves, Charles, *Royal Riviera* (Heinemann, 1957).

Graves, Charles, *None But the Rich. The Life and Times of the Greek Syndicate* (Cassell, 1963).

Green, J.R., *Stray Studies from England and Italy* (Macmillan, 1876).

Greene, Graham, *The Comedians* (Bodley Head, 1966).

Greene, Graham, *May We Borrow Your Husband? and Other Comedies of the Sexual Life* (Bodley Head, 1967).

Hamilton, Olive, *Paradise of Exiles* (André Deutsch, 1974).

Hare, Augustus J.C., *A Winter at Mentone* (Wertheim, Macintosh & Hunt, 1862).

Hare, Augustus J.C., *The Rivieras* (George Allen, 1897).

Harris, Frank, *My Life and Loves*, edited and with an introduction by John F. Gallagher (W.H. Allen, 1964).

Haskell, Arnold, in collaboration with Nouvel, Walter, *Diaghileff. His Artistic and Private Life* (Victor Gollancz, 1935).

Hopkins, Kenneth, *The Poetry of Railways*, an anthology (Leslie Frewin, 1966).

Huxley, Aldous, *Point Counter Point* (Chatto & Windus, 1928).

J.M., *Thomas Robinson Woolfield's Life at Cannes and Lord Brougham: First Arrival* (Kegan Paul, Trench, Trübner, 1890).

Jackson, Stanley, *The Great Barnato* (Heinemann, 1970).

Jenkins, Alan, *The Twenties* (Heinemann, 1974).

Johnson, Thomas H., in consultation with Harvey Wish, *Oxford Companion to American History* (Oxford University Press, 1966).

Joliat, Eugène, *Smollett et la France* (Honoré Champion, 1935).

Kellogg, Grace, *The Two Lives of Edith Wharton* (Appleton-Century, 1965).

Kennedy, A.L., *Salisbury 1830-1903. Portrait of a Statesman* (John Murray, 1953).

Keppel, Sonia, *The Sovereign Lady. A Life of Elizabeth, Third Lady Holland, with her Family* (Hamish Hamilton, 1974).

Knapp, Lewis Mansfield, *Tobias Smollett. Doctor of Men and Manners* (Princeton University Press, 1949).

Kurtz, Harold, *The Empress Eugénie 1826–1920* (Hamish Hamilton, 1964).

La Napoule Art Foundation, *Le Château de la Napoule* (pamphlet sold at La Napoule castle).

Langley, Lieut-Colonel J.M., *Fight Another Day* (Collins, 1974).

Lawrence, D.H., *Letters*, edited with an introduction by Aldous Huxley (Heinemann, 1937).

Le Chene, Evelyn, *Watch for me by Moonlight* (Eyre Methuen, 1973).

Lichtervelde, Count Louis de, *Leopold of the Belgians*, translated by Thomas H. Reed and H. Russell Reed (Century Press, 1929).

Lifar, Serge, *Ma Vie. From Kiev to Kiev*, translated by James Holman Mason (Hutchinson, 1970).

Locke, William J., *The Joyous Adventures of Aristide Pujol* (John Lane: The Bodley Head, 1912).

Lyall, Archibald, *The Companion Guide to the South of France*, revised and expanded by A.N. Brangham (Collins, 1963).

McCormick, Donald, *Pedlar of Death. The Life of Sir Basil Zaharoff* (Macdonald, 1965).

Mackenzie, Norman and Jeanne, *The Time Traveller. The Life of H.G. Wells* (Weidenfeld & Nicolson, 1973).

Macmillan, Rev. Hugh, *The Riviera* (J.S. Virtue, 1885).

Magnus, Philip, *Gladstone. A Biography* (John Murray, 1954).

Magnus, Philip, *King Edward the Seventh* (John Murray, 1964).

Mallet, Marie, *Life with Queen Victoria*, Marie Mallet's letters from Court, edited by Victor Mallet (John Murray, 1968).

Mansfield, Katherine, *Journal*, edited by J. Middleton Murry. (Constable, 1962, first published 1927).

Mauclair, Camille, *La Provence* (Arthaud, 1944).

Maugham, Robin, *Somerset and All the Maughams* (Heinemann, 1966).

Maugham, Viscount, *At the End of the Day* (Heinemann, 1954).

Maugham, W. Somerset, *Strictly Personal* (Heinemann, 1942).

Maugham, W. Somerset, *The Vagrant Mood* (Heinemann, 1952).

Maxim, Hiram S., *Monte Carlo. Facts and Fallacies* (Grant Richards, 1904).

Maxwell, Elsa, *The Celebrity Circus* (W.H. Allen, 1964).

Miguet, M., *Nouveaux Eloges Historiques*, including an essay on Lord Brougham (Didier, 1877).

Milford, Nancy, *Zelda Fitzgerald* (Bodley Head, 1970).

Mitford, Nancy, *Madame de Pompadour* (Hamish Hamilton, 1954).

Monkswell, Lord, *French Railways* (Smith, Elder, 1911).

Moore, Doris Langley, *Marie & the Duke of H. The Daydream Life of Marie Bashkirtseff* (Cassell, 1966).

Moran, Lord, *Winston Churchill. The Struggle for Survival, 1940–1965*, from Lord Moran's diaries (Constable, 1966).

Morgan, Diane, 'Mary Garden – The Forgotten Centenary', series of four articles in *Leopard*, August–November 1974.

Morley, John, *The Life of William Ewart Gladstone* (Macmillan, 1903).

Morley, John, *Life of Cobden* (Macmillan, 1908).

Morley, Sheridan, *A Talent to Amuse. A Biography of Noël Coward* (Heinemann, 1969).

Murray's *Hand-Book for Travellers in France* (John Murray, 1847).

Nagel's *Encyclopaedia-Guide: French and Italian Riviera*, original text by Paul Wagret (Geneva, 3rd edition, 1970), English version by Mrs H.S.B. Harrison.

Neave, Airey, *Saturday at M.I.9* (Hodder & Stoughton, 1969).

Nichols, Beverley, *A Case of Human Bondage* (Secker & Warburg, 1966).

Oppenheim, E. Phillips, *Murder at Monte Carlo* (Hodder & Stoughton, 1933).

Oppenheim, E. Phillips, *The Colossus of Arcadia* (Hodder & Stoughton, 1938).

Oppenheim, E. Phillips, *The Pool of Memory* (Hodder & Stoughton, 1941).

Orczy, Baroness, *Links in the Chain of Life* (Hutchinson, 1947).

Ouida, *Puck* (Chapman & Hall, 1870).

Owen, Frank, *Tempestuous Journey. Lloyd George. His Life and Times* (Hutchinson, 1954).

Parmelin, Hélène, *Picasso Plain*, translated by Humphrey Hare (Secker & Warburg, 1963).

Pearson, Hesketh, *The Life of Oscar Wilde* (Methuen, 1946).

Pelling, Henry, *Winston Churchill* (Macmillan, 1974).

Pless, Princess Daisy of, *From My Private Diary*, edited by Major Desmond Chapman-Huston (John Murray, 1931).

Pless, Princess Daisy of, *What I Left Unsaid*, edited by Major Desmond Chapman-Huston (Cassell, 1936).

Polnay, Peter de, *A Door Ajar* (Robert Hale, 1959).

Polovtsoff, General Pierre, *Monte Carlo Casino* (Stanley Paul, 1937).

Pound, Reginald, *Arnold Bennett. A Biography* (Heinemann, 1952).

Pullar, Philippa, *Frank Harris* (Hamish Hamilton, 1975).

Purcell, William, *Onward Christian Soldiers* (Longman Green, 1967).

Raitt, A.W., *Prosper Mérimée* (Eyre & Spottiswoode, 1970).

Read, Jan, 'My Dear Don Jorge', article in *History Today*, June 1974.

Reid, Sir Wemyss, *The Life of William Ewart Gladstone* (Cassell, 1899).

Retournay, Horace, *Lord Brougham et le centenaire* (Lebon, 1879).

Rigby, Dr Edward, *Letters from France etc.*, edited by Lady Eastlake (Longman Green, 1880).

Romanovsky-Krassinsky, Princess, *Dancing in Petersburg. The Memoirs of Kschessinska*, translated by Arnold Haskell (Victor Gollancz, 1960).

Seitz, Don C., *The James Gordon Bennetts* (Bobbs-Merrill, 1928).

Seroff, Victor, *The Real Isadora* (Hutchinson, 1972).

Sherard, R.H., *Bernard Shaw, Frank Harris and Oscar Wilde* (T. Werner Laurie, 1937).

Sherlock, Rev. Martin, *Letters from an English Traveller* (John Nichols, 1802).

Simenon, Georges, *In Case of Emergency*, translated by Helen Sebba (Hamish Hamilton, 1960).

Simenon, Georges, *Sunday*, translated by Nigel Ryan (Hamish Hamilton, 1960).

Slater, Leonard, *Aly. A Biography* (W.H. Allen, 1966).

Smith, Sir James Edward, *A Sketch of the Tour of the Continent 1786 and 1787* (J. Davis, 1793).

Smollett, Tobias, *Travels through France and Italy* (London, 1766).

Standish, Robert, *The Prince of Storytellers. The Life of E. Phillips Oppenheim* (Peter Davies, 1957).

Steuart, J.A., *Robert Louis Stevenson. Man and Writer* (Sampson Low, Marston, 1944).

Stevenson, Robert Louis, *Letters*, edited by Sidney Colvin (Methuen, 1899).

Stokes, Sewell, *Isadora Duncan* (Brentano, 1928).

Stravinsky, Igor, *Chronicle of My Life* (Victor Gollancz, 1936).

Stravinsky, Igor and Craft, Robert, *Memories and Commentaries* (Faber & Faber, 1960).

Sylvester, A.J., *The Real Lloyd George* (Cassell, 1947).

Tobin, A.I. and Gertz, Elmer, *Frank Harris. A Study in Black and White* (Madeleine Mendelsohn, 1931).

Tomkins, Calvin, *Living Well is the Best Revenge. Two Americans in Paris 1921–1933* (André Deutsch, 1972).

Tomlinson, Rev. John Wickes, *The Rock of Nice. Historic and Descriptive Poem* (Saunders & Otley, 1855).

Treves, Sir Frederick, *The Riviera of the Corniche Road* (Cassell, 1921).

V.B., *Monte Carlo Anecdotes and Systems of Play* (Heinemann, 1901).

Victoria, Queen, *A Selection from Her Majesty's Correspondence and Journals between the Years 1886 and 1901*, edited by George Earle Buckle, vol. III (John Murray, 1932).

Vines, C.M., *A Little Nut-Brown Man. My Three Years with Lord Beaverbrook* (Leslie Frewin, 1968).

Way, Rev. Lewis, *A Letter Addressed to the Right Rev. the Lord Bishop of St. David's for Promoting Christianity among the Jews* (Hatchard, 1818).

Way, Rev. Lewis, *A Sermon for the Benefit of the Primitive Church of the Vaudois or Ancient Albigenses and Waldenses* (Hatchard, 1823).

Wells, H.G., *Meanwhile. The Picture of a Lady* (Ernest Benn, 1927).

Westminster, Loelia, Duchess of, *Grace and Favour* (Weidenfeld & Nicolson, 1961).

Wharton, Edith, *A Backward Glance* (Appleton-Century, 1934).

Williamson, C.N. and A.M., *Berry Goes to Monte Carlo* (Mills & Boon, 1921).

Wilson, G.B.L., *A Dictionary of Ballet* (A. & C. Black, 1957).

Wilson, Robert, *The Life and Times of Queen Victoria* (Cassell, 1901).

Windsor, Duchess of, *The Heart Has Its Reasons* (Michael Joseph, 1956).

Winkler, John Kennedy, *The Life of J. Pierpont Morgan 1837–1913* (Allen & Unwin, 1931).

Wodehouse, P.G., *Pearls, Girls and Monty Bodkin* (Barrie & Jenkins, 1972).

Wood, Alan, *The True History of Lord Beaverbrook* (Heinemann, 1965).

Wright, Patricia, 'Loris-Melikov: Russia 1880–1', article in *History Today*, June 1974.

Young, Arthur, *Travels in France During the Years 1787, 1788 and 1789*, with an introduction by Constantia Maxwell (Cambridge University Press, 1950).

Young, Kenneth, *Arthur James Balfour* (G. Bell, 1963).

Index

Abdul Karim ('the Munshi'), 71
Abide With Me, 54
Adleman, R. H. and Walton, Col. G., 207, 209
Afghanistan, King and Queen of, 43
Aga Khan III, 71, 88–9, 176, 185–6
Agence Taylor, 58
air-conditioning, 157
air travel, impact on Riviera, 46–7
Aix-les-Bains, 100
Albert I, Prince of Monaco, 67, 77, 105, 112
Albert, Prince of Prussia, 85
Alexander II, Tsar, 32, 180
Alexandra, Queen, 76, 78
Alfonso, King of Spain, 86
Alfred, Prince, Duke of Edinburgh, 80
Alice, Princess of Monaco, 126–8
Alice, Princess, Grand-Duchess of Hesse-Darmstadt, 79
Aly Khan, 89
Ambrose, Bert, 110
American Express, 173
Americans and the Riviera, 42, 67–8, 99, 156, 161–79; liberating armies, 208–9
Anastasia, Grand Duchess, 182
André, François, 43
André, Grand Duke, 188
Anglican Church on Riviera, 53–7; at Cannes, 21, 85; at Menton, 28, 148;

at Nice, 16
Annals of Agriculture, 12
Ansbach, Margravine of (Lady Craven), 14–15
Antibes, 5, 18, 52, 97, 100, 143, 165–9, 194
Antier, Jean-Jacques, 19, 63
Apraxin, Count, 181
Arlen, Michael, 134–5
Arlen, Michael J., 135
Armand, Louis, 47
Arnold, Matthew, 140
Arthur, Prince, Duke of Connaught, 80, 139
Astier de la Vigerie, Baron d', 201
Astor, Lady, 102
Astrid, Queen of Belgium, 191
Attlee, Mrs C., 103
Audet, Albert, 35
Austin, H.W. ('Bunny'), 86
Avignon, 2

Baker, Ida, 124
Baldwin, Stanley, 100
Balfour, Arthur J., 92, 100–1
ballet, 37, 44–5, 185–6, 189
Ballets Russes de Monte Carlo, 185–6
Balsan, Consuelo Vanderbilt, 81, 99, 116, 170
Bandol, 124, 125
Banks, Sir Joseph, 11

Bardot, Brigitte, 212
Baring-Gould, Rev. Sabine, 54–6
Barnato, Barney, 107–9
Barnato, Harry, 108–9
Barnato, Woolf, 45–6, 109–10
Barstow, Montagu, 139
Barthou, Jean, 96
Bashkirtseff, Marie, 33, 44, 105–6, 183–4
Baxter, Charles, 121
Beardsley, Aubrey, 51–2
Beatrice, Princess, 70, 72, 79
Beauchamp, Mary, 138
Beaulieu, 52, 59, 60, 69, 73, 81, 92, 162, 186, 199
beauty queens, 157–8
Beaverbrook, Lord, 95, 98, 99, 102–4
Beck, József, 159
Beebe, Lucius, 42, 164
Belle Otéro, La, 117, 119
Benchley, Robert, 166
Bennet, Dr James H., 33, 36, 49, 56, 59, 61, 65, 70, 120
Bennett, Arnold, 40, 41, 43, 112–13, 116, 140
Bennett, James Gordon, 42, 161–2
Bernhardt, Sarah, 36, 73, 197
Berry Goes to Monte Carlo, 138–9
Bevin, Ernest, 38
Biarritz, 87
Bible in Spain, The, 53
Big Spenders, The, 42, 164
Bigge, Sir Arthur, 74
Binyon, Edward, 28
Biot, 196
Birkenhead, Lord, 95
Black Arrow, The, 121
Blanc, Camille, 112, 127, 195
Blanc, François, 36–7, 56
Bluckel, William, 117–18
Blue Train, 41–5, 164
Blum, René, 187
Bonar Law, Andrew, 95, 96
Bonnard, Paul, 195–6
Bonomi, Ivanoe, 96
Book of the Riviera, 55
Books Do Furnish a Room, 42–3
Borrow, George, 53
Boumphrey, Peter, 212
Bouryschkine, Viktor, 206
Bracken, Brendan, 99
Brantingham, Francis, 154

Bréa, Louis, 198
Brewster, Sir David, 24, 26
Brewster, Margaret Maria, 24–7, 33, 53, 180
Briand, Aristide, 95–6
Britannia (yacht), 75
Brougham, Lord (1st Baron), 5, 17–20, 32, 62, 87
Brougham, Lord (3rd Baron), 76
Brown, John, 70
Brownlow, Lord, 82
Buck, Rev. W. Armstrong, 148
Buckland, John, 7
Buchowski and Krajewski, 202–3
bullfighting, 154
Bute, Marchioness of, 4

Caccia, Harold, 101
Cadogan, Sir Alexander, 101
Café de Paris, Monte Carlo, 76, 185
Cagnes-sur-Mer, 137; Bas de, 196; Haut de, 212
Calais-Mediterranean Express, 39–45
Calais-Nice-Rome Express, 39
Cammaerts, Francis, 202–3
Campbell, Patrick, 143
Cannes, in 18th century, 2, 5, 11; growth of British influence, 18–27, 58–64; Anglican Church, 20–1, 53–4; impact of railway, 32; sport, 62–3, 147; *Gazette*, 65; Queen Victoria in, 69, 71; Edward VII in, 74–8; Duke of Windsor in, 81–5; Mérimée in, 87, 193–5; Gladstone in, 92–3; Allies' conference 1922, 94–7; Churchill in, 98–9; Hare's opinion of, 110; J. R. Green's opinion of, 122; in World War II, 132, 137, 145, 159, 199, 202–3, 208; Michael Arlen in, 134–5; development as summer resort, 156, 176; film festival, 158, 178, 211; Americans in, 168, 169, 176–8; Palm Beach Casino, 176–7; Russians in, 181–2, 188; other mentions, 51, 90, 150, 154
Cap d'Ail, 104, 106, 188, 197, 205–6
Cap d'Antibes, 99, 102, 103
Cap Ferrat, 60, 81, 130, 143, 159, 164, 174
Cap Martin, 59, 60, 79, 88, 159
Caraman-Chimay, Princess Elisabeth

de. 176

Carlton Hotel, Cannes, 58, 83, 95, 119, 147, 178, 208, 210, 212

Carnegie, Andrew, 163

Caruso, Enrico, 163, 186

casinos, *see* Cannes, Monte Carlo

Castlerosse, Lord, 102

Cavour, Count Camille, 5

Cecil, Lady Gwendolen, 92

Celebrity Circus, The, 175

Cercle Nautique, Cannes, 32, 63, 71, 75, 80, 95

Chagall, Marc, 186

Chaliapin, Fyodor Ivanovitch, 186

Chamberlain, Austen, 95

Chamberlain, Joseph, 73

Chamberlain, Neville, 101

Chamberlayne, Miss, 76

Chanel, Coco, 44

Chaplin, Charles, 43, 103

charities, 149–51, 188

Charles III, Prince of Monaco, 35

Chateaubriand, François René, 18–19

Chatterton, Lady, 23

Cherkassky, Prince, 181

Chevalier, Maurice, 84, 176

Child's Garden of Verses, A, 121

cholera, 17, 18, 122

Christian, Prince of Schleswig-Holstein, 79–80

Christie, Agatha, 43

Churchill, Odette, 202

Churchill, Peter, 200–4

Churchill, Lord Randolph, 126

Churchill, Winston, 84, 95, 98–100, 103, 104

Churchill-Wanstall, Kathleen, 80

Cimiez (Nice), 26, 60, 69–74

Citroën, André, 176

Clark, Sir Andrew, 120

Clark, Lord (Sir Kenneth), 58, 170, 171

Clemenceau, Georges, 93

Clews, Henry and Marie, 42, 172–3

Cobden, Richard, 32, 90

Coburn, Charles, 115

Cocteau, Jean, 44–5, 197

Cole, Harold, 207

Colette, 195

Collet, Louise, 194

Colossus of Arcadia, The, 44, 136

Compagnie Internationale de Wagons-Lits, 39

Connaught, Duke of, 80, 139

Connolly, Cyril, 141–2

Conquest of England, The, 123

cooking, British, 151–2

Cooper, Sir Duff, 210

Cornuché, Eugène, 43

Cornwell-Evans, T. P., 97

Côte d'Azur, origin of name, 20

courtesans, 116–19

Cowans, Sir John, 60

Coward, Noël, 106

Craig, Gordon, 171

Craven, Lady Elizabeth, 14–15

cricket, introduction of on Riviera, 62

croquet, introduction of on Riviera, 21

Cunard, Nancy, 44, 135

Curtis, Ralph, 174

Curzon, 95, 96

Cyril, Grand Duke, 188

D'Abernon, Lord, 89

Daisy of Pless, Princess, 60, 64, 78, 80, 87, 145, 182

Dalhousie, Lord, 22

Dartigues, Fernand, 157

Davies, J. T., 95

Davies, Sir Mortimer, 191

de Polnay, Peter, 46, 141–2

Debussy, Claude, 175

Delacroix, Blanche-Caroline, 87

Deslys, Gaby, 86

Devonshire, Duchess of, 15

Diaghilev, Serge, 37, 44–5, 171, 185–6, 189, 214

Dierks, Barry, 175

Dietrich, Marlene, 177

Dimanche, 130

Docker, Nora, Lady, 211

Dolin, Anton, 44–5

domestic servants, 150

Door Ajar, A, 46, 141–2

Dos Passos, John, 166

Douglas, Lord Alfred, 128

Dufy, Raoul, 196

Dumas, Alexandre, 23–4

Duncan, Isadora, 167, 171–2

Eastlake, Lady, 13

école méditerranée, 195

Eden, Sir Anthony, 100, 101

Eden-Roc pool, 168, 179

Edward VII, 20, 63, 72, 74–8, 126, 149
Edward, Prince of Wales, *see* Windsor, Duke of
Elizabeth and Her German Garden, 138
Elliott, Maxine, 99, 175
English-American Library, 65
Escoffier, Auguste, 198
Esterel, 2, 12, 55
Eugénie, Empress, 79, 87–8, 119
Evans, James, 20
Eveing News, 126–7
Ewer, Fanny, 193
exchange rates, 152
Eze, 99, 127, 182

Farina, Dr, 51
Fashoda incident, 73, 78
Faure, Félix, President, 72, 192
film industry, 158, 177, 178
Fitzgerald, F. Scott, 44, 165, 166–8
Fitzgerald, Zelda, 166–8
Foot, M. R. D., 203
football, 147
Fort de la Revère, 205–6
Foster, Lady Elizabeth, 15
Fragonard, Jean Honoré, 163, 198
Francis Joseph, Emperor of Austria, 72
Franco-Prussian War, 36, 56, 78
franglais, 66
Frederick, Robert T., 207
Fréjus, 13, 22; bishop of, 54, 123
French Revolution, 13
Fry, Wilfred T., 153

Garbo, Greta, 104
Garden, Mary, 175
gardens, 59
Gardner, Frank, 108
Garibaldi, Giuseppe, 198
Garrick, David, 14
General Irrigation and Water Supply Co of France, 61
George III, 9–10, 12
George V, 81
George VI, 83
George, Grand Duke, 182
George, Prince of Greece, 37
Germans and Riviera, 50–1
Gibraltar, Bishops of, 56
Gide, André, 140
Ginner, Dr E. Wightman, 159

Girl Guides, 149
Gladstone, William Ewart, 73, 92–4, 192
Glazebrook, Dr Otis, 173
Gloucester, Duke of, 9–10
Goelet, Mrs Ogden, 76–7
Goering, Hermann, 159
Goldsmith, John, 202
golf, introduction of on Riviera, 62
Golfe Juan, 15, 192, 194
Gordon, Duchess of, 25
Gordon, Margaret, *see* Brewster, Margaret
Gould, Anna, 164
Gould, Frank Jay, 43, 164–5
Gould, Jay, 164
Gourdon, 175
Grammont, Georges, 196
Grand Hotel, 100
Grand Hotel, Cannes, 32, 95
Grand Hotel, Cap d'Antibes, 102
Grand Hotel, Nice, 121
Grand Hôtel Californie, Cannes, 140
Grasse, 6, 8, 12, 69, 70, 90, 140, 163, 194, 198, 204, 212
Graves, Charles, 41, 43, 86, 114, 154, 200, 210
Green, John Richard, 122–3
Green Hat, The, 134–5
Greene, Graham, 143
Girmaldi palace, 55
Guglielminetti, Dr, 191
Guilbert, Yvette, 77
Guitry, Sacha, 197
Gurdjieff, Serge, 125
Gustav V of Sweden, 85–6

Hackett, Benjamin, 154
Hall, Virginia, 201
Hamilton, 12th Duke of, 105–6, 183
Hanbury, Sir Thomas, 59
Hare, Augustus, 4, 27–30, 33, 41, 62, 63, 110
Harris, Frank, 46, 76, 77, 126–9
Haxton, Gerald, 130
Hayworth, Rita, 89
Hemingway, Ernest, 166, 168
Helena, Princess of Schleswig-Holstein, 79–80
Helena, Grand Duchess, 33, 180
Henderson, Arthur, 102
Henley, W. E., 121–2

Henry of Battenberg, Prince, 79
L'Hermitage, Menton, 124
Hesse-Darmstadt, Grand Duchess of, 79
Higginson, F. W., 205–6
Highways and By-Ways of Dorset, 149
Hilton, Conrad, 178
Hitler, Adolf, 97–8
Holland Institute for English-Trained Nurses, 52
homosexuals and the Riviera, 130, 186
Honoré, Prince of Monaco, 10
Hope diamond, 164
Hopwood, Sir William, 110
horse-racing, 32, 62
Hôtel d'Angleterre, Nice, 60
Hôtel des Anglais, Nice, 60
Hôtel Beaulieu, Cannes, 159
Hôtel du Cap d'Antibes, 42, 166, 168, 181
Hôtel Excelsior Regina, Cimiez, 72–3
Hôtel de Grande Bretagne, Nice, 54
Hôtel Metropole, Monte Carlo, 89
Hôtel de Necker, Hyères, 12
Hôtel Negresco, Nice, 58, 172, 209, 210
Hôtel de Paris, Monte Carlo, 37, 41, 104, 109, 112, 137, 164
Hôtel Pinchinat, Cannes, 18
Hôtel des Quatres Nations, Nice, 11
Hôtel Regina, Nice, 98
Howard, Elizabeth, 118–19
Hugo, Victor, 18, 194
Hundred Days, 15
Huxley, Aldous, 130
Huxley, Maria, 125
Hyères, in 18th century, 11, 12; miniature railway, 41; as health resort, 52, 61, 146; sport, 62, 63; Stevenson in, 121–2; Edith Wharton in, 170; other mentions, 66, 133, 182

Ibañez, Blasco, 191
Ideal Husband, An, 128
Île St Honorat, 54, 123, 192
Île Ste-Marguerite, 119
In Monte Carlo, 191
income tax relief, 153
Isaacs, Harry and Barney, *see* Barnato
Isaacs, Isaac, 107

Isola 2000, 212–13

Jackson, Stanley, 109
Jameson raid, 73
Jérome, Prince, 118
Joel, Solly, 108–9
Joel, Woolf, 108
John, Augustus, 128
Johnson, Dr Samuel, 14
Jones, Sidney, 202
Joynson-Hicks, Sir William, 138
Juan-les-Pins, 43, 165, 168, 174
Juniory, La, 117

Karageorgevitch, Prince, 134
Karr, Alphonse, 194
Kelly, Sir Gerald, 131
Kelly, Grace, 178
Kennedy, A. L., 91
Kennedy, Joseph, 177
Keun, Odette, 140
Kipling, Rudyard, 140
Krupp von Bohlen, Gustav, 99
Kschessinska, 187–8
Kurtze, Karl, 108

La Léno, 118
La Napoule, 60, 128, 172, 201
La Provence, 193
La Solitude, 121
La Turbie, 14, 175, 205
Lagden, Emma, 193
Lamarck, Chevalier de, 192
Langley, James, 205
Langlois, Léon, 35
Lattre de Tasisigny, General Jean de, 208
Lavender Tea Rooms, Nice, 200
Lavergne, Louis Gabriel, 12
Lawrence, D. H., 124, 125
Lawrence, Frieda, 125–6
Lawrence, Gertrude, 106
Le Broq, 115
Le Cannet, 196
Le Corbusier, 191
Lear, Edward, 140
Lefebvre and Co., 36
Léger, Fernand, 196
lemon growing, 5, 29, 35
Lenglen, Charles, 64, 156
Lenglen, Suzanne, 64, 138, 146, 174
Lenin, Vladimir Ilyich, 171

Leoncavallo, Ruggiero, 73
Leopold II of Belgium, 85, 86–7, 131
Leopold, Prince, Duke of Albany, 21, 69, 80
Letters from Cannes and Nice, 24
Lewis, Sam, 113–14
Liégeard, Stéphen, 20, 193
Lifar, Serge, 189–90
Living Well is the Best Revenge, 169
Lloyd George, David, 94–8
Locke, William J., 138
London Society for Promoting Christianity amongst the Jews, 16
Loris-Melikov, General, 182
Loti, Pierre, 126
Lou Pidou, 141–2
Louis Napoleon, *see* Napoleon III
Louis-Philippe, 19, 35
Louise, Princess, 73
Lowe, F. Gordon, 146
Lumbert, H. M., 65
Lysistrata (yacht), 162
Lyte, Rev. Henry Francis, 54

Macaulay, Lord, 18
MacCormack, John, 191
McCormick, Donald, 111
McHardie, Miss, 151
Mackay, Mrs John, 164
McLaren, Agnes, 52
McLean, Evelyn, 164
MacLeish, Archibald, 166, 167
Macmillan, Rev. Hugh, 9, 52, 56
McWhirter, Ross, 213
Madge, A. E., 63, 146
Maeterlinck, Maurice, 175, 191
Magliano, Theresa, 88
Magnus, Philip, 93
Mallet, Maria, 70–3, 80, 92
'Man in the Iron Mask', 192
Man Who Broke the Bank at Monte Carlo, The, 115
Mandelieu, 60; tennis club, 146
Mannin, Ethel, 158
Manning, Henry Edward (later Cardinal), 54
Manoel, King of Portugal, 86
Mansfield, Katherine, 43, 123–5
Margaria, Count, 59
Maria Feodorovna, Empress, 181
Maritime Alps, 3
Marrakesh, Pasha of, 86

Mars, Lieutenant Alastair, 203
Marseilles, 15, 50, 208
Mary, Princess of Baden, 105
masonic lodges, 149
Massenet, Jules Emile Frédéric, 195
Mathews, Herbert, 208
Matisse, Henri, 195–6
Mauclair, Camille, 193
Maugham, Frederic, 133
Maugham, W. Somerset, 27–8, 130–4
Maupassant, Guy de, 126, 133, 194–5
Maure, Dr, 193–4
Maxim, Hiram S., 57, 67, 113
Maxwell, Elsa, 85, 131, 174–5
May, Caroline, 161
Mead, Christine, 151
Meanwhile, The Picture of a Lady, 141
Mecklenburg-Schwerin, Grand Duke of, 182, 192
Melba, Dame Nellie, 191
Memorials of Hedley Vicars, 53
Memorials of a Quiet Life, 28
Menton, Hare and, 4, 28–30, 110; plebiscite 1860, 29; lemon growing, 5; J. H. Bennet and, 33–4, 49–51; as health resort, 33, 49–51, 61; impact of railway, 33–5; Anglican Church, 28, 53, 148; hotel development, 58; gardens, 59; library, 65; Queen Victoria and, 69–70, 74; Stevenson and, 120; J. R. Green and, 122–3; Katherine Mansfield in, 124; post-World War I, 145–7; tearooms, 152; development as summer resort, 156, 158; and arts, 197, 212; and rugby football, 213–14; other mentions, 117, 149, 188, 191
Menton and Monte Carlo News, on Blue Train, 42; on post-World War I changes, 45, 145; on various celebrities, 74, 94, 101, 102, 107, 138–40, 148; development of, 65–6; on war profiteering, 110–11; on domestic employees, 150; on French food, 152; on income tax refunds, 153; attitude towards local residents, 154; promotes Menton as summer resort, 156–8; postwar publication, 210–11
Mericati, Count, 135
Mérimée, Prosper, 21, 32, 87, 193–4
Merryman, Bessie, 82–3

Metcalfe, Edward Dudley, 83, 84
Michael, Grand Duke, 40, 85, 182, 192
Milhaud, Darius, 44–5
Miller, Ruby, 102
Minangoy, André, 213
Mistinguett, 138
Mistral, The, 47
Molyneux, Capt Edward, 103, 106
Monaco, old settlement, 5, 10; in
    Napoleonic Wars, 14; cedes
    Menton, 28–9, 35; casino, 35–7,
    55–7, *see also* Monte Carlo; golf
    course, 62; threat of popular rising,
    67–8; Queen Victoria and, 69;
    Edward VII and, 75; 77; described
    by J. R. Green, 122; during World
    War II, 140, 200, 209; Grand Prix
    de, 148; *see also* Monte Carlo
Monckton, Sir Walter, 84
Monkswell, Lord, 31
Monson, Sir Edmund, 74
Mont-Agel, 62, 86
Monte Carlo, creation of 1866, 36;
    casino, 35–7, 55–7, 67, 77, 92, 99,
    103, 107–10, 112–17, 152, 191;
    disapproved of by British, 55, 60,
    69; pigeon shooting, 64; Rally, 64,
    148; Edward VII and, 75–7;
    Churchill and, 98, 103; described by
    Katherine Mansfield, 124; Frank
    Harris and, 127; described by Sir
    Frederick Treves, 149; J. G. Bennet
    in, 162; Russians in, 185–9; opera
    and ballet in, 185–6, 195; other
    mentions, 51, 67, 91, 102, 147, 163,
    175, 199; *see also* Monaco
Monte Carlo Facts and Figures, 67
Monte Carlo and How to Do It, 39, 51, 63,
    67, 116–17, 151
Moon's a Balloon, The, 143
Moran, Lord, 98, 104
Morgan, J. Pierpont, 163
Morgenthau, Henry, 177
Morny, Duc de, 118
Morrell, Lady Ottoline, 125
Mosley, Sir Oswald and Lady Cynthia,
    102
mosquitoes, 25–6, 157
motor cars, impact on Riviera, 45–6,
    59, 64
motor racing, 64, 109, 148
Mougins Country Club, 146

Mountbatten, Lord Louis, 84
'Munshi, The', 71
Murat, Prince, 118
Murder in Monte Carlo, 136
Murphy, Gerald and Sara, 165–9
Murray, John, 22, 27, 61
Murry, John Middleton, 124
My Life and Loves, 129
Mystery of the Blue Train, The, 43–4, 146

Nagelmackers, Georges, 38–9
Naissance du Jour, La, 195, 196
nannies, 150
Napoleon Bonaparte, 15, 38, 192
Napoleon III, 119
Napoleonic Wars, 14
Neave, Airey, 206
Negrin, Emile, 9
New York Herald, 42, 161–2
New Zealand, 124
newspapers, English language, 65–6,
    210–11
Nice, in 18th century, 1–5, 7–15;
    plebiscite 1860, 6; local opinion of
    English, 23–4; Margaret Brewster
    in, 26–7; impact of railway, 32–3;
    protestant cemeteries, 52; Anglican
    Church in, 54; British property and
    interests, 58–64; Book Club (later
    Library), 65; Queen Victoria in,
    71–2; opinion of Hare, 110;
    opinion of Katherine Mansfield,
    124; beauty contest in, 158; Isadora
    Duncan in, 171–2; Russians in, 180,
    183–4, 188; tearooms, 182; famous
    sons, 198; in World War II, 199,
    208, 209; postwar, 211, 212, 214;
    other mentions, 106, 128, 149, 158,
    191, 194
Nichols, Robert, 125
Nicolson, Harold, 83
Nietzsche, Friedrich Wilhelm, 191
Nijinska, Bronislava, 44, 189
Nijinsky, Vaslav, 186
Nikita, Prince, 190
Niven, David, 143
Noghes, Antony, 148

Of Their Own Choice, 201
O'Hara, Nellie, 128–9
O'Leary, Patrick, 205–7
Onassis, Aristotle, 37, 104, 191

Onward, Christian Soldiers, 55
opera, 36, 37
Oppenheim, E. Phillips, 44, 86, 131, 135–8
Orczy, Baroness, 138, 139–40, 182, 199
Ouida, 118
Owen, Frank, 95
Oxford, Lady, 32

Packenham, Admiral, 22, 25
Paderewski, Ignacz Jean, 191
Paganini, Nicolo, 191
Page, Gary, 209
Paget, Amy, 199
Palerme, Gina, 117
Palm Beach Casino, Cannes, 176–7
Paris-Lyons-Mediterranée Railway, 32
Parker, Dorothy, 166
Parry, Vice-Admiral Sir John, 138
passport control, 37–8
Paterson, General, 1
Patti, Adelina, 191
Pau, 54
Pavlova, Anna, 186–7
Pearl, Cora, 106, 117–18
Pearls, Girls and Monty Bodkin, 44
Peille, 175
Penrose, Spencer, 164
Pension Anglaise, Menton, 28
Pétain, Philippe, 197
Petrushka, 186
Pfeiffer, Pauline, 168
Philpotts, Eden, 140
Picasso, Pablo, 44, 166, 190
pigeon-shooting, 64
Pius VII, Pope, 18
Place des Îles, Cannes, 101
plebiscite 1860, 6, 29
Poincaré, Raymond, 97
Polignac, Princess Edmond de, 185
polo, 63
Polovtsoff, General Pierre, 92, 113, 187
Pont du Var, 98
Popov, Admiral, 180
Porter, Cole, 166
post-impressionists, 195–7
Pougy, Liane de, 117
Pound, Ezra, 168
Powell, Anthony, 142–3
Private Lives, 105, 106
Promenade des Anglais, Nice, 17, 33

protestantism, 20–1, 25, 52–7; *see also* Anglican Church
Puck, 118
Pullman's Palace Car Company, 39

Rabinovitch, Alec, 202
Rachel (actress), 197
railways, coming of, 31–7; sleeping cars, 38–45; postwar, 47
Rainier III, Prince of Monaco, 80, 178
Raphael, Frederic, 133
Rathenau, Walter, 96
Record, The, 20
Reid, Sir Wemyss, 93–4
Reid, Mrs Whitelaw, 163–4
Remembrance Day, 149
Renoir, Auguste, 196
resistance movement, 200–7
Reynolds, Sir Joshua, 14
Richmond Restaurant and Tea Rooms, Menton, 152
Riddell, Lord, 93
Rigby, Dr Edward, 13
Ritz Hotel, Paris, 42
Riviera News, 84
Riviera of the Corniche Road, The, 149
Riviera Palace Hotel, Monte Carlo, 39
Riviera, The, 52, 56
Rivieras, The, 41
Rivoli, Duc de, 63
Rock of Nice, The, 54
Rock Pool, The, 141
Rodocanachi, Dr, 205, 207
Rogers, Herman and Katherine, 81–2
Roper, John, 202
Roquebrune, 29, 35, 139, 191
Rosslyn, Lord, 113–14
Rothschild family, 36
Rougier, Henri, 148
Royal Navy, 67, 79, 81
rugby football, 213–14
Ruhl, Henri, 176, 197
Rummel, Walter, 171
Russians on Riviera, 32–3, 40, 180–90

SOE (Special Operations Executive), 200–4
Sagan, Françoise, 212
St-Paul-de-Vence, 167, 196–7
St Petersburg-Vienna-Nice-Cannes Express, 40
St Raphael, 52, 54, 167, 192, 195

Saint-Saëns, Camille, 195
St Tropez, 12, 55, 194–7, 208, 212
Sainte-Claire le Chateau, 170
Salisbury, Lord, 59, 71, 73, 74, 91–2
Samoa, 122
San Remo, 124, 159
Sandford, Charles, Bishop of
    Gibraltar, 56–7
sanitary conditions, 50, 60–1
Sardinia, Kingdom of, 2, 6, 18
Saturday at MI9, 206
Saturday Review, 127
scent industry, 6, 59, 194
Scheherazade, 185
Schwab, Charles M., 163
Scotch Tea Houses, 150
Scottish Churches, 25, 53, 148
Segonzac, André Dunoyer de, 196
Sella, Antoine, 166, 181
Serge, Grand Duke, 188
Shaw, George Bernard, 126
Short History of the English People, 122
Siam, Queen of, 86
Sienkiewicz, Henryk, 191
Signac, Paul, 195–6
Silberer, Viktor, 116
Simenon, Georges, 130, 191
Simmons, Reggie, 114
Simpson, Wallis, *see* Windsor, Duchess
    of
Singer family, 171, 185
Sinner's Friend, 53
skating, 64
sleeping cars, 38–45
Smith, Colonel, 110
Smith, Edward, 67
Smith, James Edward, 3, 10–11
Smolet, rue, Nice, 9
Smollett, Tobias, 1–3, 6–9, 37–8
Société des Bains de Mer et du Cercle
    des Estrangers, 36, 112, 114, 190
Sospel, 62
Spiegel, Admiral von, 189
Standish, Robert, 137
Stein, Gertrude, 166
Stevenson, Bob, 120
Stevenson, Fanny, 121
Stevenson, Robert Louis, 120–2
Stopford, Lord, 26
Straight, Whitney, 205
Stravinsky, Igor, 166, 186
Stresemann, Gustav, 89

Strictly Personal, 131
Summing Up, The, 131
superiority, attitudes of among
    British, 153–5
Sutherland, Graham, 212
Symonds, John Addington, 56

Talleyrand, Charles Maurice de, 6,
    192
Tardieu, André, 197–8
Taylor, John, 58, 59, 65
tearooms, 151–2, 200
Tel-e-Kebir, 81
Tender is the Night, 44, 165–6, 185
tennis, 21–2, 63–4, 85, 101, 146
Tennyson, Alfred, Lord, 140
theatre, 66
Times, The, 38, 57, 77, 87, 97
Toklas, Alice B., 166
Tolloush, Alexander, 1
tolls, 38
Tolstoy, Anna, 183
Tolstoy, Leo, 182
Tomkins, Calvin, 168, 169
Tomlinson, John Wickes, 54
Toulon, 31, 208
Train bleu, Le, 44–5
Travels through France and Italy, 1–9
Treasure Island, 121
Treves, Sir Frederick, 149
Tripet, 21
Trophée des Alpes, 175
Tuck, Edward, 175
Tylor, Joseph, 51
typhoid, 61

Umberto, Crown Prince of Italy, 159
United States Steel Corporation, 163

Vagliano, Athanase, 191
Valescure, 62, 85
Vallambrosa, Duke of, 32, 59
Vallauris, 89
Vanderbilt, Consuelo, *see* Balsan
Vansittart, Sir Robert, 159
Var, River, 2, 3, 17, 22, 53
Vassall, Elizabeth, 15
Vaudois, 16
Vence, 6, 125, 196, 199, 212
Ventimiglia, 39
Verne, Jules, 194
viatique, 114

Victoria, Queen of England, 59,
     69–74, 85, 88, 92–3
Victoria, Princess Royal, 78
Vigier, Baron, 59
Villa America, 166, 168
Villa Bermond, 182
Villa Eléonore, 18, 20, 76
Villa L'Horizon, 99, 175
Villa Isola Bella, 124
Villa Lou Viei, 82–3
Villa Mauresque, 130–3, 175
Villa Namouna, 163
Villa Victoria, 22
Villefranche, 67, 75, 81, 178, 180, 210
Villeneuve-Loubet, 197, 198
Vingt Milles Lieues sous les Mers, 194

Wagons-Lits, 39
Waldegrave, Maria, 9–10
Walpole, Horace, 10, 14
Walton, Colonel G., 207, 209
Ward, Lady John, 164
Way, Rev. Lewis, 16–17
Webb-Ellis, Rev. William, 213
Webster, Sir Geoffrey, 15
Weihe, Capt., 114
Wells, Charles N., 115
Wells, H. G., 41, 140
Westminster, 2nd Duke of, 106–7
Wharton, Edith, 169–71, 172
White, 'Tiger', 213
Widdecombe Fair, 55
Wilde, Oscar, 128, 130
William II, Emperor, 75

Williams, Val, 206
Williamson, C. N. and A. M., 138
Wills, Helen, 174
Wilson, Edmund, 167
Windsor, Duchess of, 81–5, 131
Windsor, Duke of, 42, 81–5, 189
*Winter and Spring on the Shore of the
     Mediterranean*, 33–4, 50
Winter in Mentone, A, 28
Wodehouse, P. G., 44
Wolseley, Sir Garnet, 81
Wolverton, Lord, 93
Woolfield, Thomas R., 20–2, 32, 53, 59
World Crisis, The, 98
World War I, 145
World War II, French mobilization,
     159; evacuation from Cannes, 132,
     137, 159; British residents who
     stayed during, 137, 140, 199–200;
     Russians' attitude towards, 188–90;
     espionage and resistance, 200–7;
     allied invasion 1944, 100, 178,
     207–10; effect on British standing
     on Riviera, 160
Worthington-Evans, Sir Laming, 96

yachting, 62–3, 75
Yarborough, Colonel William P., 208
York, Duke of, 10
Young, Arthur, 3, 4–5, 6, 11–13, 14

Zaharoff, Sir Basil, 37, 97, 111–12
Zographos, Nico, 114, 191

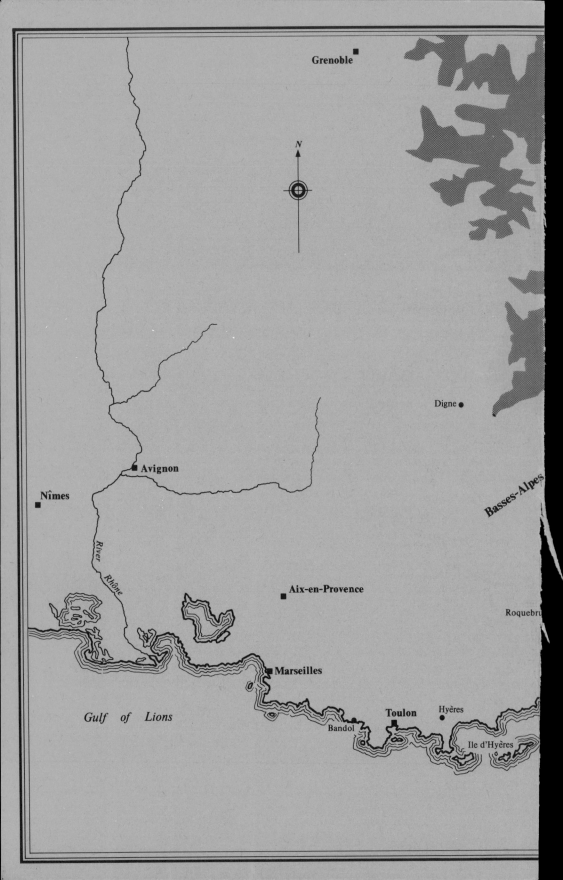